LET THAT SH*T GO

Find Peace of Mind and Happiness
in Your Everyday

Nina Purewal and Kate Petriw

Collins

Published by Collins, an imprint of HarperCollins Publishers Ltd

First edition

HarperCollins Publishers Ltd
Bay Adelaide Centre, East Tower
22 Adelaide Street West, 41st Floor
Toronto, Ontario, Canada
M5H 4E3

www.harpercollins.ca

Library and Archives Canada Cataloguing in Publication
information is available upon request.

ISBN 978-1-4434-5767-5

Printed and bound in the United States
LSC/C 9 8 7

To the loves of my life, Mike and Bianca Purewal;
and to my greatest teacher, my mom, Rita Nayar.
—Nina

To my dad, thanks for all that you do.
—Kate

To our readers: Here's to finding peace in the everyday
and letting go of the bullshit. We love you.

And to the universe: thank you.

Contents

Introduction

LIFE ISN'T ALWAYS EASY. You're trying to check off everything that's on your to-do list, but you hit the sack feeling like you haven't made much of a dent. It's one thing after another that can send you into stress mode at the drop of a hat. Whether it's the challenging circumstances around you or it's your own mind that sets you spinning, there are moments when you feel like you're running on a hamster wheel and can't get off, physically or mentally.

We know what that feels like. We, too, have faced a few life challenges and found ourselves spinning out of control, feeling as if we could barely catch our breaths. We wanted nothing more than to find a little peace and tranquility. So, we decided to take our stress pretty seriously and spent time researching, studying, and introspecting. Thankfully, we came to realize that there *is* a way out, a way to hop off that hamster wheel now and again. And we want to share what we learned with the beautiful you.

In this book you'll find more than a hundred tips to get you to a peaceful, happy place—and you'll get there without having to sit oceanfront listening to the waves, beer in one hand and book in the other. The great thing is, sometimes you don't need to drastically change your routine to find the calm. You don't need to switch jobs, or stop going to that class, or live in the mountains for years. You can find the calm by doing the things you do but just doing them a little differently—whether it's cultivating some deep breaths throughout your day or being aware of the "negative autopilot" that takes over from time to time. Finding peace doesn't have to be a huge project. As it turns out, you can actually find peace in the *everyday*.

You're probably used to hearing that you should make your diet a priority, hit the gym a few times a week, and shower daily, all to take care of that precious body of yours. But how often do you prioritize your mind? Too often we're stuck in our own heads and too busy to step back and take inventory of what's swirling around in there. Being unaware of thought patterns that might be adding an additional layer of stress to our lives can put us at risk of blowing a fuse over the co-worker who chews too loudly, the partner who's lost the remote control, or the friend who doesn't text us back.

But when you *do* take some time to make your mind a priority, giving it a good cleanse once in a while can have a positive effect on the rest of your life. Being conscious of your thoughts can help to make you less reactive to the daily bullshit that pops up. You are better able to tackle it or to accept it and let it go.

So how do you reap the benefits that come from making your mind a priority? In this book we've outlined the steps that helped us do just that. Consider this book a toolkit that will give you what you need to cultivate calm and address any obstacles that might be in your way. Our book talks about letting go of negative self-perceptions, regrets from the past, and anxieties over the future. It will show you how to reframe the thoughts that leave you feeling stressed out and overwhelmed. It will help you to stop looking at life through a narrow lens and doing stuff that's not always true to who you are.

This isn't a book that will make you feel like you need to add another "to-do" to your list. It's simply a way to reframe your perception in your daily life. Each chapter begins with an overview of a topic, to help you get into the groove. Then we'll take you through a bunch of practical tips, concepts, and examples of how to implement some peace in your daily life.

We hope that by the time you get to the end of the book, you'll be walking away with an extra skip in your step, a calm smile on your face, and a badass approach to a good life as you work to let that shit go.

CHAPTER 1

Awareness

Goodbye Past and Future Worries

It starts before you even get out of bed.

Your alarm goes off. *Here we go.* You check your phone, to find fourteen new emails that swooped in after you fell asleep. *Shit, I'm behind already.* You have a few seconds to scroll through Instagram, check the weather, brush your teeth, shower, throw on some clothes, successfully find matching socks, grab a slice of toast, and get on your way.

You get into your car with just enough time to get to work. *Phew.* As you start driving, a parade of thoughts comes marching in: *Ahh! I forgot to do the inventory report for Jamal. Wait, is my cousin's birthday on the twenty-second or twenty-third? Shouldn't have had that ice cream sandwich last night, feeling kinda sluggish. How many days do I have left for vacation? I really need to plan something soon. Ugh, I gotta file my taxes . . .*

It rambles on until—*boom!*—you're at the office. Do you even remember getting there? Where did all of that time go, from the minute your alarm went off to the moment you sat down in your chair?

Surprise, you missed it.

From the second you woke up you've been on the go. And you even managed to layer all kinds of worries on top of the basic busyness that is your life. You, my friend, might be stressed AF.

WE'VE ALL HAD MOMENTS like this—autopiloting our way from A to B while letting our mind wander in its own little world. Being on the go physically is one thing (rushing to get your kid to soccer practice, madly trying to avoid being late for lunch with a friend), but having a busy mind on top of that is another. In fact, sometimes your mind runs a hundred times faster than your body. You might not think much of it, but weighing down your already busy life with negative and unnecessary thoughts can increase your stress level. Except, it doesn't have to be this way. Just imagine if, instead of allowing your stress to build to the point of you nearly having a meltdown, you could find a way to calm your mind.

Think about that drive to work, the one in which the thought parade came marching through your mind. Those thoughts may be loud (so, so loud), but they're kind of useless. Or at least they're useless *in that moment*. From the minute you put your key in your car's ignition and fire up the engine, you can't physically do anything but drive. You can't be on your laptop pulling up a report. You can't open your calendar to confirm the date of your cousin's birthday. And you can't research a vacation or finish your taxes. All you can actually *do* in that moment is drive. So why worry about the other stuff?

When you're annoyed about something that happened in the past or worrying about the future (which of course you have the right to do and be), you're not experiencing your life *as it happens*. You're missing the here and now, the tiny little moments your life is made up of—driving your car, grocery shopping, enjoying a night out. Think of it this way: if you're always *there*, you're missing out on what's *here*.

So how do you stop your mind from racing? How do you actually stay *here*?

You start by shifting your focus. Instead of thinking through ten different things on your commute, why not try to observe the trees along the way or simply be grateful that you're heading to a place that pays you for what you do? You could notice the sweet smell of your shampoo and how it reminds you of a scent you used to wear in high school. Sure, thoughts and worries might creep in between all of that, but they will come and go—they won't take over and potentially stress you out. Each time you shift your focus to the world around you or things you're grateful for, you move away from thoughts that might make you worried or anxious. You refuse to let them take over.

When you consciously swap the challenging thoughts for more positive ones, even neutral ones, you'll notice a change. Your heart rate might drop. Your shoulders will relax away from your ears, your eyebrows will un-scrunch, and your body will feel calmer. *This* is where you can find moments of calm in the everyday.

Want to know the best part about this approach to grabbing a bit of peace? It doesn't require any drastic changes to how you live your life. Keep your routine. Hang on to your social life. Go to those gym classes. Excel at work. We're not suggesting you should stop any of that. Mostly, it's tough to be calm because of the million things going on *in your head*, not just because of how busy your life has become.

When you actively become aware of the constant swirling of your mind, you can start to do something about it. And when you learn how to calm your mind, it won't matter what you are doing physically; moments of peace can be yours.

The Pursuit of Happiness

Why is it so important to calm your mind? Simple. Because calming your mind is one of the first steps toward achieving what we're all searching for: *happiness*.

And how do you calm the mind? By living in the moment. *That's* where you can find pure happiness. The thing is, you won't find it externally, but—wait for the cheesy line—you will find it by looking within. Only you can control your thoughts and how you react to what's around you. And when you're able to move to a more self-loving, accepting, less reactive mind, you'll find you're a naturally happier human.

Think about this logically for a second. If happiness existed in objects or experiences, then the same objects and experiences would make everyone equally happy. Take coffee, for example. Our friend Tony is obsessed with the stuff. He knows exactly how he wants his beans ground, and the temperature and aroma have to be just right. His morning cup makes him feel happy, complete, and energized; he would give up beer before he gave up coffee. Nina, on the other hand, is neutral toward it. Sure, she'll grab the odd latte when she's out at a coffee shop, but that's as far as it goes. And then there's our buddy Luke. He despises coffee so much that he can't even stand to be in the room where it's being brewed. So, does happiness really reside in that cup of coffee? Clearly, the answer is no. If it did, coffee would bring the same happiness to everyone that it does to Tony, but it doesn't. You can apply this same "happiness test" to any passion: music, books, sports, a particular food. You get the gist. Ask yourself this question: Is happiness in that thing or in the act of experiencing it?

Here's another tricky thing about happiness. You can easily fall into the habit of thinking that it exists in the future. *Once I land my dream job, I'll be happy,* you might think. Or *Once I buy a condo, things will brighten up.* But have you ever followed up on those thoughts? Chances are that once you got or achieved the thing you were chasing, it wasn't long before you went back to feeling unsettled, maybe even *un*happy. The pursuit of this kind of happiness can set you off on a never-ending chase—because this type of happiness is fleeting, and it won't be long before you're thinking about the next milestone. Now that you have your dream job and a new condo, you find yourself wanting a promotion and a new couch. And once you get the couch, it's only natural to want the matching chairs. And now that your living room is all done, you're thinking the kitchen needs to be spruced up. It doesn't end. And you'll never be satisfied because there are always more things to buy or experiences that give you a high.

And we don't just look for happiness in stuff; we look

for it in people, too. To some degree that's okay: the people in our lives can absolutely be a source of happiness. But they can also evoke a wide range of other emotions. One minute you love your parents and the next you find them incredibly frustrating. You're obsessed with a friend, but then they say something that pisses you off. You love your partner to bits, and then they go and do something to make your blood boil.

So, what's the deal? If happiness can't be found in things, in the future, or in people, where is it hiding? Here's the truth:

Regardless of what is happening around you,
the only person who has the capacity to bring you
endless happiness is you.

Even the stuff that you think makes you happy is fleeting. Most external stuff comes with a built-in "peak" of enjoyment. Ever heard someone talk about the "law of diminishing returns"? It's actually an economic term, used to explain production efficiencies and such. But if you opted out of Economics 101, that's totally fine. For our purposes we'll go with the non-economic use of the phrase, which refers to how something that starts out seemingly awesome can pretty quickly fizzle out.

Take french fries, for example. Think about the last time you ordered them. The moment they arrived they were piping hot and tasted amazing. They were delicate and crispy on the outside and filled with soft, potato-y goodness on the inside. Those first few bites were bliss. You were seriously loving those fries. By the time you got to the eighth or ninth fry, though, it wasn't the same. They were still delicious, but not *as* delicious as fries one and two. Suddenly, you passed the point of maximum enjoyment. Maybe you didn't reach that point until the tenth fry or the twentieth, but somewhere along the line it happened. Even though you still had fries left, you didn't feel like eating them anymore. What's going on here? The twentieth fry has the same form (crispy outside, gooey inside) as the first. It might be a little colder, but for the most part it's the same basic fry that was making you so happy three minutes earlier. It's not the fries that have changed—it's you. Your enjoyment of them has declined.

We know what you're thinking: *Hold on a second. All those things—fries, friends, family, coffee, the promotion, the condo—do bring me happiness.* That's true . . . kind of. Those things might bring you happiness in the moment, but *you cannot depend on them for* permanent *happiness.*

You don't have to feel weird or bad for finding happiness in your new house, or your morning cup of coffee, or some fries, or a new phone. Experiencing happiness from all these things is incredible. You just need to know that they're a source of *temporary* happiness. Permanent happiness comes from within you and can be fostered through calming the mind.

It's Who You Are at the Core

And here's the bit that's really going to blow your mind: true happiness doesn't just exist somewhere within you—it *is* you. Happiness is who you are at your very core. That's why you feel *so good* when you're happy: because it is your true nature. This yearning to find happiness and peace is not about *searching* for it somewhere "out there"—it's about *unravelling* who you really are and realizing that happiness is right there, within you.

So, you might be asking yourself a few questions right now. One of them is potentially: *Where did these girls come up with this shit?* Fair enough. The truth is, we didn't "come up" with any of it; it's been around for centuries, and we'll tell you more about that as we go along, so stay tuned.

Another one of your questions might go something like *Is this for real? It sounds too good to be true. Just learn how to calm your mind and live in the now and you'll be happy? Sure.* We hear you. We were skeptical, too. Both of us come from a business background, where the proof is in the numbers. We wanted to see concrete, scientific evidence that this approach works. So, we looked at some of the many studies on the benefits of putting this wisdom into action. And we found our proof; in fact, it's *endless*. One of the most fascinating things our research uncovered is that living in the now can physically alter the composition of your brain. Neuroplasticity research supports what the ancients knew: with a little bit of training, your mind can be changed, and calming the mind can help you better manage emotions. We tested this theory by using some of the calming tips and ideas presented in this book. We did this while living our lives: working stressful corporate jobs, facing serious life challenges, dealing with the usual amount of daily BS. And guess what? We saw for ourselves just how true it is.

You might be wondering, *If happiness is a part of our*

nature, then why don't we experience it all the time? That's a good one, but it actually has a pretty simple answer, and if you've been catching what we've been throwing down, you already know what it is: we don't experience happiness all the time because there's too much shit in the way. Analogy time. Think about the sun on a rainy day. When you look up at the sky, it's dull, dark, and gloomy. On your walk to work there are puddles everywhere, the air is cool, and it's even a bit windy. You have zero access to the sun's rays. That sucks if you like the sun, but it doesn't mean the sun isn't there. It still exists, doesn't it? It's just that the clouds are preventing you from experiencing its warmth. In that same way, great peace and happiness lie within you, but when there are all kinds of stressors in the way (a.k.a. the clouds), it's hard to remember that peace and happiness are right there in front of you.

One quick note here: it's okay to have negative thoughts or those that make you sad. You're human, after all. But just remember that those negative thoughts are not who you are *at the core*. They are only a small part of you, and they will pass, just like clouds on a stormy day. In the meantime, you can work on accessing that sunshine within—regardless of the weather. You can do that by being actively present. The more present you are, the better you'll be at ditching all the crap swirling around in and outside of you, and the more you will experience the calm and happiness within.

It's time to let that shit go.

Get Off Autopilot

TAKE A WILD GUESS at what ranks as the biggest obstacle to being present. Go ahead. We'll wait . . . Okay, fine. We'll tell you. It's your mind. Your very own mind is preventing you from being able to experience life in the moment.

Do you control your mind or does it control you? If you're like most of us, it may be the latter. The truth is, you probably have very little control over your mind. So little, in fact, that you likely don't even know the next thought you're going to think. It could be:

- *Crap, I really should pee before I start this next section of the book.*
- *I can't believe Duane got that promotion last week.*
- *I'm excited about dinner tomorrow. Mmm, food.*
- *I drank way too much coffee today.*
- *That workout was a-mazing.*
- *I'm a terrible friend. Let me text him back right now.*

An article we came across stated that the average person thinks between fifty thousand and seventy thousand thoughts a day, which breaks down to between thirty-five and forty-two thoughts a minute. WTF? Forty-two? That's almost one thought every second. No wonder you hit the sack each night feeling as if you haven't had a slice of peace all day. Your mind is reeling with nonstop thoughts. And if you're not doing anything to rein them in, they can run the place. Your thoughts are on autopilot all day, errr' day. Instead of being in the moment, present in whatever you are doing, your mind is running twenty steps ahead, constantly going on about the past, the future, or maybe your epic, ongoing to-do list: *Gotta pack lunches tonight, make sure everyone has a bath, get online to check bank statements and buy a new blender, double check to see if those flights to California are still on sale, send a few quick emails, message the group chat back about getting together next week.* Blah fucking blah.

Your overactive, wandering, autopilot mind is like a monkey swinging through the trees from branch to branch to branch. In fact, this type of scattered thinking is often referred to as the "monkey mind." When you're stressed and your head is overflowing with thoughts, your monkey mind heedlessly moves from one thought to the other. And the craziest thing is that you might not even realize it, as it's all happening on a subconscious level.

If our minds had a habit of racing through happy thoughts all day every day, a restless mind might not be such a problem. But the trouble is that they tend to focus on the negative. And when we are feeling particularly overwhelmed, our thoughts are more likely to become toxic. *What ifs* and *coulda, shoulda, wouldas* creep in, and before we know it, we're beating ourselves up or worrying about things beyond our control. So not only do our minds wander aimlessly, but they also put us on edge throughout the day—and it's exhausting.

The first step in the process of letting shit go is not to make the thoughts stop but to be *aware* that they are happening in the first place. Once you do that, you can start to change your negative thought patterns and find calmness of

Become an Observer

So your mind is a complicated thing with two distinct parts: the *observing mind* and the *chatty mind*. The chatty mind is the part that you know all too well; it's the monkey mind, the one that keeps going and going and never stops. Just sit for a minute and observe it. No, seriously. Put the book down for sixty seconds and see where your mind goes.

Done? What did you observe? How many thoughts went through your head? Did you wonder, *How do I actually do this?* Or think, *I don't have time for this.* Maybe, toward the end of the minute, you even started to think about what to make for dinner. Regardless, what you did do is watch your thoughts. Doing this is how you tap into your observing mind and use it to *look* at what your chatty mind is doing, and this is the first step toward letting go of your thoughts.

Let's consider how this might help in real life.

Imagine you're stuck in a rut at work, and these anxious thoughts are ricocheting around your mind: *I have to get this presentation done by end of week, but I also need to prep for tomorrow's one-on-one with the VP. There are about three hundred emails in my inbox that I should have answered yesterday. This contract isn't going to edit itself—but I'm not a freakin' lawyer, so I don't even know where to begin. And Lisa is constantly on my ass about hitting targets. Can't she see that I'm basically buried here!*

When you find yourself having a moment like this, see if you can shift your mind into observation mode.

Calm tone this time: *There you go freaking out about work again. That presentation, emails, Lisa . . .*

In taking a moment to *observe* your thoughts, you may find that you experience a wave of calm. Switching over to your observing mind pulls you out of the panic you're experiencing and allows you to look at your swirling thoughts from a distance. Your observing mind does not do emotions. It is fact based, rational, and practical. It doesn't try to resolve your thoughts, it doesn't judge situations, and it doesn't judge you. When you switch from chatty mode to observation mode, you leave behind all the negative emotions attached to your thoughts. Using your observing mind will not totally dissolve your stress, but if you can flip over into observation mode during a really intense moment, you will find some breathing space. And in that space, you can start to let go of your panic—at least a little bit.

As a first step, let's play out some "chatty mind versus observing mind" dialogue in a few everyday scenarios. When your chatty mind starts running, here are some ways your observing mind can catch it and rein it in:

The thought: *I need to go grocery shopping.*
Chatty mind: *OMG, I have no idea when I'm going to grocery shop this week. I was thinking Sunday morning, but I don't know. Should I go on Saturday, instead? No, that's not going to work. Maybe Wednesday night before dinner. Nope, I have a late meeting. How about Friday? Nah, not Friday night. Okay, I guess I'll go on Sunday morning.* (Note that it's fine to devise a plan and

think through it once, but thinking about it over and over is exhausting.)

Observing mind: *There you go again stressing about when to go grocery shopping. You decided on Sunday morning, so there's no need to go over this again.*

The thought: *Duane got a promotion.*

Chatty mind: *I can't fucking believe Duane got promoted again. He so didn't deserve that. Everyone knows he doesn't actually do anything but talk a big game in meetings. What am I doing wrong? I can't believe they didn't give the promotion to me. I'm going to quit. They don't do much to motivate me, anyway.*

Observing mind: *There you go again getting all worked up about Duane. You like your job, and just because Duane got promoted doesn't mean that you won't soon.*

The thought: *I should eat healthy.*

Chatty mind: *I can't believe I couldn't go three days without eating chocolate. What is wrong with me? No wonder I can't lose those last fifteen pounds. I'm disgusting.*

Observing mind: *There you go again beating yourself up about what you ate. You made the decision to eat the chocolate, and you enjoyed it. Let that shit go.*

We know what you're thinking: *Easier said than done.* Right? And it's true that you might find it challenging to switch modes at first, but training your observing mind is like training a muscle. The more you work it, the stronger it will become—and the easier it will be for you to use it.

So, the next time you're having a stressful moment, take a step back, pause, and use your observing mind. At first you might only remember to do it once a week. Then once every few days. But if you keep doing it, you'll be a rock-star chatty-mind observer before you know it.

Train Your Mind to Be Present

YOU FINALLY DECIDED to go grocery shopping on Sunday morning. But now you're at the store and it seems as if everyone who lives within an eighty-kilometre radius has shown up at the same time. Instead of allowing your frustration to build in the jam-packed aisles, see if you can use this time to train your recently accessed observant mind to be present. See if you can actually *experience* a moment of calm when you're out running your Sunday errands.

Start by focusing on every action you do as you do it. Like, *really focus*. To the point of ridiculousness. Instead of walking through the aisles thinking about the party you went to last night, what you need to do at work tomorrow, or the argument you got into with your sister last week, adjust your mental dialogue to reflect what you're actually doing:

I am walking to the dip aisle to grab some hummus. Now I'm on my way to the produce section. I am picking up this perfectly ripe bunch of bananas. Now I'm walking over to get some apples. I'm opening this bag and putting five apples into it: one, two, three, four— That one's too bruised. There we go; that's better. Five. Now I'm heading over to the veggies. I'm looking at the broccoli—this bunch is too small for a salad, so I'll grab this one, instead. Now I'm getting some sweet potatoes. Let me check my list—right, I need three. Now I'm tearing off another produce bag and I'm putting in one, two, three sweet potatoes.

Don't you feel calm AF just reading that?

As you wander the store, your chatty mind will try to get the best of you. It will start to make associations based on the things you see, hear, even smell, and before you know it, your mind could go off on a tangent. One second you're reaching for a bunch of bananas, and the next you're thinking about the scarf you promised to knit for your Grandma.

Remember how you forgot to get bananas last week? Terrible mom. Don't forget to pack one in Billy's lunch tomorrow. Oh, that's right. He'll be home early because Grandma is coming over. He's going to be so excited to see her! Oh, shit. I seriously have to knit that scarf. I promised I would have it ready by the winter, and it's already November. Terrible granddaughter.

You look down at your basket, and somehow you have all the produce you need. But where did *you* go? When did you tick those items off your list?

We lose track of our actions like this all the time. Have you ever driven from home to work and wondered how you got there? Well, it wasn't your car that took you for a ride—it was your chatty mind.

When you practise using your observing mind while running errands, remember to be patient with yourself. Using your observing mind for the first time is like doing anything for the first time (playing chess, trying your hand at watercolours, using a new app): you won't be a pro on the first go. You might bounce from your observing mind to your chatty mind thirty-three times in thirty minutes. This is totally cool and totally normal. It takes time and practise to cultivate the power of the observing mind. You might also find that there are days when it's easy to tap into that way of thinking and days when it's just effin' difficult.

But each time you use your observing mind, you are training your mind to be present. And as your observing mind gets stronger, you can use it more often. The calmness it brings can be found in any situation. In fact, if you're alone at home and feeling frenzied, try saying what you're doing out loud. If you're showering, your dialogue would go something like this:

Now I'm grabbing the soap. Now I am washing my arm, and it's getting all soapy. Now I'm rinsing it. Now I'm washing my legs. Now I'm grabbing the shampoo. Now I'm rubbing it into my scalp.

This might sound ridiculous, but don't knock it until you try it. The technique works! Start with once a week. Tell yourself that, say, every Friday night you'll be present as you fold the laundry; or every Sunday you'll go grocery shopping with a present mind. Do it consciously a number of times, and eventually, you'll start to do it automatically. Menial tasks will become calming ones. You'll feel more refreshed, and you might even walk around with a bit more spring in your step. And once you start to use your observing mind automatically, you'll find that you are able to preempt any stressful or negative thoughts before they take hold, and tap into the peace that exists inside you.

Keep in mind that this is an ongoing practice. It's not like one day you get to a place where you're in observing mode 100 percent of the time and can stop working on it. It's like going to the gym: you don't stop once you're happy with how you look and feel—you keep at it, and you keep improving bit by bit. Training your mind is a continual process, but one that's so worth it when it comes to finding those moments of calm in the storm.

You Know How to Do This

BELIEVE IT OR not, you already know how to do this . . . sort of.

As a toddler, you were present all the time. You were inherently happy and full of energy because you were always in the moment. You weren't bothered by the drama that surrounded you. Your mind was clear, and you got upset for practical reasons—because you were tired, maybe, or hungry.

Toddlers are on such a high all the time, just experiencing life. Imagine if you could channel that same type of excitement to your adult self. *Wow, a worm! Look, four flags in a row! That cloud is shaped like a heart! Check out this nugget of gooey gold I fished out of my nose!*

What happens to us as we get older? How do we lose that ability to just be in the moment? Well, as we've seen, we get caught up in the world spinning around us. That crazy world creates a lot of emotional and mental stress, which in turn leads to fatigue. Think about it: you could be sitting at your desk all day, doing absolutely nothing that's physically draining, but you still come home exhausted. Why? Because mental stress takes up mental *and* physical energy. Ever had an argument with someone and been completely exhausted afterward? That exhaustion didn't come from running laps. As you go through life, your mind becomes cluttered with all the crap that's happening around you. And all that crap erodes your "born with it" ability to just *be*.

But despite the huge pile of shitty, stressful thoughts you accumulate as you move through your day-to-day life, there *are* moments when you are fully present. You know the feeling: You're so engrossed in whatever you're doing that nothing else seems to matter. You're so focused on the beauty or intensity of what is in front of you that time seems to stops. *You* just stop—or, better yet—*your mind* just stops thinking any thoughts outside of what you're focused on. And afterward, you feel fantastic.

When you're fully engaged in any activity or task, you are living in the moment, but you're doing it subconsciously. This is also known as being in a *state of flow*. You might slip into this ultra-present mode when you're playing your favourite sport, going for a run, reading an amazing book, or hanging out with your friend (and not checking your phone). It can happen when you're fully engrossed in decorating a cupcake, strumming a tune on your guitar, or piecing together a gorgeous flower arrangement.

Why do you think you love doing something you're passionate about in the middle of a stressful week? It's because your chatty mind finally shuts the fuck up.

We all tend to get lost in the moment from time to time, but the trick is to learn how to do it consciously—to bring the same kind of focus and quietness of mind you feel when you're doing something you love to moments when you are feeling really stressed, or when your mind is running out of control. If you can be as present while doing something that feels like a chore (like grocery shopping) as you are when you're doing something you're passionate about, that chore can become just as positive an experience.

The Hurricane of Life Will Forever Swirl

WE KNOW THAT'S not an entirely pleasant thought, but it's a super-important one to keep in mind. No matter how present you are in your life, there are still going to be high highs and low lows; shitty, unexpected turns and incredible, exciting ones. There's going to be hardship, and there's going to be good luck. The crazy push and pull of life will never end. Not. Ever. And no matter what you do, you're never going to reach a point where your circumstances are all good, all the time. The world just doesn't work that way.

When life is swirling around you at breakneck speed like a hurricane, you have a choice: you can either allow yourself to get swept up in it or be the calm in the eye of the storm. It's in the moments when you are fully present and using your observing mind that you move away from the hurricane's violent winds to the calm eye at its centre. There you become a witness to all that is going on around you instead of getting caught up in it.

So much of what happens in the outside world is beyond your control. The key is to look within yourself to find calm and happiness.

Let's take Laura. She's in her mid-twenties and relatively new to the working world, and was stressed to the max when she realized something had to change. She was feeling overwhelmed daily and just couldn't seem to keep up, so she decided to take steps to introduce some calm into her life by being more present (she did some of the things we've talked about here—like becoming an observer to her chatty mind and talking through some of her actions). After a few months she started to feel more blissed out on the regular. The work hurricane around her hadn't changed, but she had. She was much less reactive, and much less likely to get caught up in all the crap. She'd found the centre of her very own hurricane. And the powerful thing about being rooted in the centre of a hurricane is that when the big things hit, you're better equipped to handle them.

Like Laura, when you accept that the external world will continue to swirl and lean into your calm within, you'll reap the rewards. You might feel more relaxed in stressful work situations. You could find yourself less fazed by people who used to bother the crap out of you. And you might even start to appreciate all the good stuff in your life you may not have even noticed before.

Know That the Thoughts Don't Stop

LET'S MAKE ONE THING clear about trying to live in the present: *The thoughts don't stop—but your relation to them changes.*

It's not like you'll all of a sudden find yourself in a magical place where your mind no longer thinks stressful thoughts. So, don't be discouraged to find that your thoughts continually drift, even if it happens when you are actively trying to use your observing mind.

Asking your mind to stop thinking thoughts is like asking a child not to eat a chocolate-chip, chocolate-dipped, multicoloured-sprinkle cookie that is sitting right in front of them. It's your chatty mind's nature to think thoughts.

In fact, right now your chatty mind might be thinking, *Okay, so what's the point? If the thoughts don't ever stop, then why bother with any of this?*

Here's why: because although the thoughts themselves won't stop, when you catch them and switch to observation mode, it will change the way you *connect* to them, the way you *relate* to them, and the way they make you *feel*. Over time you'll become less and less affected by them. You'll be in control of your thoughts, instead of letting your thoughts control you.

This will happen naturally as you start to become aware of the chatty mind. Let's say a bothersome thought comes barging in—maybe about the fact that you've been meaning to clean up your bedroom for the past few days but haven't had the chance. Maybe it's the second time today you're thinking this thought. The first time it made you feel anxious and guilty. But this time you use your observing mind to catch yourself. Instead of swirling into anxious or guilt mode, you get a grip on the situation. *It's okay that you haven't cleaned up your bedroom yet,* you tell yourself. *You've been swamped, and you know it'll get done tomorrow, since you have the day off.*

Do this a few times over and you'll start to get the hang of it. At first, you'll notice you're less affected by the thoughts you might be having about menial things (the messy room, a late-night snack). They don't upset or trigger you as much as they used to. Then, eventually, the way you relate to the bigger issues in your life will start to change, too. A thought about an ongoing annoyance with your partner might still pop up the same number of times, but you'll be able to switch into observation mode more quickly. And that will get you out of a state of worry, frustration, or panic.

As you continue to use your observing mind to pull you out of your swirling thoughts, you'll start to notice a change in yourself. Essentially, you'll start to morph into a better version of you—a *happier* version. And that version—the you who has started to let that shit go and focus on being in the moment—can see things more clearly and make more informed decisions.

Put Away Your Crystal Ball

THE THIRTY MINUTES or so before Kate heads to bed is when her chatty mind fills itself with random thoughts and anxieties. She thinks about all the things that may or may not happen in the future and stressful thoughts that escaped her during the day. Kate's thoughts include but are not limited to:

- *I wonder if the guy I met on Bumble will reach out again. Does he like me?*
- *I'm worried I'm not going to meet the product launch deadline—there's just so much going on at work, but I don't feel like I'm making any progress.*
- *I wonder where I'll live when I retire.* (A productive thought at age thirty-three.)

And last, but not least . . .

- *When is everyone finally going to get on board with the changes that need to be implemented to reduce carbon emissions and save the future of humanity before the environmental crisis gets too bad?*

Think about your own worries. How many of them actually came true? More often than not, the things we worry about turn out to be non-issues. As Mark Twain said, "I am an old man and have known a great many troubles, but most of them never happened." Psychotherapists call our tendency to predict the future without realistically considering the odds *fortune-telling*. If we can't possibly know the outcome, why do we worry? Of course you can plan for the future, but worrying too much about the unknown isn't helpful.

When you find yourself tripped up by thinking about the future, call in your observing mind to shut down all the chatter. Your observing mind will allow you to stop your thoughts in their tracks by saying, *Hold up. This is just my mind getting stressed. I notice it, and I understand why I might be stressed, but really, there's no reason to go down this spiral for the tenth time.*

Looking at your worries without judging them, and realizing that they are just thoughts, can help create distance between you and whatever emotion you are feeling. And doing this can naturally make you a little less reactive to the thought. This approach has really helped Kate keep those worries in check. That doesn't mean they don't still come up or that she never gets caught up in them (remember, the thoughts will always be there), but now she knows how to acknowledge them and how to better talk herself through them.

It's important not to forget that your worries exist for a reason. They might be there to ensure you are on time for an important event, or to motivate you, or to protect you from danger. We can thank our ancestors for the part of our brain that worries; it developed millions of years ago to protect us from things like a sabre tooth tiger attack.

One way to separate yourself from whatever thought is stressing you out is to remember that your mind is bringing it up to help you in some way. Your job is then to look at that thought and determine whether you're getting worked up unnecessarily. And if you figure out that sometimes you are, that's okay, too. Give yourself a break, and don't forget that developing this kind of thinking is like developing a muscle: the more you work it, the stronger it will become—and the easier it will be to nip stressful thoughts in the bud.

Take a Deep Breath

A RESTORATIVE BREAK sounds nice in theory, but sometimes your tightly packed schedule just won't allow for it. We get it. There are times when taking a vacation, a day off, or even twenty minutes to relax just doesn't seem possible.

Okay, fine. So, you can't spare twenty minutes. But do you have five? Or one? How about fifteen seconds?

Great! We have you at fifteen seconds. It just so happens that fifteen seconds is all that's needed to find a small moment of peace in your chaotic day. You could be any-where—at the bus stop, planted in your chair at work, making dinner, or standing in line at the grocery store. Wherever you are . . .

TAKE A DEEP BREATH.

You might be thinking, *But aren't I breathing all the time?* Generally, yes. But that's not what we're talking about here. We want you to take a *real* breath. One that you're actually *aware* of. One that you're taking *deliberately*.

Throughout the day, you're likely drawing in relatively shallow breaths with your chest. When you experience negative emotions like anger, panic, or worry, your breathing tends to become shallower. Sometimes you might even *forget* to breathe. Did you know, for example, that if you're typing or reading an email, you might subconsciously suspend your breathing for a moment? Yup, it's true: we sometimes get so caught up and stressed as we open and read our email that we stop steadily breathing. Writer and consultant Linda Stone has given this phenomenon a name: *email apnea.*

Email apnea aside, the chest breathing you regularly do provides your body with the minimum amount of oxygen it needs. And that's a good thing. But there is another, better way to breathe—a way that can put you in a more relaxed state and improve your ability to cope with whatever bullshit swirls around you on a day-to-day basis. We're talking about breathing through your diaphragm, which moves much more air into and out of your body. Let's give it a try.

When you picture yourself breathing, you probably conjure up an image of your chest rising and falling. That's normal, but it's not what we want to do right now. Instead, shift your focus to your belly. Put your hand on your stomach and take a big breath in. Make your stomach inflate like a balloon as you inhale, drawing air in. And as you exhale, pushing air out, feel your stomach deflate. (You don't always have to put your hand on your belly when you do this; we just want you to notice how your body responds physically when you actually breathe deeply.) There are different views on this, but we've found that inhaling and exhaling through your nostrils as opposed to your mouth is more effective, because you will have better control over the flow of your breath. Now try doing it again, and see if you can slow the whole cycle down by bringing even more air into your stomach this time, inflating the balloon even more on the inhale and exaggerating the deflate (by pulling those sexy abs toward your back).

That's probably the deepest breath you've taken all day. How did it feel? If it felt good, try it again while sitting tall with your back straight and your feet flat on the ground; it will be even more effective. When you're not hunched over, more air can flow in and out of your body, and that good feeling gets even better. Your breath can ground you. It takes you back to the very reason you are alive. It focuses your attention inward instead of outward, which means you are relying on yourself to find that brief moment of peace, not anything in the external world.

Here are a few things you can focus on while deep breathing, instead of on whatever is stressing you out:

- Your belly inflating and deflating like a balloon.
- Slowly counting to four while you inhale, and counting down from four as you exhale. (Use whatever number works for you.)
- The air moving in and out of your nostrils.
- A mantra that you repeat in your head on the exhale—maybe even something like *Let that shit go*.

Once you've mastered the art of taking a deep breath, you can do it anywhere. It's a fantastic tool to wield when your chatty mind has the best of you or even when you just need a moment. And the best part is that you don't need anything but yourself and a few seconds to enjoy its benefits. Take a deep breath when you reach the breaking point in an argument and you're ready to explode with frustration. Find a few seconds to sneak one in right before you give a speech at your cousin's wedding or when you're about to tell a friend that you can't make it to her birthday dinner. Pause for a few seconds and breathe deeply. Or you can simply take a few belly breaths on a regular Tuesday afternoon when you're craving a moment of calm.

Taking a deep breath is also a great way to get your mind off autopilot. When you suddenly notice that your monkey mind is on its seventeenth branch and it's making your heart race, use your observing mind to recognize what's happening and then take a dee-e-e-e-e-e-e-p breath. This is also a good tool to use first thing in the morning. Taking a few deep breaths right after you wake up, before you're even out of bed, can put you in a state of calm and set a good vibe for the rest of the day.

No time for twenty minutes of relaxation? No problem. Spend fifteen seconds breathing deeply, and feel your stress melt away.

Find Peace While You Chew

HERE'S ANOTHER WAY you can work that observing-mind muscle and learn to stay in the present. And—bonus—you get to eat while doing it.

All too often we shovel food into our mouths without thinking. We eat breakfast on the go or while we're scrolling through the news of the day. We devour lunch while we're studying for an exam or in front of our laptops. By the time dinner hits, our phones are face up on the table or we're negotiating the consumption of that last Brussels sprout with our kids, who claim to be too full (but who we know could mow down a foot-long chocolate bunny, no prob).

Are we ever actually *just* eating?

Being in the moment while you eat can make the process that much more enjoyable and yummier. And there are several additional benefits. First, because you'll be more in tune with what your body is telling you, you might be less likely to chomp down more than you need. When you reach for your forty-seventh chip, you'll almost be able to hear your digestive tract moaning in agony. Second, you can enjoy an extended period of eating-induced bliss several times a day—without making a single change to your routine. Every time you sit down to eat is an opportunity to be present, and an opportunity to change the narrative of your thoughts, even if it's just for a few moments. Third, your food may just start to taste phenomenal. Maybe the same breakfast you've been eating for the past year will suddenly start to taste different. Maybe you'll experience a broader range of flavours, which burst in your mouth with each bite. Last, perhaps you'll be more appreciative of where your food came from. Was it a talented chef at a local restaurant who pieced it together, or you? And what about the farmer who produced those ingredients?

The trick is to eat your way through a meal with a heightened sense of awareness. Depending on how much time you have and how comfortable you are with the process, you might choose to pay attention for only the first couple of bites, eventually working up to an entire meal. But regardless of how long you are able to maintain your focus, you'll feel more relaxed after eating.

Let's try it.

Grab a piece of milky-smooth chocolate, or a sweet mandarin orange, or an organic kale chip—whatever floats your foodie boat. For our purposes, we'll play this out with a piece of chocolate.

Start by taking a moment to think about where the chocolate came from. Think about the farmer who planted the cacao tree and the person who plucked its pods, and then maybe all the people in the manufacturing plant who processed and packaged it for you.

Now consider each of your senses.

- **Sight:** What colour is this piece of chocolate? Does it have speckles, bubbles, or anything imprinted on it?
- **Smell:** Put it under your nose and take a whiff. Sweet? Salty? Coconutty?
- **Touch:** What is the texture of the chocolate? Where are its grooves or dips? Or maybe it's flat and smooth.

- **Taste:** Slowly put the chocolate into your mouth and put your ten thousand taste buds to work. Be aware of all the flavours that come at you and how your mouth starts to salivate.
- **Sound:** Pay attention to the crunching or chewing as you eat.

Be aware that as you slowly investigate and eat the chocolate, your chatty mind might speak up: *Why am I doing this ridiculous exercise? How will this ever help me?* And you might find yourself frustrated by the process of eating in a new way: *This is brutal—can't I just eat this already?* That's fine. Consider each of your thoughts. Let them come and go. As much as possible, use your observing mind to bring your awareness back to the chocolate.

Do this exercise on several occasions, and over time you'll notice that your thoughts might shift as you eat. You may have more moments of calm in which you focus on your food instead of that chatty mind.

Instead of focusing on: *How on earth am I going to get that project done by Friday?*
It's: *Look at all the markings on this apple. It's like it was painted by Van Gogh.*

Instead of focusing on: *My phone bill has been out of control lately. I need to look into that.*
It's: *This butternut squash soup tastes so fresh and wholesome. I gotta look up a recipe and try to make it myself.*

Instead of focusing on: *I have no idea how I'm going to handle seeing Phil tomorrow.*

It's: *I wonder who picked this delicious avocado. And who the truck driver was. Or did it come by plane?*

Of course, there's no need to be completely present for an entire meal every single time you eat. But once in a while, get cozy with your food. You'll wonder where your taste buds have been all your life.

Learn to Actually Listen

You know what we're talking about. You're out for dinner with your girlfriend and catch a glimpse of a nail-biting March Madness matchup on the TV that is conveniently situated above her head—and miss her telling you she might get promoted. Your mind wanders into the stress pool of work as your best friend reveals the details of his latest side-hustle idea. You're deep into dissecting every single moment of last night's hot date when your boss asks for your opinion in a meeting.

Cue sheepish tone: "Sorry, what did you just say?"

There's a difference between hearing and listening—and it's connected with what we've been talking about in this chapter: staying in the here and now. Hearing is generally associated with multi-tasking. You can hear and do other things at the same time. For example, you might hear the music that's playing in the background while you cook dinner, or you might hear the TV droning on in the other room while you check your email. Listening, on the other hand, demands focus. Speaking with another person requires you to not just hear the sounds coming out of their mouth but to process what they are saying. With listening you need your ears *and* your mind.

Listening—when it's done closely and intently—will make a huge difference in your relationships. At worst, you'll find you don't receive the silent treatment from your partner quite as often because they won't feel slighted or ignored; and you won't feel like a bad friend for having to admit that your mind was somewhere else when your buddy revealed his side-hustle action plan—which, by the way, he was super-excited about. At best, your relationships will flourish and intensify because you are more attentive. And when you are more attentive, you ask more questions, you're more engaged, and you might even become more compassionate.

Listening will also keep you in the present moment, and when you're more present, it's harder for chatty-mind thoughts to seep through. The next time you have a conversation with someone, pay attention to where your mind is. You might find that you're only half listening while you drift off into other thoughts or even wonder what to say next. Without realizing it, you might even find that you've started to use your phone as they're talking.

So, give this a shot: Instead of allowing your mind to dart off in different directions, try to simply Focus. On. What. They. Are. Saying. It's not as easy as you might think. While others are talking, your chatty mind loves to layer on your own experiences and consider how the topic relates to *your* life.

You might have noticed your mind performing this type of mental gymnastics the last time you spoke with a friend or co-worker about their latest vacation. If they're telling you about their trip to Thailand and you've already been, you might instinctively want to jump in and tell them about what you did when you were there. (There's a time and place for that; it's just not after the first few sentences of them telling you about their trip.) The next thing you know, you're lost in your own thought bubble, remembering how it felt to lounge on that beautiful white-sand beach with the sun beaming down on you and not a care in the world.

But, you're thinking, *reminiscing about my trip to Thailand is a good thing, isn't it?* It's true that this particular trip down memory lane isn't going to send you into a negative thought spiral (though when your friend clues in that your mind is back on the beach, they might feel as if you're brushing them off) but allowing your chatty mind to take off on its own personal journey can be stress inducing, especially when it comes to intense matters that might trigger you in a negative way. Actively listening can be a tool for staying out of your own head and learning to let that shit go.

Nina's best friend for life was undoubtedly her mom. They travelled the world together, had dinner dates on the regular, even got to a point where they timed their commutes into work so they could talk for the entire hour (obviously safely, using Bluetooth).

In 2012, Nina's mom was diagnosed with ALS—amyotrophic lateral sclerosis. Life became pretty torturous for Nina as she watched her mom slip away over the span of two years. She passed away when Nina was a few months pregnant. It was a polarizing time. Nina was eagerly anticipating the arrival of her first child but also dealing with the intense grief of losing her mother. Becoming a mom without having a mom was overwhelming on so many levels.

As many of Nina's friends started having little ones, phrases like "My mom is coming down for the week to help out," or "I'm so grateful my mom dropped dinner off for the next few days," or "Oh, my mom's so ecstatic to be a grandma!" became difficult to hear. Not that Nina wasn't genuinely happy for her friends, and not that they were being insensitive, but her own sadness took over every time she heard them refer to their mothers. These seemingly innocent conversations became an ongoing reminder of Nina's loss.

Eventually, Nina realized that she was constantly relating the circumstances of her own life to the lives of others. When she learned how to listen without allowing her chatty mind to remind her of what she didn't have, she was finally able to move back toward living a more calming life that wasn't overburdened by loss. Of course Nina still gets triggered, which is natural and okay, but listening without adding her personal context in her own head has definitely helped.

Think about the things that trigger you. Maybe every time someone talks about their "perfect" relationship it reminds you that you haven't yet found the love of your life. Perhaps your cousin climbed to a VP role in her twenties, and you feel like a career loser every time your family brings it up. Maybe everyone but you seems able to afford a dream vacation, and you feel left behind. When you hear things that make you anxious or bring down your mood, take a moment to sort out whether it's because you're digesting what's being said in the context of your own life experiences. Instead of measuring everything you hear against whatever's happening in your world, focus on what's actually being said, and let go of how it relates to you.

And here's a bit of bonus motivation: listening at work will make you smarter. When you listen with your full capacity, you're able to respond with your full capacity—as opposed to simply *wondering* what to say to sound smarter.

When It's Too Much, Mind Dump

HEARING INSTEAD OF listening, fortune-telling, letting your chatty mind run rampant—they all sometimes make us feel as if our heads might explode. We've all been there, and sometimes it's hard to wrap your head around everything that's going on. You need to release the pressure—and fast.

One way to do that is with a *mind dump*. Basically, a mind dump involves writing down on a piece of paper (or on your computer or phone) the overwhelming or negative thoughts that are rolling around in your head. The effect is similar to taking a deep breath. It forces you to slow down your mind, and it can help you to gain perspective so you can look at your thoughts in a more constructive way. It also provides a physical space for your stressful thoughts to reside in outside of your mind. As a result, the thoughts won't swirl around in your mind as much; you've released them in some way.

Writing down the things that stress you out or worry you is kind of like writing out a grocery list. When you are preparing to go grocery shopping, you might make a mental note of the things you need. You might even repeat the list to yourself over and over to ensure you don't forget anything. But as soon as you write the list down on a piece of paper or on your phone, it no longer spins in your head.

So, grab a piece of paper and write down some of the overwhelming thoughts you might have had recently. Don't judge or edit. Just write whatever comes to you. If there's a thought you don't want to write down, it could be an indication that you need to look more closely at that particular thought or feeling. Sometimes, getting out the stuff we don't want to look at can be the most helpful.

When you're done, slowly reread what you've written and take a deep breath. Often, you'll find that when you see your thoughts in writing, they don't look as bad as you might have made them out to be in your head. You may feel more empowered to tackle them or simply process them.

You can hold on to the note or, if you really want to let that shit go, you can burn or rip up the piece of paper (deleting the list from your phone works, too).

Give the mind dump a try any time you feel anxious, annoyed, or down. It's a great way to release emotions or thoughts that have been swirling unnecessarily in your head for days.

Picture the Shit Drifting Away and Visualize the Good

ANOTHER WAY TO GET some crap out of your head is to visualize it drifting off. Visualization is a powerful tool. When you picture your stresses and worries dissipating, it helps you to be less agitated by them, as well as better prepares you to tackle whatever bullshit daily life decides to throw your way.

Studies have found that visualizing an act can sometimes be as effective as the physical act itself. For instance, Dr. Guang Yue, an exercise psychologist from the Cleveland Clinic Foundation, found that people who "visualized" weight training increased their muscle strength by 13.5 percent. This is half as much as those who went to the gym (30 percent), but it was a significant result nonetheless.

Athletes frequently use visualization to achieve their goals, whether it's hitting a ball out of the park for a home run, scoring a winning goal, or crossing the finish line first in a race. US swimmer Michael Phelps credits visualization techniques for helping him win twenty-three gold medals in the Olympics.

So how do you tap into this amazing tool? And how can it help you let go of stressors that are preventing you from enjoying the present?

First, sit comfortably and start with some deep belly breathing. When you're ready, on the inhale picture a scene that's peaceful AF. Maybe it's of the last time you were in a forest, or a stunning image of nature you saw on your Instagram feed, or just a magical place you made up in your mind. Then, as you breathe out, visualize any stress you may be feeling making its way out of you. You can picture the stress turning into black smoke and floating away, or imagine it as tiny particles that gradually dissipate. You can even give it a shape and then watch it disappear.

As you breathe in and out, imagine your worries melting away. Annual report at work? No big deal. Overbooked Saturday? You can tackle it. Ongoing issues with your neighbour? Look at that shit float away. Do this for as long you like and whenever you need to. This goes both ways: you can visualize the shit drifting off—or all the good stuff coming in. Try starting with a few minutes, and take it from there.

CHAPTER 2

Self-Love

What You Didn't Learn in Middle School but Probably Should Have

WE OFTEN THINK about love as being external. We love that sport, that restaurant, that car, that TV show, that vacation destination, that song that came on at the bar and takes us back to the days of stellar '90s hip hop. All this is fantastic, but the most important type of love to cultivate is—let's all hold hands and sing "Kumbaya" now—self-love.

One of Nina's instructors, Tanya Porter, once said to her, "If we don't love ourselves unconditionally, we won't have the capacity to love others unconditionally." Say what? At first, this made Nina super-uncomfortable. Maybe she didn't love herself as much as she could, but surely she loved others unconditionally. However, the more she thought about it, the more it rang true. Think about love as a glass of water. If your glass is empty, you won't have any water to pour into anyone else's glass.

When you don't love yourself fully, your love for others can be compromised by your own emotions. You might love someone because you crave their love in return, or because you have certain expectations of their love. But when you love yourself unconditionally, there's no need to expect anything back. It's loving with a whole heart, super-freely. And quite honestly, it's freakin' liberating.

Loving yourself helps to keep you on firm ground. When you start to practise self-love, the chatty asshole in your head stops talking so much, and you begin to get to know yourself better. This can help you in a couple of ways: you can make more informed decisions about what you want and need, and you can avoid taking external feedback or comments too seriously. At the end of the day, you just start to enjoy yourself more. And that's an awesome thing, because guess who you get to spend the rest of your life with? The amazing you.

When Kate kicked off her mission to find more peace, she was so inspired by all the wisdom she was reading that she felt like she was having one of Oprah's "aha moments" every single day. Revelations like *Of course self-compassion for others and self is the key to happiness!* Or *That's so true—I should definitely treat my worries like a mother would a crying child.* It occurred to her that self-love is something she should have been taught at a young age. Why hadn't anyone taught it in grade school, or at least high school and university? The more she thought about this gaping hole in her education, the more it kind of blew her mind. Because this shit's important.

Of course, some people do learn self-love along the way. Maybe they have parents who teach them, or a friend who recommends a life-changing book. But it wasn't part of Kate's curriculum up to that point. Knowing how to be less of a jerk to herself could have been helpful as she finished school and prepared for her working life.

When Kate went to New York after graduation to work for a global ad agency, she had a difficult time adjusting. She was extremely hard on herself. Negative thoughts flew through her mind day in and day out. She was an account executive, a role that required strong attention to detail, which wasn't her strength. At that time, her ability to converse nicely with herself was weak. She would arrive at huge, sweeping generalizations like *I'm a terrible at this*, *I'm not smart enough*, and *This job is too good for me*.

Now, part of what she was saying to herself was true— Kate wasn't the best at her job—but to say she was blowing things out of proportion is an understatement. She wasn't the top performer at her firm, but she also wasn't the worst; she was even promoted at one point. A little bit of self-love could have enabled her to have a chat with herself and say things like "You know you're doing amazing. You just graduated from one of the top universities in the world and were chosen from among thousands who applied for this job. Even if you don't feel great, there are many options out there that could be better suited to you."

Most of us know how to do this, but sometimes we forget to check in with ourselves. We might let the negativity run rampant until we're in crisis mode, hitting our max stress point at work, potentially resulting in tears in the bathroom or taking it out on our partner. When you get to know yourself better, you can have kind convos with yourself on the regular, and address the chatty mind. And when you do that, you realize that you're not so bad at all. Life isn't a cakewalk, so on top of everything else that's going on, why beat yourself up?

It's worth pointing out that the negative thoughts that pop into your head might not be your fault. Maybe you were told something over and over again as a child, by a parent or a mean teacher. You're also bombarded with ads that have uber-gorgeous people who make you think everyone is smiling and super-happy all the time. And, of course, everyone's living their best life on social media. Baby announcements, engagement photos, successful work updates—all of this can make you feel as if you're not up to snuff.

And so, the negative thoughts come marching in, accompanied by their perfect emotional companions: jealousy, sadness, annoyance, frustration, and a whole host of others. Now, these lovely emotions may not always be your fault, but they are your responsibility. What we mean by this is that no matter who's made you feel crappy about yourself, and regardless of how that thought came into your head, it's *your responsibility* to decide what to do with it.

The key is to look at the thought without judgment. It might be a really tough one, say, *I don't think I'm worthy of this relationship.* Hold that thought, and then use your observing mind to figure out whether it's a true statement or just something your nasty chatty mind has decided to let loose in your head (keep reading, and you'll find some exercises that can help you sort this out). Once you do this, you'll be in a better position to tackle that thought, because you've actually acknowledged it. So massive kudos to you if you go ahead and try it out, because that's no easy feat. Seriously, this is one of the hardest steps!

As one of Kate's inspirations, Jay-Z, says, "What you reveal, you heal." It's not easy to reveal the shitty things we might be saying to ourselves—it's sad, hard, and a struggle at times. But once you acknowledge those things and release them, a big chunk of your healing has begun. And that's what this chapter is about: revealing the negative thought patterns that have been kicking around in your mind for years without you even knowing it, and replacing them with something so much better: self-love.

The Records You Play

If you hang around a jerk for a long time—one who keeps saying things like "That's not funny," "You're so awkward," and "Get it together"—you might start to believe what they're saying. If you do have dick friends like that and you haven't already done so, it might be time to eject them from your life. Funny thing is, you might have sent them packing fifteen years ago, but those things they said still pop into your head when you're triggered by something. What's that all about? Well, it's because those things are sitting in your subconscious, just waiting for their moment to pounce.

When you calm your mind—like you learned to do back in chapter 1—you'll be better equipped to deal with these nasty thoughts. Once again, we want to remind you that we're not suggesting that all negative thoughts and worries will forever disappear. What we *are* saying is that when you calm your mind by being aware of these thoughts, you'll be better equipped to handle negative thoughts when they arise, and look at them objectively (a.k.a. start to let that shit go). And from there you can start to reframe the thought by CSI'ing the shit out of the story you're telling yourself about it. Where did the thought come from? Is it true? How did it get into your head? As you investigate your thought, you might come to a conclusion about it—could be positive, negative, or neutral. It almost doesn't matter, because guess what you did in the meantime? You started to *observe* it. By chatting with yourself nicely and gently, you took a big step, one that will naturally make you feel better and allow some of the bad stuff to start floating away.

What you're basically doing here is jumping off that harsh, self-talk merry-go-round. You're letting go of the pressure to be that perfect *someone* right now (that is, be a perfect mom, the best employee, et cetera) in order for the *situation* to be better right now (that is, to be content and happier). You get to just be you, and to love the perfectly imperfect person you are.

You've got the capacity to do this. Think of how nice you are to Sanjay (your boss), June (your grandmother), or Mark (your local barista). Take that ability to be kind to others and start using it on the most important person in your life: YOU. You deserve to be spoken to like a sweet angel sent straight from the gods. Why? Because you have a tremendous amount of value and deserve to enjoy your time here on Earth.

When you don't recognize the impact of your thoughts and find yourself feeling crappy for no good reason, it could be that you're playing the "you're not so great" record on

Repeat without even realizing it. As you begin to calm your mind (and quiet the chatty asshole), you can hear your thoughts loud and clear and stop them in their tracks, and begin to be a better friend to yourself. This self-love thing is a life journey. It won't happen overnight; it might even be an ongoing practice, because things that make us question ourselves are always going to come up. That's okay. As you strengthen the self-love muscle, you'll naturally get better at it.

A word of warning: Self-love isn't all bubble baths and chill Netflix moments (though this is definitely part of the process). It's also having uncomfortable conversations with yourself, and maybe even letting go of someone or something that doesn't jibe with the remarkable person you are. That's all part of the process. When you start to get to know yourself better, you begin to know what you like and what you don't like—and it becomes easier to say no to shit you don't want to do (or people you don't need in your life) and pursue what you are meant to. It becomes easier to be happy.

Self-Love Is Selfless

BEFORE WE START kicking your negative thought patterns to the curb and introducing some much-needed self-love into your world, we need to clear up a great misunderstanding: namely, that self-love is selfish. There are many people out there who have a hard time putting themselves first, thanks to the heaping doses of guilt that have somehow gotten associated with taking care of ourselves (more on that shortly). But the truth of the matter is: self-love is selfless.

Don't believe us? Let's look at how self-love can work.

It's Sunday morning. You're still lying in bed, but your mind is racing through the day's to-do list: *I need to make breakfast, hit the grocery store, take the dry cleaning in, buy Alicia's birthday gift, make basketball-themed peanut-free, gluten-free cupcakes for Joey's bake sale tomorrow, help him finish that school project, tidy the house, and whip up some dinner. THEN I can put my feet up and dip into that wine.* Sound familiar? So, here's a question for you: Why are you always last?

What if, instead, you started your jam-packed day with a trip to the local café, where you grab a latte and read a stellar book for thirty minutes before you hit the grocery store? How do you think the rest of your day would go? Instead of waking up and potentially jumping into anxious mode, you'd be doing something small for yourself that would have a positive impact on the rest of your day. Self-love is not about escaping the things you need to do or even pushing them off until the next week. On this particular Sunday, you are still going to tackle your to-do list; you're just going to give yourself a sweet little breather first.

Grabbing that bit of me time will get you into a calm and happy zone, which will have a trickle-down effect on the rest of your day. You'll be able to go with the flow if the dry cleaner happens to be closed or there's no coconut flour left and you need to look up a quinoa-flour cupcake recipe, instead. And you might be less inclined to snap at Joey when he decides to practise his drumming, or freak out at your partner for not defrosting the chicken. Why? Because you gave *yourself* some love before giving it to everyone else.

That was a single-day sample. Imagine if you made sure your cup of love was full on an ongoing basis? You wouldn't constantly be trying to give and give and give while running on empty. Trying to give when your cup has only a few drops left leaves you frustrated, exhausted, and fed the fuck up. You become annoyed at the world at the drop of a hat. But when you make sure you fill your cup before anyone else's, you'll feel lighter and happier—and you'll approach life from a place of *wanting* to give, not *having* to give.

If you don't have time for a thirty-minute coffee break to start your day, try a different approach. Fill your cup by doing little things for yourself throughout the day—like taking a few belly breaths in the morning before anyone wakes up, calling your bestie on the way to work for a quick chat, or buying yourself some essential oils.

Self-love is selfless because the universe is a happier place when you love yourself first. When you love yourself, you remove some of the clouds we talked about in chapter 1 and make it easier to access the sweet sunshine that lives within you. And when you can tap into that sunshine—and the moments of calm it brings—your whole day gets better.

Ditch the Self-Love Guilt

LET'S JUST AGREE to get rid of the self-love guilt already. Guilt is a horrible emotion. Actually, it's a waste of an emotion, because it's entirely self-inflicted: *I should have finished that deck last night. I wish I had more time to talk my friend through his troubles. I work too much and don't spend enough time with my partner. I don't work as hard as other people in my industry.*

With your chatty mind taking you on a constant roller-coaster ride, there's no need to add guilt to the mix. That's like asking you to not wear your seat belt *and* keep your hands up as the coaster whips through its peaks and troughs. Why would you do that to yourself?

Here's a different approach: When your observing mind realizes you're feeling guilty about something—particularly if that something happens to be treating yourself to a bit of self-love—give your chatty mind a "Shut the fuck up." Straight up. There's no need to water this message down.

Nina's mom always used to say, "Do your best and leave the rest." Preach. All we can *do* is our very best. We can't intellectually, emotionally, or physically do more. You can't possibly give everything 110 percent. So, use your judgment. If you know you're being the best employee, parent, friend, or teammate you can be, then leave it at that. And feel good about it to boot.

When you get rid of the guilt, you'll find being in the moment (and all the good stuff that comes with it) that much easier. So, the next time you're at the spa or out with your friends, just enjoy it and let the guilt shit go.

We're Assholes to Ourselves

NOW THAT THAT little issue is all cleared up, let's get back to those negative thought patterns that often plague us. It's entirely possible that you have no idea just how horrible your internal dialogue can be. Some of us, often with great difficulty, have let go of toxic people in our lives. It's a good step to take, a necessary step, but it's not enough. A dangerous type of toxicity can lurk closer to home. Have you ever stopped to think about how toxic *you* can be to yourself?

It's in the little things. What happens when you post something on Insta that doesn't immediately get tons of likes? Do you find yourself thinking, *Nobody likes it. I knew this photo wasn't that good. Why don't I get as many likes as Simi?* Have you ever spoken up in a meeting, totally confident in what you were about to say, only to have it not come out quite right? *I'm such an idiot. Why did I even bother?* What about when you look in the mirror? Is your first thought a negative one? *I need to lose weight. Age is starting to catch up with me.* Or just a downright *I'm so freakin' ugly.* Toxicity can also come in future forms. Your friends are coming over for dinner; you're running late, grabbing the ingredients and thinking, *Shit, I always scramble, and then the dinner is never good enough.* Or maybe your first emotion after you swipe right is *This girl is so not going to dig me.*

Of course you're going to have negative thoughts about yourself from time to time. That's totally natural. Sometimes negative thoughts can motivate us to make a positive change, or allow us to realize we need to change our thinking, or both. But look at it a little more closely:

How often are those negative thoughts cropping up, and what are they preventing you from doing? More importantly, who are they preventing you from being?

Once you start paying attention to your negative autopilot, you'll likely realize there's a bit of a broken-record thing going on. Your chatty mind tends to pipe up with the same thoughts, or types of thoughts, over and over again:

- *I'm not good enough.*
- *I'm not attractive.*
- *I'm not smart.*
- *I'll never get my finances in order.*
- *I suck at relationships.*
- *I'm not worth this success or love.*
- *I'm a terrible_____* [*friend/parent/son/employee/ et cetera . . .* fill in the blank].

The sneaky thing about these negative thought patterns is that they are often subconscious. They're so embedded in you that you sometimes don't even realize you're thinking them.

And as we mentioned, they've likely been around for years, even decades. They might stem from something a parent said to you, or simply the way they made you feel. Maybe that parent was always dismissive (instilling in you a lack of self-worth), or compared you with someone else (making you feel not good enough), or held you up to some ridiculous standard (which has turned you into a control freak or perfectionist). It's not their fault, though; they didn't know any better. They are wired based on how they were raised. Besides, this is not about the blame game. And parents aren't the only source of negative thought patterns. They could have come from a sibling who always criticized you, a nasty coach who made you feel an inch tall, or a shit friend who pushed you down in order to pump themselves up.

Once you start to tap into your observing mind, you'll begin to notice something. A lot of the negative you say to yourself about yourself:

a) probably didn't come from you; and
b) isn't true.

That's an important first step. But things will really start to improve when you ante up the self-love and realize, *Fuck, yeah, I'm pretty great.* Self-love is one of the best tools we have for fighting back against negative thoughts. If negative thoughts can fill your mind, why not the opposite? Why not dispute whatever your chatty mind is going on about; or even better, crowd out those negative thoughts with reminders of how fab you are?

Reality-check time: We're not suggesting that everyone constantly tell themselves they're perfect or big themselves up into something they're not. That would produce a bunch of emotionally coddled, potential cocky assholes unaware of their weaknesses. But everyone deserves to love themselves. Unconditionally, flaws and all.

Sure, you're going to fall off the wagon now and again—and that's okay. Self-love gives you a bit of a break from that shitty, exaggerated negative self-perception autopilot and allows you to start changing the thoughts and emotions that feed it. Sounds good, right? So, here's how it's done.

You Said Whut???

THE FIRST STEP in breaking your toxic thought patterns and making some room for the delicious self-love you need is to be *aware* of what you're telling yourself. What *are* the recurring thoughts swirling around in your head?

You may think it's your action-packed day that leaves you exhausted, but the mental tirade you subconsciously unleash on yourself is likely the bigger culprit. Remember back in chapter 1 when we talked about toddlers and their amazing, unending energy? Sure, that's partly due to their age, but they also love themselves unconditionally. They don't know any better. Mentally, they are free and always in the moment, which means they aren't wasting energy on any of the bullshit that can suck the life out of us older human beings.

You can tap into a bit of that freedom by getting a handle on the negativity that's weighing you down. Start a list of your negative self-thoughts (if you're having trouble getting started, see page 60 for some fun examples). You might begin with just two or three. That's fine, but don't stop there. As you go about your week, try to catch yourself when a negative self-thought creeps in and then add it to the list. Use your observing mind to make yourself *aware* of the not-so-nice things your chatty mind loves to tell you about yourself. Also, make a note of the thought patterns that are *constantly* recurring—the ones that crop up, say, when you look in the mirror, or when you're prepping for a big gig, or just in general.

You can also start a second list: one that includes the emotions associated with your negative thoughts. You'll know what these are; after all, you're used to feeling them. A few examples: sadness, fear, victimization (Nina's specialty), anger, anxiety, panic, worry.

As you're writing your lists, take a moment to reflect on what happens when you think these negative thoughts or feel these emotions:

- What do these thoughts or feelings do to you physically? (Racing heart? Shallow breath? Low energy?)
- How often are you having these thoughts or feeling these emotions? (Every week? Every day? Several times a day?)
- When do these thoughts or feelings occur? (As you talk to a certain person? Before bedtime?)
- What are these thoughts or feelings stopping you from doing or achieving? (Success? Calm? Happiness?)

Writing down and analyzing your negative inner thoughts and feelings may not be a ton of fun, but the exercise will make you realize what an asshole you can be to yourself. We once did a workshop in which a marketing director realized that if anyone in his life talked to him the way he talked to himself, he would cut those people out of his life!

Maybe you've had a similar realization. If so, you're off to a terrific start. But you're not done yet. You need to follow up, to push ahead, to keep going. And you can do that by transitioning from a Negative Nancy to a Positive Peggy.

Shift Thoughts from
Negative Nancy to Positive Peggy

So now that we're aware of our negative thought patterns, let's do something about them. Go back to the list of negative thoughts you made in the last section. Now write out a positive replacement for each one. What does a positive replacement thought look like?

Negative thought: *I am dumb.*
Replacement thought: *I have a university degree and am doing well at my job.*

Negative thought: *I am fat.*
Replacement thought: *I am a curvy goddess.*

Negative thought: *I am not worthy of love.*
Replacement thought: *There are a ton of people who love and care about me, and I am totally worthy of it.*

Before you get going, here are a few caveats and rules:

1. It's important to remember that the intent of a positive replacement thought isn't to make you complacent. It's not meant to encourage you to sit back and accept things you can change. For example, if one of your negative thoughts is *I suck at my job*, your replacement thought might be *If I wasn't good at what I do, I wouldn't have got promoted*, or *This role doesn't feel right anymore; I'm going to*

make a change. A replacement thought can absolutely be action-oriented.

2. Do *not* suppress emotion. *You need to let that shit out before you can let that shit go.* If you're having a rough time or have just had a shit-day, acknowledge it: cry it out, work it out, talk it out, sweat it out. There's no need to revert to a replacement thought, when what you really need is a good release. What we're trying to address here is the autopilot negative thinking that's been taking over for years.

3. Where it makes sense to do so, start your replacement thought with *I*. For example: *I am smart. I am worthy. I am good enough. I am beautiful.*

4. This is not about coddling yourself or telling yourself shit that ain't true. Being honest with yourself is always the way to go, but don't badger yourself over and over again for not being a perfect human.

There's no need to come up with replacement emotions, because as you change your thoughts, the emotions associated with them will naturally shift, as well.

Let's play out a scenario to see how this works.

Say your negative thought is *I'm a bad mom*. Here are two replacement thoughts to consider:

1. Standard response: *I am a great mom and I'm doing my best.* (Some backup, if you need it: Being a mom is fucking hard. You have to juggle parenting, house stuff, being a partner or single mom, daugh-

ter, and friend, and, on top of all that, kicking ass at work. Don't be so hard on yourself, girlfriend.)

2. Action-oriented response: *I'm going to make quality time a priority.* In this case, maybe you carve out time for a special one-on-one activity with your child every so often. Or perhaps you spontaneously forgo piano practice one night and get some together time by surprising the family with a dinner out.

As you incorporate Positive Peggy–thinking, remember to accept that you won't be great at everything. And that's totally cool. You can't always be firing on all cylinders. Maybe your house isn't always spotless, or your kids eat a shit-dinner from time to time, or you meet that deadline on Friday at 7 a.m. instead of Thursday at 5 p.m. It's all good. Why are you holding yourself up to a ridiculous standard? Do you know anyone who actually does it all? (Side note: Nina's aunt Sweety once said to her, "What is this ridiculous thing your generation says about being a 'good mom'? When we were moms, we were just that—a mom, not a 'good' mom or a 'bad' mom or a 'helicopter' mom or a 'tired' mom. We were just moms!")

Going forward, when your observing mind catches your Negative Nancy chatty mind spewing out absolute crap, combat it with a Positive Peggy replacement thought. It might feel mechanical at first (*But I don't* feel *worthy*, or *I don't* feel *smart*, or *I don't* feel *like a good mom*, et cetera), but slowly those negative thought patterns will start to break down—which will have a profound effect on your self-love and, of course, your happiness!

You're Being Viewed
Through Multiple Lenses

AS WE'VE SEEN, one of the worst things about the negative thoughts that bring us down is that, oftentimes, they aren't even true. Have you ever been in a situation where you say, "I look terrible in this dress," and someone responds, "Are you crazy? You look gorgeous!" What about "I played an awful game last night," and your teammate says, "You killed it! We wouldn't have gotten so close to winning without you." Or maybe you've just performed a few tunes. You step off the stage saying, "That was one of my worst performances," only to have a good friend in the audience assure you that you "rocked it up there!"

We know you've heard this before, but it's worth repeating: we're our own worst critics. We're all for self-improvement and giving yourself a good ass-kicking once in a while, especially if it serves as self-motivation, but to be constantly badgering yourself is just not cool.

The thing is, our self-perception is just that: perception. And everyone has a perception of you, so who's to say who is right and who is wrong?

Let's pretend that you live in a town with a town square, and in the middle of that square stands a sculpture of seven mystical unicorns. Gathered around the sculpture on this totally make-believe day are ten super-talented photographers, each of whom is allowed to submit one picture for an upcoming show. Once developed and framed, each picture will be absolutely beautiful in its own regard but completely different from the others. One might be a panoramic shot of the entire sculpture. Another might be focused on the rainbow unicorn that inspired the photographer. And another might be a close-up of a single unicorn horn. Each photographer will come at the assignment from a different angle.

Similarly, everyone sees *you* from a different angle, through their own lens. To your kids, you're the rock-star dad. At the gym, you're that sexy meathead. To your partner, you're a sweet teddy bear. And at work, you're a jerk to some and a freakin' genius to others. Through your own lens, you're a stellar dad who could stand to bulk up a bit more, who treats your partner really well, and is nothing special at work.

Which version of you reflects the truth?

Our sense of judgment is derived from our own experiences. Hate spinach? It could be that your mom used to make seven-year-old you eat every last bite before you could leave the dinner table, even though it was your least favourite vegetable. And adult you goes to a dinner party and is put off by delicately wrapped spinach in filo pastry. That same conditioning—ancient or otherwise—is at work in people's judgments of you. Their own pasts have shaped their current opinions and likes. Maybe someone feels really close to you after only a few interactions because you remind them of their sister. For that very same reason, maybe someone else can't stand you. Or maybe someone thinks you're hilarious because your jokes remind them of their uncle Ted, but someone else isn't a fan and finds your jokes offensive.

And this judgment thing ain't a one-way street. It's also at work in how you perceive others. Have you ever met someone you initially couldn't stand, only to eventually realize that they're actually totally cool, and you get along really well? Your initial judgment was based on your own lens and biases. Perhaps their mannerisms reminded you of a guy you found rude in university. But then you got to know them better and realized they weren't like that at all.

And get this: younger versions of yourself might even have biases toward present-day you. Kate recently got into mushroom hunting, and she knows for sure that her twenty-year-old self would have judged that too "granola." Current Kate doesn't care. She thinks mushrooms and nature are fucking miracles, and will proudly mushroom-hunt while snacking on granola.

What we're saying is that people's thoughts and judgments of you come from different vantage points and more often than not don't really have much to do with you. On some level we all know this, but it's easy to forget, and even easier to get offended or to judge what is going on in the moment.

The important thing to remember is that the perception you have of yourself isn't up to Uncle Ted's son, since you can't control what he thinks or why he thinks it. It's up to you. Only *you* have the ability to look at the thoughts you have about yourself, question them, and decide what you want to do with them. And that's why shifting your self-judgments to something more positive or neutral can have a powerful impact.

Practise at the Dinner Table

HERE'S A CHEEKY WAY to become more aware of the many versions of you. Next time you have dinner with your extended family, take a moment to think about how each person perceives you.

The sweet doll your grandmother sees when she looks at you is probably far from your stepbrother's perception; in his eyes, you're a bit of a tyrant. Your aunt might have an issue with your progressive outlook, while your uncle finds it refreshing.

You can do this anywhere: around the boardroom table at work, in the change room after practice, at the neighbourhood dog park. The more you do it, the more you'll come to realize that everyone has a different perception of you—and that's okay. You can't control it. It's also important not to take it upon yourself to make up stories and figure out why certain people see you the way they do. That's a complete waste of time and energy and, quite frankly, a losing proposition. You'll never know why they are the way they are, so don't get hung up on it. Just know that you are your own sweet-ass unicorn—and that everyone is snapping their own pictures of you.

Let that shit go, and remember, the only lens that matters is your own.

Negative Thoughts Have Impact

LET'S PAUSE HERE for a moment and delve deeper into the secret life of negative thoughts. We know they don't do any favours for your mental health, but could it be that negative thought patterns are even more toxic than they seem on the surface?

Dr. Masaru Emoto was a Japanese researcher, photographer, and entrepreneur who wanted to prove that words and thoughts had an effect on the molecular structure of water. Throughout the '90s, he conducted a series of experiments. He took water from the same source and put it in separate bottles, and then he labelled the bottles. There were many bottles and many labels, but here are just a few:

- Love and Gratitude
- Peace
- Thank You
- You Disgust Me

But Dr. Emoto did more than just label those bottles: he put the *intent* of the label into each bottle, too. He showed pictures, played music, and offered prayers to the water, in accordance with what it said on the bottle.

Side note: Did you know that only a very tiny percentage of your communication comes via words? The rest is in the tone of what you're saying, or is completely non-verbal. Your facial expression, body language, eye contact, posture, and, importantly, *intent* are all factors in how you communicate. This is why two people can say the exact same thing to you and it can *feel* entirely different. It's because the intent and emotion behind the words are different. For example, both your mom and your ex could say, "Congrats on purchasing your first home!" Mom's words would probably come out all ecstatic and proud, while your ex's . . . well . . . there might be a tone of bitterness at play. And if the same sentence is said differently, you, of course, will receive it differently. #goodvibesonly.

But we digress. Back to Dr. Emoto and his experiment. After some time, he looked at the water from the bottles through a microscope. He wanted to see if words and intent had indeed had an effect on their molecular structure.

The results were astounding:

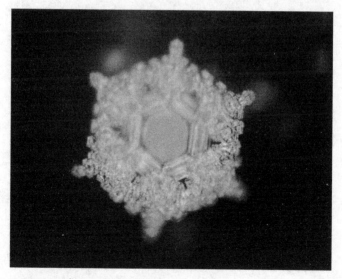

1. Love and Gratitude

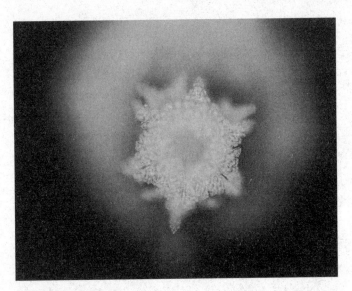

2. Peace

3. Thank You

4. You Disgust Me

The water crystals in the bottles bearing positive messages were stunning, translucent in colour and snowflake-like in shape. The water crystals in the "You Disgust Me" bottle, on the other hand, were totally disfigured and discoloured. They barely even looked like crystals.

Why are we going on about some experiment on water? Well, we felt it was important to share this with you because 70 percent of your body is made up of . . . *water*. In other words, every time your chatty mind decides to pick something off Negative Nancy's list and whisper it into your ear, you are essentially turning your molecular snowflakes into warped piles of broken-down shit.

Unfortunately, there are no physical indicators of words and intent, so you can't even see what you're doing to yourself—or how others are affecting you. If you're in a physically abusive situation, there's "see it with your own eyes" proof of your pain, which can give you the ammunition you need to get out. But when the abuse is verbal, you can't *see* it—and this can leave you questioning whether it's real. *Am I really being controlled or manipulated, or is it just me?* Although deep, deep down you know if something doesn't feel right—not just with a partner but with a friend, family member, or maybe even a co-worker—it can be hard to see what's happening without physical proof.

This is where your self-love talks (which are, of course, part of using your observing mind) can help. You'll go from a Spidey sense of *Hmm, something's up* to knowing that it's a self-love blockage: *Ah, I'm talking shit to myself again, and here's what I'm saying,* or *This person is not saying anything outright mean, but for some reason, they aren't making me feel great.*

What you say to yourself is powerful. What others say to you is powerful. What you say to others is powerful. Not just the words, but the intent and energy behind what is being said. Love, compassion, hate, anger—they're all felt. So, use your observing mind to be aware of what goes on. You just might see things you didn't see before.

Negative Thought Patterns Are like Crack

As if their stealth ability to change your molecular struc-ture isn't enough to deal with, it turns out that nega-tive thoughts and their resulting emotions are addictive. Counterintuitive, right? We hate that we think or feel a certain way, and yet we can't stop.

Believe it or not, you get a chemical rush every time you think one of your beloved negative thoughts, and after a while your brain and body get used to it. This is why you sometimes just can't help yourself. In fact, you can become so addicted to the rush that you subconsciously create situa-tions in your life that allow you to experience it.

Ever notice that people get into patterns of dating, where they choose the same type of partner, even when it's obvious that this sort of person isn't good for them? Or maybe they keep switching jobs but run into the same issues? We've been there. It's because *we can't help it*.

Dr. Joe Dispenza is a physicist who believes that each of us has unlimited abilities and the potential for greatness. He educates on how we can rewire our brains to achieve this. When it comes to negative thoughts, he explains, it's as if the cells in your body are yelling up to your brain, *SUP? We haven't gotten our fix today*. And your brain listens. It subcon-sciously makes sure those asshole cells are satisfied by trot-ting out some tried-and-true classics—you know, the ones that include (but are not limited to) sadness, anger, worry, and *You're not good enough*.

Nina was pretty klutzy in her day. Rarely would she come home without some sort of toddler-like food stain on her clothes, and she would always have scratches on her arms and legs from banging into things or falling down stairs. Her friends can attest to some stellar laughs at Nina's expense, but she didn't mind; her klutziness made her laugh, too.

Dr. Dispenza's take on this situation is that Nina subconsciously created those moments for herself. Why? So that every time a drink would spill or a pillar would be bumped into, her cells would get a nice rush, and she would say to herself, *See, you are a klutz!* She once even gently tapped the car in front of her at a red light as she was waving to friends in the car beside her. Nina assumed that klutziness was just a part of who she was—until she realized it was a pattern. As soon as she figured this out, she gave herself a talking to: *It's okay to be careless sometimes,* she said, *but I don't need to label myself a klutz.* Those tendencies still creep in now and again, which is totally fine, but these days, Nina gets a thrill from going out and *not* being the one who wipes out or walks into a glass door.

Dr. Dispenza emphasizes the importance of positive self-thoughts, even intention setting. In fact, he wakes up every morning and decides how he wants his day to go. More often than not, what he envisions for himself manifests. He claims we all have the ability to do this.

Our thoughts are important. They create our future. You've all heard the phrase "So you think, so you become." It's fucking true. So, resist the urge to take a hit of those toxic chemicals, and next time Mr. Chatty tries to tell you that you're a certain way, step up and challenge him. You just might surprise yourself.

Pretend You're in a Court of Law

ONE WAY TO CHALLENGE thought patterns is to pretend you are in a court of law. Make a case against the jackass in your mind that's saying nasty things.

Let's use John as an example of how this works. John is twenty-nine. He began his career in finance but then decided to switch to the start-up world. He's working as a VP at a tech firm, but it's been two years and the company hasn't gotten to scale. On a fairly regular basis, John says something like this to himself: *Ugh, my career is in shambles. Why aren't I in a better place at this age?*

All right, that was pretty mean, but let's first gather the evidence and make a case against it.

The evidence in review:

- John's interest in tech sparked him to leave a cushy finance job to pursue his passion.
- John's experience in finance helped the start-up attract $100,000 in funding from investors.
- John's never been so fulfilled in his career, nor has he ever had such autonomy and responsibility.
- Most tech companies like his don't make it past the first year, and the industry is known to have many ups and downs.

Standing in front of the judge once the evidence is presented, Chatty Mind (a.k.a. the plaintiff) will say things like "Your Honour, we do believe that John is indeed sort of a loser. He can't excel in start-ups, and on top of that, he's falling behind his friends like an idiot."

OUCH! The plaintiff is a real dick.

Now here comes the defence (mounted by John's observant mind):

"Your Honour, for the past eight years, John has worked his way up the corporate ladder. He's continually been promoted, and his income has steadily grown. This in itself proves that John is capable of driving revenues and is respected by his peers.

"I'd also like to point out that a career spans between forty and fifty years. These two years represent only 4 percent of that. To say a career is in 'shambles,' when we're looking at such a small portion of it, would not be a fair statement.

"In addition, John has proven his capabilities by attracting $100,000 from investors—a difficult feat for many start-ups. While the start-up has not yet scaled or reached its initial profit targets, it's important to note that most start-ups like his don't last beyond year one.

"Last and most important, John made the decision to leave his stable job for one that better matched his passion and provided more autonomy. His job is more fulfilling and challenging—which is precisely what he envisioned for himself. Thank you, Your Honour."

Did you catch all that? Not exactly the profile of someone whose career is in shambles, is it? When the defence made a case by gathering evidence and putting it into perspective, it allowed us to reframe the situation.

The next steps are up to John. Whether he wants to stay at the start-up or not is still in play, but now he's in a less emotionally reactive state and therefore better equipped to decide about his future.

If you're having a hard time serving as your own defence counsel, ask someone close to you. They'll tell you the truth and help put things into perspective. And when they respond by enumerating all the wonderful things about you, really try to soak in what they are saying. So often we get compliments and don't actually *receive* them—we tend to deflect them. For instance, when someone compliments you on how great you look in your new outfit, you might say, "Oh, I got this for thirty bucks" or "Yeah, not sure if my shoes go," instead of just smiling and thanking them. They are telling you that you have great style, so try to take in the compliment instead of deflecting it. The compliment was meant for you to receive, and accepting it with a simple "Thank you" can help boost your sense of self and give your negative chatty mind a reality check, because it's not in one ear and out the other—it's being received.

So, the next time you have a negative thought, get all lawyerly on its ass. Gather evidence, analyze it to see if the thought is true (hint: it's probably not), and make a case for the defence.

Brush Out the Grooves Your Mind Makes

IF ALL THIS is feeling . . . well . . . difficult, that's because it is. Walking around with not-so-pleasant perceptions of yourself takes a toll. These negative thought patterns are like grooves in your mind—and they keep getting deeper and more ingrained as you continue to validate them. Stopping that process by replacing the negative with the positive isn't easy work. It requires constant mental effort to tell yourself something you don't (at first) inherently believe—especially since those grooves can be pretty damn deep. Some have been with us for a few years, and others for as long as we can remember.

An analogy Nina picked up during her studies can help make this clearer. Think back to when you were a child, maybe a few years old. Your parents purchased a new home, and let's assume this was back in the glorious '80s, so it featured wall-to-wall carpet. The next step was to furnish this home, so along came the appliances, TV, beds, bookshelves, et cetera. Your parents bought a floral print sofa and a loveseat for the family room.

Fast-forward thirty years and imagine that the sofa and loveseat are still there. If you were to finally haul them out of the family room, what do you think you'd see? Grooves in the carpet from the furniture's legs—deep, sunken-in, round circles, eight in all. Even if you tried to brush up the pushed-down carpet, it would not easily rise.

Some of the belief systems you have about yourself are, like that sofa and loveseat, decades old. Vintage. This sounds cool, in a hipster kind of way, but it isn't really. All it means is that this "furniture" has been sitting in your brain's family room for so long that you've grown accustomed to the view, and the grooves created by the legs have sunk deeper and deeper into the carpet. Those grooves have been there so long, in fact, that it can take a ton of time and work to brush them out—and to start thinking of yourself in a healthier way.

Replacing your negative thoughts for a day, a week, or a month is just the beginning. It takes constant effort and awareness to change these thought patterns and create new ones. Be patient with yourself and the process. Your chatty mind is used to being in control of your self-perceptions—and clouding the lens you see yourself through—so it's going to take some time to get it in check and let that shit go. But if it means you're finally able to heal and treat yourself better, it's totally worth it.

Update Your Software

SOMETIMES IT'S HARD for us to even hear the thoughts running through our head. Your chatty mind is running so fast that you're not sure where to start. One way to settle the dust so you can see what's going on is to update your software. We'll explain what we mean.

If you've ever had a computer freeze up, you might have encountered the marble of doom—the colourful, spinning pinwheel that shows up when you've got PowerPoint, Excel, and Word open while you're simultaneously trying to watch YouTube and edit your calendar. *Okay,* you might think, *it's just here to remind me that the computer is working hard to keep all those programs running. It will pass.* If you see the marble of doom on your screen once a week, it's probably nothing to worry about, but when you start seeing it multiple times a day, you know something is up. A quick Google search will tell you that you probably need to update your software.

One of the psychotherapists who run our stress workshops, Alison Fosbery, says humans are just like computers: when too many programs are open—when we're doing a million things without rest—our bodies and our minds can start to break down. And when that happens, we, too, need to update our software.

It's not hard. You can update your software through various acts of self-care. Take a walk, have a nice long soak in the bath, enjoy a chat with a friend, or relax and watch TV. You might even want to try meditating. Whatever method you choose, a bit of self-care goes a long way toward relaxing your system and helping you be better prepared to take on stressful situations.

Treating yourself to a software update is a way to relax your system so that your chatty mind won't be agitated when challenging situations or negative thoughts come up.

Relaxing Is Productive

Too often, we feel we have to be productive all the time, even on our days off. There's pressure to check out the cool exhibition that's in town, make dates with friends, or see the band that's coming through on tour. All these activities can be enjoyable, but when we overbook ourselves in the name of having fun and forget to wind down, we end up still feeling stressed come Monday.

Kate can attest to this. Having worked in high-stress corporate jobs for most of her twenties, she felt that being productive gave her value. Getting promoted, taking on the tasks no one else wanted to do, and trying to be the most-well-liked employee made her feel good. Her desire to be busy spilled into her personal life, as well. She felt she always had to have something exciting planned for the weekend, and she would go to parties she didn't really want to attend, because she'd told someone she would be there. With her calendar so packed, she didn't have time to relax. When she did try to chill out, it was difficult to unwind, and she often felt guilty for not "doing something."

The problem with Kate's lifestyle was twofold:

1. Kate was seeking validation outside of herself (a no-go for happiness, as we've discussed); she felt that being busy meant she would be seen as more productive.
2. Kate wasn't taking time to heal her system by allowing her mind and body simply to relax.

If you, like Kate, feel you need to be productive all the time, you two aren't the only ones. These days we're bombarded with messages like "Work hard, play hard" or #hustle. We're constantly made to feel we're never doing enough.

The tricky thing is that we know having a high rate of productivity can be useful. It can help you improve your standard of living, for instance. But there needs to be a balance. By all means keep working hard, ticking things off your to-do list or being the badass boss you were meant to be. Just make unwinding a priority, too.

It may seem counterintuitive, but relaxing *is* productive. It helps to slow your breathing down, relaxes your muscles, and contributes to repairing your system when it's running on overdrive.

Think about what you do to relax, and then think about how you can bring some of those peaceful moments into your month, week, even day. Maybe this means listening to relaxing music, taking a nap when you feel like you need one, reading a good book, or just sitting around in your jammies and chilling out. Instead of seeing these activities as "lazy," try to see the productive value in them, instead.

Relaxing can help your brain calm down and be less reactive to stressful stuff when it comes up, especially negative thoughts.

Treat Yo' Self

YOU PUT A LOT of work into that dinner you made for your vegan friend. And you figured out your niece's favourite Disney character so you could put together a perfectly themed gift for her birthday. But what about you? It's easy to forget to take care of wonderful you. It's time to be self-less and treat yo' self!

Self-love is about your thoughts, but it's also about actions. Reminding yourself that you care with a tiny treat can be a nice little perk-me-up. It's also a friendly reminder that you've got your back.

Think about what you might have done for yourself yesterday. Pat yourself on the back if you did something, no matter how small. If you didn't, try for something tomorrow. Try to squeeze in a bit of self-love with something that perks you up. Maybe it's a cappuccino with whole milk instead of skim or almond, or saying no to another office get-together, or scheduling a massage. Your day doesn't need to be all about giving it away to everyone else. Don't get us wrong: happiness does come from helping others, but you also have to remember to *treat yo' self*.

Talk to the Little You

USING YOUR OBSERVING MIND to catch your negative thoughts and replace them is fantastic. It also doesn't hurt to dedicate some time to visualizing the process. It can make the experience much more powerful.

Remember that fifteen seconds we negotiated in chapter 1 for belly breathing? If that's still all you've got, that's cool. But if you have five minutes, ten, even twenty, give this a try:

Close your eyes and take a few big belly breaths. Picture yourself running in an open field as a child, a time when zero shits were given. See yourself in detail: the colour and texture of your hair, your little hands and feet, your innocent smile.

Now have your current self approach your child self. Look how cute little you were. Give your child self a big hug filled with unconditional love, and feel your child self hugging you back. Tell your little self that they are perfect just the way they are, and have your little self remind *you* that that perfection is reflected in the person you've become today.

Remember that a lot has changed since then, but kid you is still who you are at the core. Let go of all your negative self-perceptions. Within you, you have the world's love, which is all that you need.

You might think this exercise is cheesy AF. We know. It feels weird at first, but connecting with that inner child can be uber-healing.

Give Some Good Lovin' to Others

ONCE YOUR GLASS of water is full—that is, once you've given yourself enough sweet-ass love to get to an emotionally positive place—it doesn't hurt to share a bit with others. Bonus perk? Doing this can also help *you* feel good.

Here's how it works:

Shut your eyes and take a deep breath. (We know you're already a pro at that!)

1. Think of someone you are very close to. Envision them in detail—their face, their smile, the genuineness in their eyes. Imagine yourself giving them a big hug and telling them just how much you love them.
2. Now think about someone in your life who needs some love. Maybe they're going through a rough time. Picture them overcoming whatever massive battle is ahead. Think of them smiling and happily enjoying life.
3. Next, think about someone you are indifferent to: your dentist, the neighbour a few houses down, the owner of your new favourite restaurant. Picture them in a joyous state, pulling out teeth (or whatever) while feeling super-accomplished and content in their practice.
4. Now think about someone you find challenging. Put yourself in that person's shoes for a moment. Send them love and happiness and wish them well. (As hard as this is, what you're doing here is letting

those toxic emotions go, which will help you move forward. More on this later.)

5. Now that you've done a round of goodness for others, think about yourself, happy, and healthy, and achieving all that you want.

Give yourself a nice pat on the back for the work you have done, and remind yourself that you're pretty fucking awesome.

CHAPTER 3

Acceptance

*You Can't Control the Number of
Instagram Likes You Get*

So much of the shit that happens in life is out of your control. That hurricane we talked about earlier? A big chunk of that whirling mess is caused by what's happening in the world around you, not by you yourself.

Let's start small. Say you're on your way to an important meeting, but the highway is closed because of a huge accident—not within your control. The stand-up comedian you've been pumped to see is in town while you're away—not within your control. You plan a much-deserved vacation to Jamaica and it pours rain there every single day—not within your control. You can ladder up to big things, too: someone you love becomes ill—not within your control.

This is the game of life, and we've already noted that it's effin' hard sometimes. Understanding that a whole ton of stuff is out of your control is a stellar first step to living a more peaceful life.

So, what *can* you always control? Your reaction to what's going on. One of our favourite quotes comes from composer Irving Berlin: "Life is 10 percent what you make it and 90 percent how you take it." Another way to look at it is this: Life is like a really long stint at a blackjack table, with a dealer dishing out random cards. It's up to you to figure out how to play them. When absolutely nothing adds up to twenty-one, it's easy to blame the dealer or get into a funk. Remember, though, that the only person who can play out those cards is you. *You* get to choose your reaction to everything that is happening around you.

So how do you manage this? Let's go back to one of the situations we outlined a few paragraphs ago. You're in that car on the highway, knowing beyond a shadow of a doubt that you are going to be late for your meeting. The anxiety starts to bubble up inside you. You picture yourself sneaking into the boardroom and cringing as all eyes turn to watch your walk of shame. At every red light you hit, you burst out with a "Fuck! No!" It sucks—there's no denying that. But there is nothing you can *do* about it. So, instead of panicking, remind yourself that in this moment it's up to you to decide how you respond. You could focus on what's around you, play some tunes, even take a deep belly breath at every light. The way to let that shit go is to manage your reaction as best as you can and breathe through the ride. Once you get to your meeting, you'll be a heck of a lot calmer. You'll walk in, feel all eyes on you, and own it. You'll apologize, and everyone will go about their business. And who knows? You might actually be only five minutes late and enter as everyone else is walking in, too. So maybe it wasn't that big of a deal after all.

Being accountable for your emotions means you get

to be sad, frustrated, or angry. These emotions are totally okay and are all needed at some point. But the key to letting shit go is to not *stay there*—especially when the situation is beyond your control. Sure, our emotions kick in when someone is rude AF. We get mad, upset, or annoyed—and rightly so—but once you let yourself feel all of that, you need to decide how you are going to feel for the next five minutes, or hour, or beyond. Do you want to be steaming all day? You can if you'd like; that's entirely up to you. Alternatively, you could get mad, feel it, and then choose to get . . . that . . . shit off your shoulders. What do you think is going to feel better in the long run?

We'll grant that this is far from easy when it comes to the big stuff. Suddenly, with no warning, you lose your job, or something horrifying happens to a loved one. Whatever the case may be, intense shit is flying around, and it's out of your control. When this happens, it's helpful to address what is going on emotionally and ensure you're well supported. With the heavy stuff, it's almost as if you need to go through the first four stages of grief—denial, anger, bargaining, and depression, or whatever intense emotions naturally come your way. Those feelings are important when it comes to getting to the last stage: acceptance. Be gentle with yourself and honest with your emotions. Acceptance might take months, years, even decades, and that's okay. This process is not about "getting over it," because we never really get over the toughies. We just learn how to live with them. Trust us when we tell you that one of the hardest things to do in life is come to terms with something horrible that happened that was out of your control.

It Is What It Is

We've established that life is full of things that are out of our control. And realizing this, as it turns out, is uber-liberating. Once you get past the idea that you can control every single situation you find yourself in, you'll start to become less affected by whatever negative emotions that situation brings up. You'll be able to say, with more conviction, "It is what it is."

It would be hard to find someone who hasn't regretted a past action or worried about something in the future. Regret and worry are uniquely human traits. You don't see your dog regretting the container of cookies he tipped over in 2011 or worrying about what his life will be like when you decide to have a child. This type of past-and-present thinking tends to fit into some broad categories. Depressive thoughts are often associated with the past (*I wish this hadn't happened to me* or *I should have reacted differently*), whereas anxious thoughts live in the future (*When is this going to happen? How is it going to happen?*).

Believe it or not, this past-and-present thinking, which as we've said is part of your human makeup, is intended to lead you in the right direction. For example, a caveman's memories of being bitten by a snake would cause him to be more cautious of where he stepped. And planning for the future determined how he would secure his next meal. But the problem today is that we take this thinking far beyond the practical. If you're in the past or future too often, wishing that something hadn't happened or hoping that something will, where are you not? The present. The here and now. You're missing out on what's right in front of you.

Acceptance can help with that. It's a particularly effective way to deal with the need to control that's lurking behind those past and future thoughts and to get to a super-peaceful headspace. Non-acceptance—whether associated with the past, the present, a person, or an event—can be a non-productive time-suck, as well as emotionally exhausting.

How? Consider this. Most of us grew up with an idea of what certain relationships should be like. The media told us, *This is what a dad is like, a mom, a friend,* et cetera. So, what happened when your reality didn't match up? You got frustrated, or angry, or sad.

Maybe you wanted a quiet stay-at-home mom, like the ones you saw in the sitcoms you used to watch after school, but your mom was a corporate badass who never stayed home and baked cookies. You may have spent time being resentful, never realizing that she showed her love in lots of other ways. Or maybe you long for a friend who calls and texts more often, but they're so laid-back that's it's just not them. When you're together, though, you have magical chill times. Carrying around resentment and anger—emotions that spring from trying to manage how other people should behave—is exhausting. You can't control that shit, so why not let it go and enjoy the relationships you do have, instead?

Jenna and Ashley have been BFFs for fifteen years and shared all the amazing ups and shitty downs life has to offer. They've always been there for each other. Jenna is a lawyer—a real type-A personality—whereas Ashley is a creative and easygoing kind of lady.

One thing Jenna grapples with is that Ashley can be

a little loosey-goosey on the planning front. She'll forget plans or switch something up at the last minute, and she's constantly fifteen or twenty minutes late. Each time this happens, Jenna takes it as a slight, although it often has nothing to do with her and is more about Ashley's time-management skills. It's not Ashley's forte to always be on time, but she's brilliant in so many other ways that make her an amazing friend. But because Jenna is type-A, she can't help but notice these things, maybe more often than other people would.

This is what Jenna needs to remember (and the fact that she and Ashley have been besties for fifteen years suggests that she does): there comes a point where you just have to accept people the way they are and appreciate what they *do* bring to your relationship. It might not always match up with what you think an ideal relationship is *supposed* to look like, but that's okay.

Of course, you still need to set boundaries around how you want to be treated, but when you give people the benefit of the doubt and don't *expect* them to be perfect, your relationships become a little easier. And because you're focusing on what that person *does* offer, there is more room to love all the great things they bring to the table. You're no longer wasting your mental energy on unrealistic expectations. Remember, when you realize you're responsible for your own happiness, a shit-ton of pressure is lifted off your shoulders.

When you try to control how you want life to go, things can get messy. True happiness is not in having control over every aspect of your life; conversely, it's in knowing that you actually *don't* have control over every tiny detail. When you learn how to let go of control, you experience mental freedom.

Start with the small—like how many Instagram likes you get. You can't control it. Yes, you can use hashtags and tag people, but at the end of the day, the likes are unpredictable; they are out of your control. Accept it, and move on. It is what it is.

This can be a bit harder with "big picture" stuff. Often, we have a plan in mind. Maybe it's a pretty typical one—say, what society portrays as "normal": get a degree, travel, find a job, do a graduate degree, get married, have kids, blah-blah-blah, retire, travel, have grandkids. It's cool to have a plan, but sometimes life gets in the way, and things go a little sideways. Your plan may or may not look anything like the above. But it panned out in another beautiful way that you couldn't have predicted. It's when we spend too much time trying to resist—*But wait, this isn't the way I pictured it*—that we get hung up or upset.

Control Can Be Toxic

THE MORE YOU try to control things in life, the more thrown off you'll get when they don't go your way.

Keri has been picturing her wedding since she was fourteen. As she got older and found a partner, she continued to add to this vision. She knew she would walk down the aisle with Pachelbel's Canon playing, that it would be a summer wedding with a purple colour scheme, that her dress would be strapless, that a live band would play three different genres of music, and that she'd hire a photographer who knew how to take good candid shots. She was lucky enough to find a partner who let her plan it exactly the way she wanted, so off she went. The expectations escalated to the point where she was constantly picturing exactly how the day was going to go.

Keri's big day finally arrives and she's bursting with anticipation. Unfortunately, the weather is shit. She's walking down the aisle to Pachelbel's Canon in the dress she picked, but the service is indoors, not outdoors like she'd always envisioned. And then she gets a call: the band is going to be two hours late due to unforeseen circumstances, so she and her partner have to enter the reception hall to a song played off her brother's laptop instead of to live music. And then—the icing on the cake—one of her bridesmaids gets so drunk that she gets messy and passes out early on in the reception. Another good friend has to deal with her, which means they both miss most of the reception.

Throughout the day, Keri has two choices:

1. She can remember that this is one of the most important days of her life, one that she's been fantasizing about for twenty years. What matters most is that she found and is marrying her incredible partner. Knowing this, she can do her best to say "Fuck it" to all that doesn't go her way and continue to have a blast, making memories to last a lifetime.

2. She can be miserable and decide that her big day has turned into a disaster. She can try to smile and muster her way through, and then she can spend the next few months in a state of severe longing and regret that it all didn't go the way she expected.

There are a million things Keri can focus on in order to choose option 1: the fact that she's marrying the love of her life; the fact that she could afford this grandiose event in the first place; the fact that all her friends and family came out to support her. She can even appreciate all the little details that *did* go as planned. Wishing that it had gone any other way is just a waste of time and energy for Keri.

Of course, her attitude in the moment is not going to be 100 percent option 1 or option 2. Even if she is, for the most part, sitting in option 1, she might have moments where she feels bummed out. That's okay; she worked hard to make this day perfect, and she's allowed to be disappointed about a few things going sideways. But if she's mostly in option 2 territory, thinking the wedding didn't go *exactly* as she planned, it means her need to control everything has hijacked her special day.

You're probably saying, "Okay, wedding day. It makes sense that Keri would want to make a big effort to get out of a shitty mood. There's lots of money at stake, it's a meaningful day, and she would want to make the most of it."

But what if you treated *each day* as if it were just as important for you to switch gears—just as important as your birthday, or graduation day, or retirement day? What if each day when little things didn't go your way, you could just go with option 1 and say, "Fuck it—it's all good"? Imagine how much happier you would feel.

The fewer crazy expectations you have of exactly how life should unfold, the more you will be able to enjoy the good shit. The reality is that sometimes things will go according to your plan and sometimes they won't. The moment you realize this is the moment you are free from the shackles of control. Accept that you can't predict when shit's going to hit the fan, but remind yourself that you can't predict the wonderful things that will come your way, either.

It's important to note that *control* is different from *planning*. You have to plan in life. Want to go on vacation? You have to choose a destination, research flight options, decide which flight you want, find a place to stay, and pay for it. Do all that and—*boom!*—your trip is booked. All within your control. But next comes the part that is out of your control. That flight gets delayed due to an ice storm, or it's outright cancelled because not enough people purchased a ticket. You could catch your very first case of pneumonia a few days before you're scheduled to leave, or have to attend a funeral. And ouch, you didn't buy cancellation insurance. All out of your control at this point.

When things don't go your way, it's easy to get anxious or pissed off. And maybe, if it was something you really cared about, it's worth steaming over a bit. That's fair; you need time to process your emotions. But just know that how long you want to hold on to those emotions is entirely up to you.

Acceptance comes not only from accepting what is in front of you but also from accepting the emotions that come with it. Lean into your observing mind and become aware of what you're feeling. Ask yourself if whatever you're upset over is really something that means a lot to you, or whether it's just a small annoyance, not worth ruining your day over. This simple act can help you to separate yourself from whatever shitty feeling you've got going on.

So the flight was delayed and you missed the horseback-riding excursion you'd planned for the first day of your vacation. You're allowed to be pissed, but how you deal with the rest of the vacay is up to you. The moment you realize this, you can make a choice to switch to an "ah well, there's nothing I can do" mode—because nothing you do will bring back that missed vacation day, and dragging out the pissed-off-ness is only hurting you. The quicker you can get to a place of peace and acceptance with things that aren't worth giving too many shits over, the less time and energy you'll waste in a negative headspace.

Remember, our lives are made of little moments that all add up. If we choose to make each one of them awesome by shifting our mood and accepting what's in front us . . . well, that can add up to a pretty stellar life.

Cheesy Sayings Have Deep Meanings

YOU MAY HAVE heard of the Serenity Prayer, or seen it painted on a rustic wooden plaque at a decor store:

> *Grant me the serenity to accept the things I can't change,*
> *The courage to change the things I can,*
> *And the wisdom to know the difference.*

Nina first heard this verse about a decade ago. *Cool,* she thought. But one day a light bulb went off: shit, this saying is powerful. Essentially, it's telling us to break down the situations in our lives into the parts you can control and the parts you can't. Turns out this is wise advice, because this type of dissection can bring you closer to sweet acceptance.

For example, let's say you've found your dream job. It's exactly what you want to do, your team is stellar, you have good work-life balance and lots of autonomy, and you love the company, but . . . your commute absolutely sucks. You're schlepping an hour across the city twice every single day. Neither you nor the company is going to move. And you'd never leave the good thing you have going on. Given all that, the commute is not something you can control. So, getting pissed off, frustrated, or annoyed at how long it takes you to get to work is a waste of time and energy. What you can control is how you react to the situation. Instead of giving in to the negative emotions and feeling your blood boil all the way to and from work every day, why not spend your commute doing things you enjoy? If you're taking public transit, read a great book or take a nap. If you're driving, listen to a podcast that inspires you or music that pumps you up, or simply be present during your drive.

Thoughts about things you can't control are classified as *dead thoughts*. They don't propel you forward, so what's the point of thinking them? When you don't waste headspace on dead thoughts, you won't grudgingly sit on the highway each day pissed off at traffic that never fails to delay you. Granted, it is annoying, but once you've acknowledged that the commute is totally out of your hands, you'll more easily be able to focus on the good in the situation—that is, the job you absolutely love.

If you *can* control a certain aspect of a situation, by all means *do*. But if it's completely out of your hands, it's time to say goodbye to those unproductive thoughts.

To help you out with this process, here are a few examples of things you can't control, and things you can.

What You *Can't* Control

- the number of Instagram likes you get
- who is in your family
- the weather
- how others perceive you
- how other people live their lives
- your flight being delayed
- the restaurant running out of your fave orders
- whether your hairdresser is working today
- teachers going on strike
- that mean person at work

- the stock market
- the housing market
- the wireless not working
- a power outage while you're cooking
- when your friend texts you back

And, of course, some of the heavies:
- natural disasters
- someone you love getting sick
- someone you love dying
- something serious happening to you

What You *Can* Control
- your ability to get out of a situation—job, relationship, residence, et cetera
- what you decide to eat
- how often you shower
- where you go on vacation
- what clothes you wear
- what career you choose
- how to style your hair
- having tea or coffee
- who you choose as your friends
- the way you treat others
- what books you read
- how to spend your money
- what shows and movies you watch
- your attitude
- the way you perceive a situation

Say Goodbye to Dead Thoughts

IT MAY SEEM a little crazy to make a list of something that, on the surface, seems so obvious, but it's amazing how often we forget the things that are and aren't within our control. So, we find it helpful to remind ourselves now and again. And we wanted to remind you because once you have a general sense of the things you can and can't control, you can start applying that knowledge to your life. Use the Serenity Prayer as a guideline to help you assess your life situations.

Make yourself aware of the things in your life that you can't control (if you're stuck, revisit those lists we just provided). And don't limit yourself to just one area of your life. Think about your personal situations (relationships, health, et cetera) and your professional situations (your company and the people you work with, the school you attend, and so on). Then, ask yourself if you're stressing about any of those things you can't control. If you are, remind yourself that these are potentially dead thoughts, and it might be time to let that shit go.

The next time your chatty mind unleashes a heaping load of worry about something that is out of your control, call on your observing mind for backup. Use it to tell yourself that there's *nothing you can do*. Picture yourself saying goodbye to that dead thought, realizing that it no longer has control over you, and watching it drift the fuck away.

It's Neither "Good" Nor "Bad"

THERE'S A FAMOUS Taoist story about a farmer.

One day his horse, which he heavily depends on, runs away. Upon hearing the news, his neighbours come to visit. "This is such bad luck," they say sympathetically.

"Maybe," the farmer replies.

The next morning the horse returns, bringing two wild horses with it. "How wonderful!" the neighbours say.

"Maybe," says the farmer.

The following day, the farmer's son rides one of the new horses, but because the horse is untamed, the young man is thrown off and breaks his leg. The neighbours again come to offer their support. "This is so terrible!"

"Maybe," answers the farmer.

The day after, military officials come to the village to draft young men. Because the son's leg is broken, they pass him up. The neighbours congratulate the farmer, because his son can now stay and help on the farm. "Such great news," the neighbours exclaim.

And the farmer says—let's say it together now, "Maybe."

This farmer had an incredible ability to accept whatever cards life's blackjack dealer threw his way. He knew there was absolutely nothing he could do about his horse running away or his son getting hurt, so he kept his cool. He didn't worry about what was coming next. He remained calm, regardless of whether things went well or didn't.

If you can master the art of accepting things the way they are, it's easier to remain calm in the eye of the hurricane. You'll be less reactive to the stuff that's happening around you, be it positive or negative. In fact, like the farmer, you might even stop labelling things as "good" or "bad" and instead start applying the mantra we touched on earlier: It is what it is.

When we accept things the way they are and don't try to change them, a tremendous amount of anxiety is lifted. Some things suck, and that's okay. Sometimes you feel shitty about them and don't want to be positive, and that's okay, too. The more you can let go of wanting things to be different than they are, the better you will start to feel. And sometimes, as the farmer found out, there might even be a silver lining waiting for you down the road.

Maybe this has happened to you or someone you know: your Prince (or Princess) Charming calls it off after a year, kinda out of the blue. *Are you serious? Now what? I thought I was going to marry this person. I can't believe I have to go back to being single. I can't possibly swipe through any more people. This is the worst day of my life.*

You're in a funk for a few weeks or months, and then you get yourself back to a good place. Suddenly, a friend introduces you to a friend, whose cousin is super-cute and single. Before you know it, you're in an even stronger relationship. You had no idea this type of connection could even exist. You're on date seven, hanging out poolside, listening to some fab tunes, and laughing your asses off together. In that moment you think, *That breakup was the best fucking thing that could have ever happened to me.* It all came full circle.

Silver linings don't necessarily happen overnight. They can take months to show up, even years, but if you look for them hard enough, they'll be there, often staring you right in the face. Even the toughest situations have them. Tragedy, as heart-wrenching as it is, can give you perspective. It makes you looks at life differently—and cherish each moment as precious and beautiful. And, quite frankly, that is the greatest gift you could possibly ask for. Of course, not at the expense of the tragedy you've just experienced, but that's something you can't control, so why not try to find the silver lining?

Sit in the Silver

It's okay to sit in whatever shitty emotion you're feeling when a horrible thing happens. It fact, it's really important. Like we said, you need to let that shit out before you can let that shit go. Do what you need to do to address what's going on internally. But when you're ready, it doesn't hurt to take a moment to seek the silver lining. It might take years, even decades, to get to the point where you feel you can do this, but it's a way to make peace with what you've endured and perhaps give it a bit of an explanation. It can also be incredibly healing; finding a silver lining could mean that you live the rest of your life differently.

One of our good friends, Rob, had a stroke at thirty-eight. He was in great shape, played hockey regularly, ate pretty healthy, and was one of the happiest, funniest, and most laid-back guys we know. Definitely not a stress-bucket. The stroke was unexpected, to say the least. Rob ended up in the ICU. Those early days weren't easy on him; his wife, Lisa; or their two young kids. But thanks to his lucky stars, he made it through.

Fast-forward a few months. Rob—still deep in the difficult process of recovery (upcoming heart surgery, unexpected seizures, and his body still not working quite the way it once did)—was taking his four-year-old daughter, Naomi, to her first swimming class. It didn't go so well. Scared of getting her face wet and going underwater, she cried through the whole class, and kept telling Rob that she couldn't—and wouldn't—do it. The following week, her fear and anxiety were still firmly in place; her instructor called her name to come to the pool, but Naomi wouldn't move.

Instead of making her go in, or turning around and heading home, Rob sat Naomi down for what he thought would be a little pep talk as they watched the other kids swim. But one sentence led to another, and the chat turned out to be one of the most beautiful and intense heart-to-hearts this dad-daughter duo had ever had. "Promise me," he said, "that if something is difficult, you will push through and never give up. Daddy is never going to give up, and neither should you." By this point, they were both in tears. They promised each other that, together, they would never give up. Naomi wasn't going to give up trying to put her head underwater, and Rob was never going to give up on fighting for his life.

Of course, not having the stroke in the first place would have been the ideal, but that wasn't in Rob's control. So, what's the silver lining here? The conversation he had with his daughter would not have been as meaningful and deep if not for his stroke. It would have been a comment in passing—a "You really need to put your head in the water next time, honey" kind of thing. Instead, it turned into an unforgettable moment in both their lives. Not too long after, Rob had "Never give up" tattooed in Japanese on his chest, over his heart. His relationship with his kids and Lisa, and the way he looks at life, will never be the same again. He's grateful for each moment and lives with more purpose than ever, knowing how precious life can be.

Consider Malala Yousafzai—she's a remarkable example of someone who found the silver lining in her tragedy and turned it into an awe-inspiring movement. In 2012, at the age of fifteen, Malala was shot in the head by a Taliban gunman in an assassination attempt as a result of her activism for female rights. She miraculously survived, and continues to advocate for human rights and girls' education. She is the youngest recipient of a Nobel Prize (for Peace) and has been labelled the "most prominent citizen" of Pakistan. Talk about an inspiration.

Some people believe that everything happens for a reason. It's a liberating thought. We can't possibly know what the future holds, but we can have implicit trust that the universe (or whatever you want to call that blackjack dealer throwing down your cards) knows what it's doing and that your life is unfolding as perfectly imperfect as it's meant to.

A word of caution here: finding a silver lining when something sucky has happened doesn't mean that you're suddenly "over it," nor should you be. When you lose someone you love or experience tragedy, no silver lining is going to magically wipe away the sorrow and pain overnight. You may still have moments of heartache, sadness, or longing, and that is completely normal.

What the silver lining will do is provide some healing. It will offer you perspective on what's transpired and allow you to find purpose in it all. You'll spend more time focusing on the mountain you climbed as opposed to the valley that got the best of you. Your heart might feel a little lighter, and you might not hurt quite as often. You might even find that you have a new strength and deeper understanding. Like Malala's, your challenges might intensify

Embrace the Unexpected

NINA HAD AN EPIPHANY while she was talking to her cousin Avi about his relationship. He was all excited, telling her how the next ten years were going to go: "First, we'll get engaged, and then married. We'll take a few months off to travel, and then, after two years, we'll have a child. After that we'll buy a house and—" Nina stopped him in his tracks as something hit her like a ton of bricks.

She, too, had planned out her entire life when she was in her early twenties. But now, listening to her cousin, she found herself considering how the decade since had turned out. It came as a bit of a shock to realize that her thirty-five-year-old self was *nothing* like what her twenty-five-year-old self had pictured she would be. Life had unfolded in the most beautiful way, hardships and all, but not in the way she'd expected.

Back in her mid-twenties, Nina had envisioned herself climbing the corporate ladder; instead, she'd followed her passion and became an entrepreneur. She'd thought she would move to the city; instead, she fell in love with the nature trails and wild birds behind her house in the boring burbs. She'd definitely thought her mom would be around until she was a hundred; instead, she was gone when Nina was thirty-three. So there Nina found herself, completely without warning—someone her once-upon-a-time self wouldn't even recognize.

It's cool to picture how you want the future to go. Envision what you want. The sky's the limit and intention setting is a powerful tool. Plan for your future, but do so with the knowledge that it might not go *exactly* the way you expect it to go.

Life can be full of the unanticipated, so the best way to deal is to grab your surfboard and ride those crazy waves. Sometimes the tide will be calm and easy to navigate; other days you'll be working your way through a fucking tsunami, undertow and all. And the switch can happen gradually or suddenly. One day you're happily feeling the light breeze while you walk the trail behind your house, reflecting on how amazing your life is, and the next day you're told your mom has two to five years to live.

Think about what you envisioned for yourself ten years ago, and then think about your life now. It's almost certain that some things didn't go the way you expected them to go. But look closer. Are there things you didn't plan for that you're pleasantly surprised about? Make it a point to acknowledge those things and be grateful for them.

It can be hard when things don't go the way we plan, and it's important to feel whatever it is we feel (sadness, frustration, anger) when that happens. But once we've gone through those emotions, all we can do is surrender to the situation.

Practise the Art of Surrender

SURRENDER IS BASICALLY the crux of letting shit go.

Once you surrender to life, you will feel a huge weight lift from your shoulders. Unfortunately, surrendering ain't easy. It's not like you get to a point where you master the art, earn your magical shit-shield, and live the rest of your life knowing nothing can ever touch you again. It's a process, and with each life challenge you face, you'll need to learn to surrender again—over and over and over.

Surrender happens when you get to that point of acceptance we discussed earlier. When you've let go of regretting the past or wishing it was something it's not, and you've also let go of expecting the future to play out a certain way.

This doesn't mean that you say "Fuck it" and give up. Rather, you give 'er. You still run those stairs like Rocky, double-fist-pumping to your favourite pump-up tune. You push forward and go for what you want. But you do all this while surrendering to life. There's power in surrender. Because once you surrender, you have no expectations. You're putting your best out there, and whatever comes to you comes.

You've no doubt heard about people whose lives fall into place once they surrender. Like the couple who get pregnant the minute they stop trying to have a baby, or the band that get their big break after they finally decide to just play for fun. It happens all the time. Why? Because these people are no longer "forcing it"; they're letting it be. They're releasing future worries and raising their middle finger to unnecessary regrets. They're easily surfing those waves.

Expectations Cause Frustrations

IF YOU HAVEN'T picked up on this yet, here's a big reveal: expectations are a bitch. The more expectations we have of life, the more room there is for disappointment.

We all want certain big things in life, and that's fair, but the more time we spend in "expectation mode," the less time we spend in living mode. And, of course, expectation mode keeps us in the future, not in the here and now.

Expectations come in many forms. Maybe you have them about your job (*I'd better get promoted next month*), your coffee (*Can't wait for my perfectly brewed decaf-hazelnut-latte-with-coconut-milk-extra-hot*), or how others treat you (*I hope she's nicer to me next time*). But sometimes the promotion comes in six months instead of one, or the coffee isn't extra-hot, or that person carries on giving you 'tude. Let that shit go!

We're not telling you to stay if you're working your ass off and your employer is taking advantage, or to keep going to a coffee joint if they never get your order right. And we've already touched on what to do if a person isn't treating you the way you deserve to be treated. You need to practise self-love, remember? Know your worth, but loosen up on the reins a little, and just watch how happy you'll become.

Being in expectation mode takes up *a lot* of energy, and it's typically negative. If you're in expectation mode at work, for example, you won't be spending 100 percent of your timing kicking ass and allowing your natural skills and passion to flow. Nope, you'll be spending 50 percent of your time kicking ass and 50 percent of your time complaining, worried, anxious, and frustrated—in other words, in dead-thought mode. So, instead of coming up with a fresh new social media strategy, or a plan to kickstart a company-wide environmental initiative, or an update to an old, unproductive process, you're huddled in a supply cupboard, bitching to your work confidant that you haven't gotten promoted, or not speaking up in a meeting because your head is swirling with angry thoughts. That's definitely not going to get you promoted any faster.

Dialing back on your expectations will allow you to be super-content with whatever does come your way. Your energy will shift, and you'll start to attract even more sweet goodness. And when things do come through, you'll be ecstatic (*Fuck yeah, I got a promotion!*) versus relieved, frustrated, maybe even entitled (*Fucking finally, I got that promotion*).

So, stop forcing yourself to stick to some arbitrary script that you created for yourself (maybe a long time ago), and start allowing the goodness to flow to your rock-star self. Surrender to life, and accept that not everything is within your control. If you can do this—instead of resisting the things that are "off script"—you'll be amazed by what unfolds.

What You Resist Persists

HAVE YOU EVER been annoyed with someone for not doing something the way you wanted it done? (Hands up on our end!) Ever noticed how each time it happens you get a little more agitated?

There's a saying "What you resist persists." This can be applied to anything: something you're not addressing about yourself, something about someone else, something about where you are in life. You get the idea. The upshot is this: the more you resist dealing with whatever that thing may be, the more it seems to bubble up and frustrate you.

Let's take Samantha as an example. She's in month three of a new relationship. Things are going well, but she's mildly annoyed at the way her boyfriend, Tommy, reacts when she confesses her problems. For example, whenever she brings up something she wants to offload, like her prof's impossible twenty-minute online quizzes or her sister's need for the spotlight, she doesn't feel supported in the way she expects to be. Tommy listens, makes a few remarks, and offers his input, but not in the cheering tone she's used to hearing from her best girlfriends or her mother.

Now each time Sam starts to dive into an issue, she finds herself waiting to hear how Tommy responds. When it's not in the way she likes, she gets annoyed, and she immediately starts to play a particular soundtrack in her head: *He doesn't care. He's not supportive. What a dick.*

But Tommy comes from a family who (like so many) didn't talk about their issues in such an open way. It's not that he doesn't want to be there for Sam or that he doesn't care; it's just not something he's used to.

Samantha can't change Tommy. That's not to say we shouldn't give Tommy the chance to better understand how Samantha wants to be heard, or improve on how he can support her. What we're saying is, Sam can't control exactly what's coming out of Tommy's mouth when she's opening up. The more she expects a certain kind of response, the more annoyed she'll be when she doesn't get it. And the more she resists really looking at the issue (and just relies on her tried-and-true soundtrack), the more it will persist in their relationship.

Sam could keep this shit bottled up, which might lead her to conclude that Tommy's a jerk. Or she could bring it up by telling him how it makes her feel (not heard, not cared for, et cetera). It's possible Tommy has no idea he's making her feel this way. Maybe he thought his input *was* enough. But once he's aware of Sam's feelings, he can do his best to support her better. The rest is up to Sam. She can let the issue go, by keeping in mind that he's doing his best. And she can remind herself that Tommy's not her best friend, who's so good at giving advice that she should be a therapist; or her mother, who's tone is so soothing. Tommy is her boyfriend, who comes with his own set of strengths, and if they've made it to the three-month mark, there are probably a lot of things that she loves about him. She can choose to focus on them while they work together to sort out the rest.

At the end of the day, it's up to you to decide how you want to react to someone and how you want to see a situation. The more you hang on to internal assumptions (which are sometimes completely off base) and the more you resist accepting how someone truly is, the more pissed off you get. Remember that most people are doing the best they can with the tools they've been given in life up to now. This perspective can be freeing.

So, don't resist that agitating thought or the annoyance that's brewing up inside. The longer you go without addressing it, the more pissed off you'll be. Take a look at it, see what you can do about it, and let go of what you can't control about the situation. From there you can slippity-slide into acceptance—a much more peaceful place.

Stop with the Storytelling

ONE IMPORTANT WAY you can succeed in getting to that place of surrender and acceptance is to be aware of the thoughts behind the emotions you're feeling.

Let's say you had plans with a friend on Thursday night. On Wednesday, that friend finds out their favourite artist is doing a solo show on Thursday; another friend has tickets and has invited her to go. She texts you and asks if it's cool if she ditches your Thursday night plans. Ouch! Suddenly, you're feeling rejected. You think she's not making you a priority, which means that she doesn't care about you. But that's just a story you're telling yourself. The truth of the matter is that the situation has nothing to do with you and everything to do with her passion for art.

At this point, though, you can react in one of two ways:

1. *WTF! We had plans to hang out! She doesn't prioritize me, and she doesn't value our friendship. Maybe I did something to upset her.* (The storytelling approach.)
2. *Oh, awesome! I'm so happy for her! We're going to hang out on Friday, anyway, and she did just spend last weekend at my parents' place.* (The reality approach.)

Next time someone upsets you, take a moment. Sometimes, the situation has *nothing to do with you*. Of course, if someone is constantly putting you on the back burner, it's time to check your self-love. But more often than not, their actions are the result of circumstances and have nothing to do with how they feel about you.

Don't Compare Yourself to Others

You know that comparison game we play all too often? *But Daniel has his own boat, and Julie has 4K followers, and my high-school ex married a bombshell!* It's brutal—and one of the best ways you can kick yourself right out of whatever state of peace or calm you've managed to attain. Daniel, Julie, your ex—so what? You have *no idea* what people's lives are really like. They might be amazing or mediocre, or they might suck. You'll never truly know—and that's a good thing, because *it doesn't matter.*

Think about this for a minute. Don't all of our lives fall into each of these categories at times: amazing, mediocre, or sucky? No one has a perfect life. No one that you know. No one that you follow on Instagram. No celebrity, or athlete, or world leader. There's so much that goes on behind the scenes, beyond what you see on social media or hear at the odd dinner out. What's important is how you see your own life. What's important is not letting someone else's success make you feel shitty about yourself.

There are probably times in your life when you're acing it, and people think, *D-a-a-a-a-a-amn, they've got their shit together!* But you know what it took to get you there. You definitely had bumps along the way—or cliffs you had to fucking mountain-climb the shit out of to get back on top.

When you measure your baseline according to others, you are putting your happiness in jeopardy. Devin's a happy guy, with a great job and a lovely family, but he measures his financial success by comparing himself to his friend Alim. One day, he finds out that Alim made millions in the cryptocurrency market. *Boom!* Devin's self-confidence takes a nosedive. But why? If Devin is happy in his own life, what does it matter what Alim has?

One way to stop comparing yourself with others is to think about all the great things you have—and to acknowledge that there are probably people who think *you* have the perfect life. Recognize what's stellar about your life, and embrace it. Maybe it's a great relationship, or a hobby that makes you super-happy. Whatever. You've got something great going on, so embrace it. It's also worth keeping in mind that the person you're comparing yourself with may have something you want, like a crap-ton of money, but they might be envious of you because you don't work nearly as hard and get to spend so much quality time with your family. When you compare, you often focus on just one aspect of a person's life. Look at the big picture, though, and you'll realize that everyone has their own challenges. If you're wishing for the best parts of everyone's life, know that you're basically comparing yourself with someone who doesn't exist, or who only exists in fairy tales—though even Disney princesses have shit to deal with.

Remember the lists from earlier in this chapter—things you can control and things you can't? Well, you can't control the stock market, and you sure can't control what happens in other people's lives. So just focus on yourself and let the comparing shit go.

Get Grounded

IF YOU FIND YOURSELF in panic mode over something that happened in the past or about how something will go in the future, grounding yourself is one way to calm the fuck down. Even if you are experiencing what you think might be a panic attack, this tool can help. By leaning into all your senses and becoming acutely aware of them, you can get out of your swirling mind and back to the present.

Let's say your chatty mind has you spinning out of control, so much so that you can physically feel its effects: racing heart, shortness of breath, maybe even a bit of dizziness. Apply the grounding process. Take deep belly breaths as you ask yourself the following questions:

- *What do you see?* I see the side table in front of me with the lamp and books on it. I see a window and the bed I'm sitting on.
- *What do you hear?* I hear birds chirping outside and the drumming of my air conditioning.
- *What do you feel?* I feel the sheets on my bed, my pyjamas, my pillow.
- *What do you smell?* I smell the shampoo in my hair, the cream I put on my hands.
- *What do you taste?* I taste my toothpaste and the saliva in my mouth.

By homing in on your senses and breathing deeply, you're grounding yourself in the present moment and turning away from the intense chaos that your chatty mind has created. We're not saying the swirling thoughts will completely disappear, but your powerful attachment to them will subside.

Next time you're in freak-out mode and can link it back to what's going on in your mind, try the grounding process. It will take you to the centre of the hurricane for a moment and help you breathe your way back to a calm state of mind.

CHAPTER 4

Perspective

You Are Made of Fucking Stardust

ONE WAY TO mitigate the stress ride your chatty mind loves to take you on is perspective. Perspective can cultivate gratitude, and that's some powerful goodness. It can take you right out of rumination and set you surfing on a wave of stellar feelings.

We'd like to start this chapter by asking you to write out a list of things you stress about on a day-to-day basis (don't judge your stresses as you're doing this). Maybe it's finding matching socks, or figuring out what to cook for dinner, or worrying about how you're going to get through your massive to-do list. Whatever. Grab your notebook and pen or your phone's Notes app, and give it a go.

We're serious here; this is going to help you. Go for it.

Okay. So now that that's done, jot down your daily stress level, on a scale of one to ten. Got it? Awesome.

Often, we look at our stresses from a micro perspective. Think of a funnel. We tend to stress about things that are near the bottom of the funnel, the little things. No one is judging. We're all entitled to our stresses, and they're all relative.

What perspective does is take us closer to the top of that funnel. Suddenly, we're looking at life from a macro perspective—in other words, we're seeing the big picture. And when we look at life from a macro perspective, great things start happening: we start giving fewer shits about the little things; we feel as if we're on top of the world more often; and we're just happier and calmer.

When we get caught up in the micro perspective—*Ugh, I forgot my lunch at home. I have a huge project that's due. My kid won't eat broccoli without melted cheese. I haven't gone to the gym enough this week. My sister-in-law is visiting, and I need to wash the sheets*—we forget the macro. We forget what's really important in life. We don't mean to; it just happens. And it happens to everyone, all the time.

Of course, day-to-day stress is natural. We're not saying that you can't or shouldn't stress, but ask yourself how often you're stressing and what you're stressing about. Stress is on the rise, and it can be super-unhealthy, both emotionally and physically.

So, what can you do about this? How can you avoid wearing yourself out with worry? That's where perspective comes in. When your chatty mind issues you a one-way ticket to Stressland, lean into your observing mind to start thinking big-picture thoughts: *I'm so grateful that I have running water. I'm glad I'm in good health. I love my friend Aria; she's always there for me when I need her. Look at those trees that filter the air that I'm breathing.*

If you're going through something challenging in life, you might naturally and involuntarily be sitting in the macro; big life events tend to provide perspective. Or maybe you're someone who always thinks big picture. In that case, kudos to you. For the rest of us, though, macro thinking takes *effort*. It often doesn't come naturally because we're caught up in work, a relationship, or concern over when the hell we're going to do our taxes. But when we make an effort to take a big step back and be grateful for the macro, our perspective changes for the better.

Have a look back at your list of daily stresses and the number you wrote down to represent your stress level. Let's say you jotted down an eight or nine. Ask yourself if it's *really* an eight or nine, or if lots of things—way worse things—could happen before it gets to eight or nine? For a moment, let yourself think about the worst possible thing that could happen to you. *That* is a stress level of ten. Everything else is relative. Look at your list again and remind yourself of far worse things that you've been able to overcome.

When you're looking at life through a big-picture lens, your stress levels take a big step back, too. You think about everything you're grateful for and—*boom!*—life isn't so bad at all. It's actually fucking amazing. Now your stress level of eight or nine starts to feel more like a four or five. That's a perspective change in action.

Another great way to gain perspective is to use your observing mind to notice what percentage of your thoughts is focused on what you *don't* have versus what you *do* have. You might not have the latest phone, or the vacation you're yearning for, or even that gig you wanted, but what do you have? Your health? Your family? Food, shelter, water? How often are you grateful for those things? Once you start focusing on what you do have, it's easier to sit in the macro because, at the end of the day, it's all good.

Putting things into perspective can have a massive impact on your mood. And it doesn't matter whether we're talking about the small stuff (the snazzy ballpoint pen you use, your soft toilet paper) or big things, like being grateful for your family and friends or simply being alive.

Think on that last statement for a moment. Do you know that the chances of winning the lottery are about 13.9 million to 1? Pretty dismal odds, which is why many of us choose not to bother playing the lottery, but they actually *rock* when compared with the odds of being born. Author Dr. Ali Binazir attempted to quantify this probability. After running the math, he came to the conclusion that the odds of you existing are almost *zero*. It's beyond a miracle that your parents met, decided to have a kid, and that the 1 in 100,000 eggs from your mom and 1 in *4 trillion* relevant sperm from your dad collided to make you (the probability of just that happening is 1 in 400 quadrillion). If you think about it, you've already won the lottery: you're alive, and that's a miracle in itself!

And even your lovely parents can't explain why we're all here on a blue dot, floating in space. There's the big bang theory, of course, and incredible advancements in science have given us a more in-depth understanding of the world around us, but that doesn't mean our circumstances are any less miraculous. As we grew up, we were taught about the great progress humanity has made, which is astonishing. But there's so much out there that physicists, biologists, and doctors will admit to having no clue about. How often do we think about what we *don't* know?

Realizing that there's a lot you still don't understand— like what's beyond our galaxy—can actually make you feel tiny and beautiful. Just you on your own, not even taking into account all the things you *do* have.

We all go through phases where we're overly focused on the frustrating aspects of life—the project that's due, the annoying cyclist who went through the red light, the ten pounds we can't seem to shed. Your chatty mind loves these phases (it's responsible for them, after all). So, when you notice yourself caught up in the chatter, take a step back. Look at the clouds, the trees, the birds, and the miraculousness of even a squirrel. The dude is jumping from branch to branch thirty feet above the ground like it ain't no thing. As Stephen Hawking once said, "Look up at the stars, not down at your feet." If you're looking down at your feet, you're seeing only the problems that revolve around you. In that state of mind, you'll miss all the magic. And there's so much magic—around you, above you, below you. Change your lens and you'll be able to see it.

The Miracle of You

Here's a little crazy fact for you: we are literally made of stardust. A survey of 150,000 stars confirmed that humans and our galaxy have about 97 percent of the same kind of atoms. Your body is made of some of the same components as those twinkling things in the sky.

Sometimes, big things happen in our lives that remind us of what a miracle it is to be alive. Two of Kate's good friends, Dylan and Oliver, passed away as a result of gun violence ten years ago. Six years later to the day, their other friend, Andrew, died unexpectedly. The tragic events hit Kate and her group of friends like a ton of bricks. What? Why? Who? It was heart-wrenching to see the families in such sorrow. The loss was unimaginable. These were three extremely bright lights who had brought so many people together; their loss shocked and saddened us all.

There were a million things these remarkable friends taught us: how to be a nice person; not to take things too seriously; to resist gossiping; to enjoy what you do; to consider friends family; to laugh and not to stress; to always sign emails with "love you." Dylan even introduced Kate to yoga a decade ago, before it became really popular in North America. What the tragedy also taught us, in an extremely difficult way (once some of the shock and sadness started to settle), is that being alive is a sweet, unbelievable gift.

When bad things happen—especially then—we tend to step back and think big picture. We hug the ones we love a little tighter, and maybe even say "I love you" more often. We stop stressing about the small stuff.

You might experience these moments of perspective from time to time, whether as a result of a personal tragedy or because of something you read or heard in the news. It's profound, and you never want to forget the feeling. Then, all of sudden, you're back to your routine, and that macro perspective has slipped through your fingers. You're annoyed about the waiter getting your order wrong, and you get pissed off about being pissed off about ridiculously stupid shit. We all do it. That's okay—you're human. But you can cultivate those feelings of gratitude, and use your observing mind to get into macro mode any time your mind is stuck in a chatty zone. Macro will take your mind away from the minutiae and remind you of what a joy it is to be here.

In this chapter we'll lead you through some ways to get yourself into macro mode. Once you start cultivating that macro perspective, it will strengthen the more often you use it, just like a muscle. Before you know it, you'll be going from micro to macro in a snap, and experiencing more and more moments of *Fuck yeah, my life is amazing!*

Shitty things will still happen. That hurricane is never going to stop swirling, but when you see life through a micro lens, you're allowing the clouds to come rolling in and fog up your day. Switching to the macro view is another way for you to access the amazing sunny part of yourself that is filled with pure goodness, and to not get bogged down with the crap. It'll leave you knowing—deep down—that so much about your life simply rocks.

Get Cozy with the Macro

WHEN YOU ACTUALLY start to think about it, you'll realize there are a shit-ton of ways you can look at life from a macro perspective, but let's start by taking things way beyond you. In fact, let's take things way beyond humans in general. Have you ever been camping, or to a place way out of the city, and looked up at the stars? Did you see the Milky Way, maybe even the northern lights?

Next time you're in nature, channel your inner park ranger and notice the miraculous surroundings. You'll soon find yourself in awe of what you see. Here are some things to chew on:

The Universe
- The sun rises and sets in perfect order *every single day*.
- The distance between Earth and the observable universe is 46.5 billion light years.
- There are an estimated one billion trillion stars in the galaxy. That's 1,000,000,000,000,000,000,000—which is coincidentally about the same number of grains of sand on all the beaches on Earth.

The Greens
- A tiny little brown seed can grow an entire green plant with luscious red tomatoes.
- Trees carry water from their roots to their leaves.
- If you plant a zucchini seedling, you know you're going to get zucchinis, not cucumbers or peppers—it's freakin' brilliant.

The Wildlife

- A spider can make a silk web that's twenty times its size.
- Tiny little wasps can create a massive paper-like nest.
- Sea otters hold hands while they're sleeping so they don't drift apart.
- Octopuses can use their arms to smell and taste.
- Wood frogs can completely freeze in the winter and then thaw in the spring.

Crazy, right? You've heard the phrase "Wake up and smell the roses"? Well, try it. Investing brainpower into reflecting on the great mysteries and perfect order of the universe takes you *way* out of the place where your chatty mind rules, and into a place where you can really start to appreciate all the magic that blackjack dealer has to offer.

Think to Back in the Day

SOMETIMES WE'RE SO wrapped up in our day-to-day lives, running from one place to another, that we tend to forget how amazing life is here in the modern world. The appliances and technologies available to us are miraculous. From plumbing systems to planes to computers—it's endless. Keeping that in mind can help you get into a grateful mood.

Think back twenty years. We were in high school then, and using pagers (!) to notify our friends of our whereabouts. You had to find a pay phone, put in a quarter, text your friend the number of the pay phone, and then patiently wait for them to call you back. The most exciting thing we could do with our land lines was a three-way call. These days, we can call our friends halfway across the world and *see their faces*. WTF? Back in the day, that would have been considered some crazy *Star Trek* shit.

There are tons of examples just like this. Present day, if you're away on a trip halfway around the world, Wi-Fi makes it easy to stay in touch. In the 1800s, when people left the country for a job far away, they simply had to accept that they wouldn't be in touch for days, months, or years. The only way to communicate was through letters. Some parents didn't even see their children for years. Now you can text your best friend about your office crush, screenshot from their profile pic included, and receive instant feedback on how to make the next play.

Think pre–Apple Music, or even pre-Napster. Over twenty years ago, we had to wait for our favourite songs to come on the radio during the "Top 6" at 6. The second a song started, you'd quickly hit Record on your giant stereo system. This took great skill—the goal was to not end up with the DJ's voice at the beginning and end of each song. Once you created your mix-tape masterpiece, you could listen to it on your boom box, but if you wanted to find a particular song, you had to rewind or fast-forward. Now, with the click of a button, you can access any song you want, throw on your headphones, and jam out.

Fun fact: cars weren't invented until 1886. If you're a millennial, that's your great-great-grandparents' era. Now we can hop on buses, get our mangoes delivered by trucks, even fly across oceans. A trip from Europe to North America in the seventeenth century took almost two months by boat. Today, a plane can make that trip in about eight hours. Next time you're grumbling about the dry in-flight chicken, remember that you are *in the fucking air*—like, 35,000 feet above ground.

Ever heard your parents say, "You know, back in the day ..."? When they break that one out at the next family dinner, pause and get curious about how they used to live. Maybe ask a few questions about how they made phone calls, got to school, or listened to their favourite tunes. It's really cool to think about how far we've come. Take a moment to be grateful for the hard work of previous generations and how it's helped to create the amazing accessibility of life today. You can even write down the technologies you're grateful for—the ones that help you in your work and your personal life. When you're having a bad day, one in which it's difficult to find the macro view, you can take out this list and use it to help adjust your lens.

Perspective Can = Success

IN THE SAME MONTH that her mom was diagnosed with ALS, Nina got the promotion of a lifetime—to be the general manager of a start-up. She had worked in several senior roles, but she'd never had such responsibility. She wasn't quite sure how she was going to handle it all, but right away, something magical started to unfold. Over the two years that her mom was sick and Nina held this role, she was uber-successful—more so than at any other time in her career. Her team *quadrupled* its profits. Of course, this was the result of the team's amazing work. But for Nina, it was about perspective.

During that difficult time, Nina's chatty mind was entirely dedicated to the reality that her mom was dying. She stopped with the professional self-doubt and achieved a laser focus at work. She needed to get her shit done so she could get home to chill with her mom. And as soon as she got into her car at the end of the day, all she could think about was seeing her mom and spending as much time with her as she could.

Her usual chatty-mind thoughts were long gone: *Should I have said that in the meeting? How are people reacting to that slightly aggressive email I sent? We'd better land that client for the third year in a row or it's going to fuck up our P&L.* It didn't matter if she was doing something for her team, the clients, or the global CEO—she put the same effort into it all. She gave each moment her best. She was able to do this because, all of a sudden, she had fewer shits to give about the little stuff. Life and death matters were staring her in the face. She still loved what she did. She worked super-hard, was incredibly passionate about her role, and adored her team, but work stress was nothing compared with what was going on at home.

That perspective gave Nina the ability to get out of her own head—to get herself out of the way and just do her thing. For once, it didn't matter what people thought or how she was perceived (issues she'd struggled with her entire career). All that mattered was that she was highly accountable and putting her best foot forward. For the first time, she was able to let the rest go.

When you look at life from the macro perspective, things tend to fall into place. It's not that you stop caring; it's that you let the small shit go and focus on what really matters.

Cultivate the Oneness

YOUR DRIVE TO BE someone unique is great, as long as it doesn't fog your ability to see the similarities you share with everyone else on this planet. Our physical structure is the same; we all popped out of a mother; and we all live on Earth and breathe the same air. Oh, and we've all experienced the same emotions—down in the dumps, anger, jealousy, sadness, embarrassment, you name it. When you find yourself feeling some of these feels, think of the billions of others who have experienced the same thing. It's an instant reminder that you aren't alone. We're also all striving for happiness—which is a pretty big common denominator.

The next time you're walking down the street, make a point of seeing the similarities between you and those around you rather than the differences. If you catch yourself making a quick judgment about someone—say, on their outfit or behaviour—just stop for a minute and remind yourself that they are a person with two eyes, a nose, and a mouth, just like you. They, *too*, are made of fucking stardust.

Frustration with other people often stems from difference. Maybe you like to talk problems out, but your co-worker prefers to go quietly about their work. Or you're a neat freak, while your partner lets clothes pile up all over the bedroom. Focusing on what you have in common can change your perception and diffuse your annoyance. Sure, other people have their own points of view and habits, but they still have hundreds of attributes that are similar to yours.

You come from a lineage that spans millions of years. Your looks and personality might be different from that of your ancient ancestors, but you are not a different species. Your DNA is similar to your parents, your great-great-great-grandparents, and millions of other humans. Seeing that oneness—as opposed to the differences—connects us, which in turn cultivates more genuine emotions, like relatability, empathy, and love.

Your Body Is a Temple

ANOTHER WAY TO FOCUS on the macro is to think about how incredible your body is. Have you ever spent a moment in awe of your body and how it works? It's literally the highest form of technology in your house. You might be in love with your latest gadget, but just know it has nothing on the technology of your bod.

Ever torn your ACL (anterior cruciate ligament) playing football, or even broken the index finger on your dominant hand in a stupid mishap? Have you ever had a stomach ache, or really bad heartburn? If your body isn't functioning in an optimal way because of injury or illness, you may find yourself feeling really grateful for the times when it is working as it used to. But here's the thing: your body works pretty damn perfectly most of the time, and you barely stop to acknowledge it. So how about you do that now?

Here are a few facts to consider:

- Your heart beats on average 115,200 times a day—that's forty-two million times a year.
- Your lungs and respiratory system allow oxygen to be taken into your body, while also enabling it to get rid of carbon dioxide.
- The network of your blood vessels is so long it can circle the globe twice.
- Your liver can regenerate itself with only 25 percent of its original tissue.
- Your kidneys filter half a cup of blood every minute and remove waste and extra water via urine.

- Your brain has approximately eighty billion nerve cells, which is more than ten times the number of people living on this planet.
- Your nerve cells communicate using neurotransmitters that send messages to all parts of your body, which enable you to:
    » walk to the bathroom
    » brush your teeth
    » shower
    » feed yourself
    » get to work
    » use your phone
    » talk to people

Let all the above sink in, and realize that you have a full-time staff of cells working daily to keep you alive.

If you don't have time to look up at the stars, like Stephen Hawking recommended, go ahead and check out your feet. Wiggle your toes and appreciate the miracle inherent in the fact that your brain can make your toes wiggle. Take a breath and wonder over how your body knows how to breathe. Feel your heartbeat and be grateful it's on beat 33,387,296 of the year.

Waking Up Is a Fucking Miracle

HAVE YOU EVER woken up just happy to be alive? Perhaps this happened after you witnessed a tragic event on the news, or attended the funeral of someone who passed unexpectedly. But what if this was the first thought you had *every* morning?

Not so long ago, we listened to a lecture by the famous yogi Sadhguru. He said that one of the things we take most for granted in life is our own mortality. We all have a start date and an end date; that's a fact. He brought this up not to instill fear or make us worry but rather to inspire a feeling of gratitude for simply being alive.

If you wake up in the morning, he went on to say, it's a sheer miracle. Why? Because 150,000 people won't. That's right. Every single day, 151,600 people won't wake up. This is the global daily mortality rate, which is roughly the size of a small town. The simple act of opening your eyes when your alarm goes off, it seems, is something extraordinary. So, what if you and the five people you love the most wake up each morning? This, Sadhguru says, is the greatest blessing you could ever ask for. And he's right. This is 100 percent true, but also so quickly forgotten.

So, consider this: What if your first thought in the morning wasn't *What time is it? Crap, let me grab my phone* (which leads to seeing three texts, five notifications, and a whole slew of Instagram posts you couldn't resist checking)? What if, instead, your first thought was something like *I'm just happy to be alive*. And what if, on top of that, you took a moment to be grateful that the five people you care most about are alive and well, too? What if you spent a few seconds giving a nod to your lucky stars?

After we heard Sadhguru's lecture, we did this religiously for two months. The trickle-down effect was phenomenal. Suddenly, the little things didn't seem so serious, and we found ourselves smiling a whole lot more. Being more appreciative when we talked to our friends and families, and a little less mentally rushed in the morning.

The thing is, when you wake up with a macro perspective thought, it has an impact on the rest of your day. This really helps you switch into the observing mind setting. If you're just happy to be alive, how stressful can that meeting or school project really be?

To see this perspective difference in action, let's look at a scenario in both micro and macro modes.

$$* \quad * \quad *$$

Micro Mode

You get in your car after a super-stressful and exhausting day at work. The entire way home, you're pissed off at Dan in finance; what he told you in his office was totally different from what he said in that meeting. You're also overwhelmed about the new expense-reporting initiative Nikhil kickstarted, and you're freaking out a bit about your year-end review with Anya, your boss. You're all worked up, so the road-rage situation is also starting to bubble. You get home in time to have dinner with your family, but you can't really focus because your chatty mind is still droning on about work.

After dinner you check your email to see if Anya needs anything and—*boom!*—you end up having a thirty-minute post-dinner date with your laptop. That makes you even more pissed about work than you already were, and you find yourself wondering, not for the first time, why you took that job. You can't focus on your family for the rest of the night; you're too worked up about all that transpired today and worried about how you're going to handle things tomorrow. You hit the sack, and the next thing you know your alarm is buzzing and the whole shit-storm starts up again.

Macro Mode

You get in your car after a super-stressful and exhausting day at work. You decide to leave work at work, and take a few deep breaths to release the bullshit; after all, you're in the car and there's nothing you can physically *do* about work at this point. You listen to a hilarious podcast or put on some music that makes you smile and has your head bopping. You laugh to yourself about the totally redic conversation you and Nikhil had about that famous YouTube cat. You get home and have dinner with your famjam. You talk about your team's playoffs, which are coming up, and a sweet piece of art you've had your eye on. Your head is clear because it hasn't spent your entire commute swirling in work stuff you can't control.

Because you're a badass worker with a huge sense of accountability, you check your email to see if Anya needs anything. Yup. You see a request, so you address it; after all, it's par for the course. You work through it quickly and efficiently and put your laptop away. Then you go back to enjoying your amazing family. You hit the sack feeling good about what you've accomplished, and wake up ready to tackle the workday.

✳ ✳ ✳

In both those scenarios, you were *doing* the exact same thing: getting in your car after work, driving home, having dinner with your family, addressing a pesky work issue, spending more time with your fam, and then heading off to bed. The *only* difference was what was going through your mind. We get it, scenario two sounds perfect, and it's not always like this, and of course you'll be better at it some days than others. But just acknowledging your chatty mind, and making an effort to calm it and enjoy what's in front of you, can have a great impact on the rest of your day.

Each moment of your day, *you can choose* what to focus on. Your life will be drastically different if you keep the big picture in mind more often. You'll be happier, no doubt, but there can also be other cool side effects. Your creative abilities might flourish because you're not always operating from a stressful headspace. And you might be less exhausted because your thoughts are neutral and positive instead of negative and overwhelming (remember, negative thoughts can weigh you down and drain your energy).

Thinking with the macro is a great way to find moments of peace, and it doesn't require you to change your routine in any way. It's just a matter of deciding what you want to focus on.

Love the Little Luxuries

THOSE FUZZY WARM FEELINGS you get from putting things into perspective can come from the smallest things— which makes it easy to find a plethora of stuff to be grateful for.

Here are a few things you can think on during your day:

- As you shower, think about your amazing plumbing system, and how your city spent decades building the infrastructure that makes this daily ritual possible.
- In the kitchen, think about the mug that holds your coffee or tea. Was it a gift? Did you buy it? Smile at the magical miracle that is your favourite hot beverage.
- After work, take a walk in your neighbourhood and think about all the great stores or restaurants near you. Think of the people who spend gruelling hours busting their asses in their businesses to put a smile on your face.
- As you watch Netflix after dinner, remind yourself that only ten years ago you might have had to consult a TV guide to find out when your favourite show was on, and then wait for it to start on channel 2. If you don't have a subscription service, just think of the millions of shows you can watch on YouTube for free and at your own leisure, not at whatever time the network thinks is best. Go back further and feel grateful to even have a TV or a laptop to watch stuff on.

- When you go to bed, think about how safe you feel and how others might not be so lucky.

If you really take the time to think about it, there is *so much* shit to be thankful for. You can probably think of something for most hours of your day. And when you feel thankful more often, you'll find you're in a better mood, and more easily able to brush off small grievances.

Give with Gusto

GIVING BACK and doing things for others makes you feel fan-fucking-tastic. You're helping to put a smile on someone's face, and that can put everything into perspective.

Kate's friend Raul sponsored a Syrian family this past year, and she's been helping out a little bit. Each time she sees them she's reminded of the heart-wrenching tragedy this family has been through. They had to leave their home and start all over in a country where they don't yet fully speak the language. Their experience often puts some of Kate's own challenges into perspective, and being able to make the kids and family smile fills her up like a cup of sunshine.

Studies have found that people who volunteer generally live longer. The reasons aren't entirely clear. Is it giving back? The perspective that volunteering provides? A sense that life has more meaning? We're not certain, but the benefits are obvious. Maybe volunteering is as good for us as that green concoction we buy at the fancy juice bar down the street—and quite possibly less expensive.

What are you passionate about? Have you watched a documentary lately that left you feeling inspired, or steaming? Why not use that excitement or frustration to fuel something positive, something that can make someone else's life better? In the process you could end up taking your mind off your own worries.

Giving doesn't have to be in the form of volunteering; it can mean giving to your friends, loved ones, or someone you just met. They say that people who give for the joy of it are generally happier. Kate's dad is like this. He constantly gives, no questions asked. It just brings him joy. He's always offering to pick people up from the airport, is happy to go for a coffee with anyone who wants to know more about his industry, and will always bring the host of a dinner party a small gift. This giving nature helps him to keep stress at bay, as he's always focused on others.

Dr. Elizabeth Dunn from the University of British Columbia conducted a study in which money was given to students. Half were asked to get something for themselves, and the other half were asked to get something for someone else. The group that spent money on someone else reported higher levels of happiness.

Even the business world is learning that helping others can be a pathway to happiness and success. In his research, Adam Grant, author of *Give and Take: Why Helping Others Drives Our Success*, found that giving was the key to driving increased productivity and creativity. We typically think of financial incentives as the big motivators in the business world, but Grant discovered that when employees feel that they're aiding others and being of service to them, it can help them feel good about themselves and their work.

So, give with a whole heart, and watch your levels of gratitude and happiness accelerate. The great part about it is that you're not just helping others—you're helping yourself, too.

Say What You're Grateful For

NINA AND HER HUBBY, Mike, developed a game called "Five Things." It's been one of the greatest gifts in their relationship.

Here's how it works:

If one person is on day two or three of a grouchy mood, the other one says, "Okay, *five things*!" And then it's non-negotiable; the mopey person has to immediately respond with five things they're grateful for. It could be anything: the basics (food, shelter, water), family, health, a good job, a vacation, each other—the possibilities are endless.

It's really not hard to come up with five things you're grateful for in life. And when you do—when you really think about and list them—it shifts your mood. Every thought you think releases brain chemicals, so why not put some positive vibes out there? No, it's not going to work like a light switch and completely change your mood, but something inside won't feel quite so shitty anymore.

Of course, there's one caveat: if you happen to be in "let that shit out" mode, you might want to take a rain check. Remember what we talked about in chapter 2? If you're having a rough day or going through something challenging, you need to let the emotion out or sit in the shittiness for a while. This might not be the time to call out "Five things."

You can create different types of lists of five things—for work, for school, for a person. And, of course, your list (or lists) can keep changing. Maybe you refresh it every month, just to stay on top of the whole gratitude thing. However you decide to go about it, write down your list and stick it on your bathroom mirror. Then, each morning, give it a read as you brush your teeth. You might just notice a slight pep in your step for the rest of the day.

Zoom Out

A GREAT WAY to get out of your head and gain perspective is to step out yourself. Focus on the billions of other humans who are on this planet. Sounds weird, but it's an exercise that can take you right out of a negative thought pattern. So, the next time you're experiencing a bout of frustration and need a moment of calm, try this:

Take a few breaths and think about all the other people who are physically surrounding you. If you're in an apartment building, think about the tenants on each floor and what they are up to. If you're in your house in the burbs, think about the people in each home in your neighbourhood, maybe cooking dinner or chatting with their buds. Think about all the people out on the street, in the restaurants and cafés, and in the park. Let your mind zoom out and reflect on all the amazing people who make up your town or city, and how they all might contribute to the way you live. Then zoom out to your country, continent, and planet—and then to the galaxy beyond.

It sounds cheesy, but remembering that you are part of something bigger than yourself can have a calming effect. It gets you out of your own head and makes you realize that you are not alone. There are billions of people here, all going through life and trying to figure it out.

Cultivating perspective is a powerful tool, so be aware of which lens you're using to look at life. The further out you go, the more beautiful your life will feel.

You Once Wished for What You Have Now

TOO OFTEN WE GET into a job we're all excited about and then, a few months later, end up frustrated and cursing our boss. Or maybe we were once ecstatic that a landlord picked us out of so many applicants for the apartment we're in, but now we want something bigger.

It's human nature to want more, and sometimes this propels us to do more—whether it's to change jobs or save up for a larger living space. But if you're stuck in that place of "want" all the time, you're not getting to enjoy what you have in front you.

Even small things that we wished for can bring us joy, though we sometimes lose sight of that. Let's say you've just purchased an iPhone, the most recent model, and you picked up a really sweet-looking case while you were at it. Every time you open your phone you get a rush of excitement. You're happily making new wallpaper and adding your favourite apps. Basically, you're in love. Now fast-forward eight months. The email you've just spent fifteen minutes composing won't send because you're out of storage. Your screen may have a few tiny nicks. And that case you loved so much is cracked. It's still the same phone, with pretty much the same capabilities, but it doesn't bring you the same happiness you had on day one. Suddenly, the thing that so excited you just a short while ago is frustrating AF.

Take yourself back to the day you bought your phone. What amazed you about it? Maybe the fact that it does almost everything your computer can? Or the 12-megapixel camera? Or the Retina HD Display? When you remember the things that had you initially swooning, you get a little burst of gratitude that makes you feel all warm and nice. You're focusing on what you *do* appreciate about your phone as opposed to what you don't.

Have a good look at what's around you right now, and then take yourself back to the time when you wished for it. Think about those moments when you were longing to get into the school you're now in, swiping through Tinder about to give up on love, or in a bidding war over your house.

If you find yourself annoyed and frustrated, and continually *wanting* the next thing—whatever that might be—this can be a great way to snap out of it. Remind yourself of all the things that made you want what you have now. And don't forget to take a moment to appreciate the things that pleasantly surprised you about what you got. It could be in the tiny little details—the storage closet you hadn't discovered when you bought the house, or the coffee machine you didn't know your shared studio had when you decided to rent it.

This conscious appreciation will remind you of just how amazing the present is, and take you out of past- and future-tripping. And that will make you *so* much happier.

CHAPTER 5

Authenticity

There's Only One Magical You

THERE IS NO ONE ELSE on this planet who is meant to do what you are here to do. There really is only one magical you. Your intellect, your personality, your favourite foods, temperament, passions, your very essence is yours alone— different from any of the other 7.6 billion humans on the planet. You might have parents, siblings, and friends who are similar to you, but no one is exactly the same. This is, of course, obvious, and yet it's not something we consciously think about on a day-to-day basis. But there is great power in embracing everything that's different about ourselves, right down to the way we sneeze or how we hold a pen.

The more you own who you are, the less you'll be bothered by your shortcomings. And when you live your life as your most authentic self, owning even the not-so-perfect stuff—that's freedom, amigos. You'll feel more content, happy, and inwardly confident. You'll also be depriving your chatty mind of some of the shitty content it loves to chew on, so it won't be able to get the best of you quite as often.

Being your authentic self is not always an easy path. In fact, sometimes the process of "owning it" is downright brutal. It might mean you have to pipe up about things that are important to you, potentially at the expense of offending other people or not fitting in. But once you're focused on making that shift, the pieces of your life might just start to fall into place in a way that they haven't before, and you could even end up inspiring others to do the same.

More than twenty years ago, Ellen DeGeneres came out on national television. She told the world she was gay. She simply felt it was the right thing to do—to be authentic to who she was . . . who she is. It was something that had never been done before, so this wasn't about being fearless; in fact, she was scared to death. Can you imagine the courage it took? She also didn't do it because she actively wanted to be a spokesperson for the gay community (though she ended up happily accepting that role). She did it because she wanted to *speak her truth*. She had no idea of the impact her decision would have. The media turned it into a complete shit-storm, and people didn't quite know how to handle it. On the one hand, there were those who despised her for speaking her truth, and who said all kinds of nasty, unrepeatable things about her. On the other hand, though, and more notably, there were those who embraced her. In the days and months following her coming out, Ellen got to see first-hand how owning her truth had a profound impact on so many people, and most important, in her own life. Some fans opened up about wanting to commit suicide before she came out, and shared their stories of how alone and misunderstood they'd felt. Her words and actions gave millions hope, not to mention the confidence to stand in their own truth.

Fast-forward two-plus decades. Ellen is now one of our most-loved daytime talk show hosts. She has a heart of gold, gives back to communities all around the world, and has people laughing their asses off daily. Barack Obama awarded her the Presidential Medal of Freedom (if you haven't seen the video, check it out; it's a real tear-jerker). Coming out wasn't easy. There was the backlash bullshit, and her original show got cancelled, and the other networks shunned her. But she pushed through. And because of how she owned her truth, she genuinely made history. She inspired many to live authentically and continues to do so, and she achieved amazing personal success. It all worked out in the end.

It's not always easy to speak your truth or stand up for what you believe in. Especially if you know you're going to be swimming upstream. But at the end of the day you'll be respected for it by those who matter to you. And for those who don't, or those who aren't a fan of your point of view? Well, what they think and feel isn't on you. As is commonly attributed to Dr. Seuss, "Be who you are and say what you feel, because those who mind don't matter, and those who matter don't mind." Wise words.

You Do You

Sometimes it takes a while to find out who you are. Nina saw an incredible grief counsellor, Rebecca Daum, the year her mom died—the year Nina was expecting her first child. Rebecca told Nina that the grief process might not even set in until her daughter turned one, since the first year of motherhood is a crazy triple-threat cycle of diapers, feeding, and sleep (or lack thereof). And that's exactly how it panned out. Nina's daughter turned one and *it* began—the shock, the sadness of losing her mom. As if that weren't enough, even things she thought she'd dealt with in the past were bubbling up to the surface and causing anger and disappointment. It all hit her like a ton of bricks.

Nina knew it was time for some serious soul searching. Her theme song for the next two years became "Over," by Drake—specifically, the two lines in the chorus where he talks about "doin' me." After years of autopilot, maybe even suppressing things, it was finally time for Nina to just do Nina. As she jammed out to this tune, she took some pretty serious steps on this journey. She went to meditation retreats. Watched TED Talks on how to heal. And she read wellness books galore, just to start. It was tough, but also incredibly healing. Nina quickly realized that finding her peace would be an ongoing journey, not one with a final destination. As the modern poet Rupi Kaur writes, "you do not just wake up and become the butterfly—growth is a process."

You are not going to get to a place where you have it all figured out. Remember that the hurricane is going to keep throwing things your way, good and bad. And *that* means you're never really going to stop learning about yourself. It's a process—a hard one at times—but when you start peeling back the layers and piece together who you are at the core, it's the aha of all aha's, the final frontier, the point of no return. And it fucking rocks. The more you uncover, the more authentic you get. And the more authentic you are, the truer to yourself you become.

It's important to be your authentic self with the big things, but don't forget the small stuff. Let's say you're at a concert, sitting up in the balcony. Your favourite tune comes on, and your instinct is to jump out of your seat and dance. But you hesitate when you notice that all the people around you have their asses planted. You've heard the expression "Dance like no one is watching"? Here's your chance. Or maybe you're out with friends for dinner. Every single one of them orders a salad. You ate super-healthy this week and had been planning on treating yo' self tonight. Suddenly, though, you feel self-conscious about wanting a loaded burger with sweet potato fries, and when the waiter arrives, you make a last-minute swap to the pear-and-walnut salad for fear of being judged. *Why?*

If you're like most of the human race, you have a tendency, now and again, to be hypersensitive to what others might say—be it about an Instagram post, what you feed your kid, what you choose to wear, or how you do your hair. But you really have to ask yourself what's more important to you: being who you want to be or being who you think others want you to be. Getting up and dancing the night away at a concert—and sucking all the enjoyment you can get out of it (given the expensive seats)—is so much more fulfilling than sitting on your butt just to avoid some judgy comment that someone might make in passing about how extra you're being. Who cares? That person will be on to their next thought in no time, so you do you and forget the rest.

Embracing Your Superpower

So many of us have parts of ourselves we've been taught not to love. We try to hide that aspect of ourselves or just refuse to accept it. Here's the thing, though: these traits may be the very thing that makes you the amazing you that you are. What's more, they could actually end up helping others or inspiring them to be who they are, as well. It wouldn't be an interesting world if we were all robots. Imagine if every musician looked and sounded the same, and every artist put out similar work. Snoozeville. We are each unique, and that's a good thing. And when we embrace the unique qualities in ourselves and in others, we let things go a little more.

Kate's unique trait is her sensitivity. She easily cries watching movies and the news, quickly picks up on other people's emotions, can be easily offended, and sometimes feels overwhelmed at big get-togethers. In our society—especially in the business realm, where she's spent a third of her life—these traits aren't often praised. She's been told to "toughen up," to not be "so sensitive," and to "get over it." She's heard these things at work, and from her partners and friends.

It got to the point where Kate didn't want people to find out how sensitive she truly was, so she often hid this part of herself by pretending to not care. When we don't acknowledge our real feelings, they tend to bubble up in other ways. (Remember, what you resist persists!) By stifling her sensitive side, Kate brought resentment and anger into her relationships, and ended up feeling misunderstood.

It wasn't until Kate realized that her sensitivity was also her strength that she began to reframe things. In many ways, her ability to be sensitive to other people's emotions actually helped her in her job and relationships. By understanding her bosses' and colleagues' needs, she was able to deliver great work autonomously. She didn't need as much guidance as others, since she intuitively got where people were coming from. And she was a great marketer and entrepreneur, because she could easily pick up on trends and develop material she knew her audience could relate to. In her friendships and partnerships, she could sense when others might be off their game and offer better support.

Recently, Kate made an interesting discovery. She learned that a psychologist named Dr. Elaine Aron has been doing research on sensitivities, and that the highly sensitive person, or HSP, is actually a thing. Turns out this trait is found among 15 to 20 percent of the population (and also found in animals). Psychologists speculate that it might exist in some members of a group to help protect others from dangers they can't perceive because they aren't sensitive to them. Kate dove into the research. Realizing that there were other people out there like her opened up a new area of self-discovery. She now sees sensitivity as her superpower—a perspective that wouldn't have been possible had she not accepted and owned this trait.

Often, a perceived weakness can also be a strength. The key is to embrace that "weakness" as part of the unique, magical person you are. When you do this, you're less likely to feel awkward when you make mistakes or take things too personally. You're aware of the stuff you're not great at and unfazed when someone else points it out. You accept it as part of who you are, or make a conscious choice to improve on it, or maybe even spin it to see how it can serve you better.

If you're a recovering perfectionist like we are, this process isn't easy at first. We have this mentality in our culture that strength is demonstrated by not showing signs of weakness or admitting mistakes. But from a psychological perspective, this actually isn't helpful. When we're not aware of our own "flaws," we're less likely to improve on them. Also, opening up about who we truly are—mistakes, flaws, and all—helps to build social connections.

And—big bonus here—being your authentic self will help you ladder up to more peaceful moments in your life. Why? Because when who you are at the core lines up with who you're being inside and out, it means there's less internal conflict swirling around inside you. Remember, it requires time and patience to start figuring this shit out. But once you take the first few steps, there's really no going back. Each day you spend in your truth moves you closer to the authentic you you're meant to be.

It's Okay to Run Upstream

WHY IS IT sometimes difficult to really say what you mean or do what you want to do?

It can be hard to decipher our truth. Humans are hard-wired to want to feel like they belong, and following the group can make that easier. It's even part of our biological makeup, because our ancestors realized we were more likely to survive together than alone. This is undoubtedly true—there is indeed strength in numbers, and as a collective we've accomplished extraordinary things—but sometimes the herd can lead us down the wrong path.

History provides tons of example. Take gladiators. In Roman times, they used to beat one another to death as a sport. People would fight animals, or each other, *for entertainment*. Imagine going to a FIFA World Cup match knowing that some of the players would perish. It's bananas, but back in the day, people embraced the spectacle. They turned out in droves and cheered as the blood and guts flew. This went on for around six hundred years, and *millions* of people died. There must have been someone in the crowd who thought, *Hey, this shit's kind of fucked up*.

Sometimes human beings will blindly follow the herd until a few people start piping up to say, "This is not right." It was less than a century ago that African Americans had to drink from separate water fountains, sit in a different place on buses, and go to different schools. It's shocking and disgusting to even think about. Thankfully, a united group of passionate, strong-willed people—including the visionary Martin Luther King Jr.—stood up for what they believed and put a stop to that shit. Their efforts resulted in a slew of new legislation—the Civil Rights Act, the Voting Rights Act, and the Fair Housing Act. These laws helped to stop discrimination in employment, public areas, and housing, and also protected African Americans' right to vote. Looking back from today's vantage point, it's hard to comprehend how we ever thought segregation was acceptable, but a lot of people did—and a lot of others went along with the prevailing mentality. Until they didn't. Those people weren't afraid to swim upstream. And thank God for that.

You know your truth, starting with the small stuff (like how to just be you at a dinner party) and progressing up to the bigger things (like agreeing to disagree about what aligns with your moral code). Knowing what's important to you can be tough to figure out. Honouring what's important to you can be even tougher. Sometimes, following the herd is the easy way out. But living a life that aligns with who you are feels a heck of a lot better.

Speak Your Mind,
Even If It Makes Your Voice Shake

WE OWE THIS EXPRESSION to Maggie Kuhn, who advocated for senior citizens. Maggie fought for their rights, social and economic justice, and mental health. She was way ahead of her time, and felt strongly about speaking up for what was right.

One of the most challenging parts of owning your truth is finding the confidence to say what you want to say, even in front of naysayers. You might be rooted in a belief system that you can discuss openly among your social group—people who are on the same page as you—but what happens when you're in a room with people with whom you don't see eye to eye?

When you speak your mind, you might experience emotions like fear, anxiety, worry, excitement, and empowerment, not to mention physical symptoms like a racing heart and sweaty armpits. These are all good things, because saying what you believe is true can indeed make your voice shake. Ellen DeGeneres said that when they were rehearsing for the "coming out" show, she couldn't say the line "I'm gay" without tearing up. And even in the final edit you can see how emotional it was for her.

When you finally stand in who you are, you are no longer living as someone you're not. You are giving yourself permission to be you. And that's a powerful thing. Your voice shakes because maybe, on some level, you know that being you sometimes means others aren't going to be happy. But you are not living your life for others; you are living your life for badass you.

When you do muster up the courage to own it, shaky voice and all, make sure you give yourself a pat on the back. That shit ain't easy.

Speaking your truth gets rid of all the chatty-mind clutter that results from not speaking it. It also helps you to avoid the pent-up emotion that accumulates when you want to speak out against something but feel you can't. Have you ever left a get-together where someone made a mean comment and you thought *I wish I'd spoken up*? Did you spend the next few hours stewing, and crafting the perfect response for "next time"? When emotions and thoughts like those aren't swirling around in your head, there's more room to be present with yourself. And you know this by now: being present equals being happy. And being happy feels pretty good.

The Word Should *Is Dangerous*

SHOULD IS ONE of the unhealthiest words out there. We talked a bit about this back in chapter 2, where you learned how to tap into some self-love goodness and feel less obligated and guilty. And that's super-important. But we need to revisit the topic here because of the other baggage that comes along when *should* enters your headspace. *Should* takes you away from who you want to or are meant to be. *Should* pushes you to be more like someone you're not. *Should* is some toxic shit.

There's a children's book by Ginny Tilby called *You Should, You Should!* It's about a hippopotamus who lacks confidence. He meets a whole bunch of animals that tell him that instead of doing his hippo thang, he should be hanging from a tree, walking more gracefully, pecking instead of chomping, or cultivating more spots. He tries all these things and gets himself into an unholy mess. Finally, he realizes he's pleasing everyone else at the expense of being true to himself. He finally marches to the beat of his own drum and is so much happier.

We can learn a thing or two from that hippo. How often do you do things because you feel you *should* do them as opposed to really wanting to do them? Do you feel like you do a whole crap-ton of stuff to satisfy the *should*s of others?

Cut that shit out. Unconditional love is just that—unconditional. If people feel you should be someone else in order for them to like or love you more, that's a red flag.

But—big *but* here—it's also important to understand the intention behind the *should*. Is it coming from a place of love? Maybe your partner suggests that you should take a day off and relax given all the stress and pressure you're under. Or perhaps a good friend says you should watch a show because it addresses topics you're passionate about. These types of *shoulds* are harmless and all good.

But clearly, not all *shoulds* fall into this well-intentioned category. Below you'll find a list of the more toxic variety. After reading it, you might realize just how often these types of comments are being said to you.

A List of *Shoulds*

- You should be making $X by age X.
- You should have a house by now.
- You should have a family with X kids by now.
- You should start eating this way.
- You should buy a car (or not buy a car).
- Your child should be acting like this.
- You should keep trying to make your relationship work.
- You should be more active on social media.
- You should celebrate Valentine's Day.
- You should start doing this type of exercise.
- Your poo should ideally look like this.
- You should go for that promotion.
- You should adhere to this superstition.
- You shouldn't leave your cushy job to start your own business.
- You shouldn't be so serious all the time.
- You shouldn't laugh so much in these scenarios.

Fuck the Sholds

Now, LET'S TAKE all of these *shoulds* and give them the middle finger. They are putting a tremendous amount of pressure on you, and you just don't need it—especially since, when you look at each one closely, you'll see that even though you're saying them to yourself, they might not necessarily have *come* from you.

Should thoughts are tricky that way. Likely, they came from a colleague, or something you saw in the media, or even your parents. Sometimes you can trace the *should* back to a specific person or event, and realize, *Oh yeah. These* shoulds *came from my dad, those were from my last workplace, and these are from my ex.*

Keep in mind that some kinds of external pressures can help you be a more civilized human being. You *should* be nice to your boss. You *should* spend time with your kids. You *should* do your best to remember your aunt's birthday. So, sometimes you listen to these *shoulds* because they help you. They help you not get fired, or avoid tensions. These things matter. But when you're adhering to *shoulds* that don't matter to you, it can lead to feeling crappy and not good enough. And that's when you know it's time to take a step back.

At the end of the day, what is important to *you*? What kind of person do you want to be? What are your values? You know the answers to these questions, and when you're really clear about all that, and follow through with what's important to you, the *shoulds* will quiet down.

Take Tyler, for example. He thinks he should be able to buy a house by now, but so far, no dice. This *should* has been following him around for the past four years. During that time, he's been making good money, but he just doesn't have what he needs to make it happen—not yet.

This doesn't mean Tyler will never be able to afford a house; it's just that he can't do it right at this moment. He lives in a city where housing prices are continually on the rise. Of course, if he wanted to make the house thing happen, he could do it by working extra hours or taking an extra gig here and there. But Tyler has to ask himself a few questions: Is a house that important to him? What are his values, and how have they shaped the past four years?

Tyler's a social kind of guy. He likes to spend his weekends with friends, and he appreciates the flexibility his job offers. So, in fact, the way he's been living his life is actually *in line* with what he wants (time with friends, for himself, to enjoy weekends, et cetera). Taking an extra gig that would cut into this time would go against his values. He'd be honouring the *should*, and not who he is inside.

The idea that he should have a house by this point in his life might have come from his friends, or his siblings, or something he read somewhere. You know where it didn't come from? From Tyler himself. Tyler needs to assess whether he really *wants* a house, or if he just feels he *should* have a house. Knowing that the whole house issue is coming from a *should* could take a huge weight off his shoulders.

When you dig deep into your own value system and really get in touch with what's happening there, you are better able to analyze stressors and determine if they're worth fussing over. Once you do that, you'll get closer to your truth and be able to obliterate the dreaded *should*.

Go ahead and write your own list of *shoulds* (see the previous section if you're having trouble getting started). Then do three things:

1. Figure out where the *should* might have come from.
2. Decide whether it's important to you.
3. Let go of the *should* if it's really not important to you, or take some steps to make it happen if it is something you truly want for yourself.

It's Okay to Say No

WHEN YOU'RE DOING THINGS just for the *should*, you're messing with your authentic-self boundaries. There's an Oprah SuperSoul Conversation with Reese Witherspoon and Mindy Kaling (yas, these three queens!).

At the end of the podcast Oprah asks, "What's the lesson that took you the longest to learn?"

Mindy kicks off with "That it's okay to say no."

Reese says she was going to say the same thing.

Oprah agrees that this was the case for her, too.

They all say it's something they continue to work on.

When you say no, you're setting up a boundary for yourself. Often, you feel as if you can do it all. You say yes to that extra project that's handed to you at work, feel like you need to cook an entire dinner for a party of fifteen from scratch, agree to drinks after baseball practice even though you're exhausted. What is it about saying no that inspires guilt? If you can do it all, go for it, but if something inside you doesn't feel right after you've just taken on the next thing, pause a moment. If it's nerves that are bubbling away inside you as you wonder whether you can actually do it (*I really want to make thirty jars of antipasto to hand out for Christmas, but I'm not sure how it will turn out*), then go for it. You got this! But if it's *I can't believe I just committed to coaching the school volleyball team on top of teaching responsibilities . . . I kinda felt pressured, and I don't really even like volleyball!*—then use your observing mind to acknowledge that and dissect those thoughts. Did you say yes because on some level you *want* to do it, or did you say yes out of *obligation*?

Take the time to understand why you said yes. Listen to your gut—it might have clearly been screaming at the top of its lungs, asking you if you're crazy. Perhaps that's why your heart was racing as you were nodding. Of course, there are some things we might feel are okay to take on: someone unexpectedly resigns and you need to fill in for a few weeks to get things rolling. Ajay's dad has the flu so you agree to pick Ajay up and drop him off at school this week when you drive your own kid. But if it's something you absolutely don't have to do and you are taking it on because you don't want to disappoint anyone or it might come across as if—heaven forbid—you can't handle it all, then it's time to reevaluate. You're letting the *should*s have the reins.

If we are putting a desire to impress others over our own sense of peace and well-being, then that ain't good. It means we're prioritizing other people's approval and emotions over our own. And remember self-love: we need to make sure *our* cup is full. There are nice ways of saying no, and if someone truly cares about your well-being, they will understand. If they don't, well, there's nothing you can do about that. It might be uncomfortable, but what's worse? Discomfort or constantly running on empty?

Learning to say no is a hard but powerful thing. It makes you feel more grounded in your authentic self, because it means you're doing things for you. It might be something you always have to work on, but check in with yourself from time to time and make sure you're doing all those added things in your life for the right reasons—and because you want to, not because you should. In other words, get comfy with saying yes to saying no. It will only do you good.

Don't Give Your Power Away

IF YOU DON'T OWN your badass self, you might be making it easy for someone else to take the wheel. It doesn't have to be one specific individual—maybe it's a particular person in your family, and another one at work, and another in your circle of friends. There are people around who love the idea of controlling others. Sometimes they don't even mean to. And the ways in which it happens can be subtle. Maybe they're pressuring you to go somewhere or believe in something they believe in, and because you're not firm in where you are, you unintentionally allow it.

Some of these people have a subconscious radar for those who will be susceptible or easily swayed. Realizing that this is happening to you can be a big wake-up call. Start to make some shifts and changes by questioning yourself. *Do I really want to go to this event? Do I truly believe in this principle?* If you don't, then stand in your truth. We talked in the last section about having to do things out of goodwill that don't float our boat, but that's not what we're talking about here.

Deep down, you'll know when you're handing over the wheel. You might start walking on eggshells around certain people or overanalyzing how they might react to something you do or say. You might put them on a pedestal for some reason or crave their approval. Or maybe you don't really like them at all and are confused by your own behaviour.

If you feel this happening, just remember, you get to decide how to live your life—no one else—so embrace that and stand in your power.

Get Out of the Too-Many-Shits Zone

SOMETIMES WE FIND OURSELVES stressing over bullshit. Maybe we're bothered about what someone said, or think we *should* have said something differently, or feel pressured to be living our lives in a different way. What gives?

Being your authentic self means living your life in line with *your* beliefs and embracing who *you* are. There are things in life that are worth stressing over, and deep down you know what those things are. If something is truly worth it and aligns with your values, it will feel manageable and purposeful, even if it can be overwhelming at times.

Mark Manson, author of *The Subtle Art of Not Giving A F*ck*, has some insight into what happens when we tap into our true selves. "Essentially, we become more selective about the fucks we're willing to give," he says. "This is something called maturity. . . . Maturity is what happens when one learns to only give a fuck about what's truly fuck-worthy."

The good news is that we tend to know in our gut when we're giving too many shits over the wrong things. How can you tell if you've crossed into the too-many-shits zone? You simply ask yourself if what you are stressing over is something that's important to you, or something external and out of your control.

If it's the latter—say, someone's opinion of you—it falls clearly into the no-shits zone. Why? Because it's outside of you. It has nothing to do with who you really are. It doesn't matter.

Let's say you've got a crush. You text the object of your affection, but they don't text you back right away. The thought-swirl begins: *I shouldn't have said that. Maybe I should have been funnier, or coyer. Maybe I should have said something more interesting.* Whatever you said in that text is unique to you. Don't second-guess it. Your personality—quirks and imperfections and all—is why your friends love you, or why your colleagues and acquaintances asked for your number or added you on Facebook. Don't undermine yourself by questioning who you are.

The time you spend trying to figure out what other people are thinking is time spent in the too-many-shits zone. You have no way of knowing. And even if you did, it doesn't matter. What you do know is who you are at the core and what makes you amazing. (And you know this because you've been working toward self-love, right? If you need a refresher, revisit chapter 2.) As you embrace who you are and own what you say and do, you're less fazed by incidents that might have once made you question yourself. The internal thought parade switches gears from *Why didn't they text me back?* to *I know who I am, that text was just perfect, and I love all parts of myself, even if I'm left on "read" by this person for eternity.* Or, better yet, you don't think about the non-response at all. You send the text and let that shit go.

The key to staying out of the too-many-shits zone is to catch your chatty mind in these moments and realize what's going on. And then—instead of giving in to the guilt, or pressure, or whatever other negative emotion your chatty mind has let out to play—use the chatty mind's patter as an opportunity to embrace every single part of yourself.

Stop with the "I Feel Bad Because . . ."

HOW OFTEN DO YOU use the phrase "I feel bad because . . ."?

Life isn't simple these days. We are overscheduled, over-worked, and overtired most of the time. Often, we're pulled in so many directions that we end up feeling bad that we can't be everything to everyone. Think about how this plays out in your own life. When you're at work, you may *feel bad* that you're not at home with your kids, and when you're finally at home building a Lego farmhouse, you *feel bad* that you're not working on the endless to-do list sitting on your desk. Even something as necessary and simple as a doctor's appointment has you *feeling bad* that you're going to get into work late. But we can only do what we can. Beyond that, we have to let that shit go. Like we said in chapter 2, guilt is a self-inflicted emotion, so saying "I feel bad" just adds more clutter to your already racing mind. It also takes you away from being in the present moment, because you're wishing something else for yourself. But here's the thing: it's likely that nobody even cares or is concerned about what you are doing. Your boss is busy playing Monopoly with her family after work; she doesn't care that you're not tackling your to-do list at 8 p.m., and that while you're at the office, your kids are having a blast eating freezies at recess. It's all good.

You have the right to feel good and do the things you want to do. In fact, this not only helps you live a life you really enjoy but also positively affects those around you. If you know you're putting your best foot forward managing all that you have going on, then there's no room to feel bad. If anything, you can feel pretty stellar about yourself and your ability to work full-time, volunteer, play a sport, cook, call your sibling, talk your friend through that challenge, and give yourself a bath.

Use your observing mind to become aware of every time your chatty mind pipes up with an "I feel bad because . . ." Give it a good old f-off and yourself kudos for doing all that you do.

Say Sorry

WHEN YOU START doing your own thang and saying no to stuff you don't like or want to do, you'll inevitably piss some people off. That's okay, but it's not a licence to be a jerk (obvs). If someone close to you points out something you did that unintentionally hurt them, own up to it. Just say you're sorry. It's important to take responsibility for who you are, especially if it caused pain to someone you care about. This also antes up your personal integrity.

Kate's brother Cam recently called her out on always being fifteen minutes late (and chewing with her mouth open too much, but that's another story). He prides himself on being on time, as most great humans do. At first Kate got defensive, and she began to counter with examples of instances when she'd been entirely punctual. But then she realized he was probably bringing it up because he found it kind of annoying, maybe even disrespectful. With this in mind she owned it. "Yeah, you're right," she said. "I could get better at this. It's something I'm working on. I didn't mean to be rude." Done. Argument defused.

Kate knows she's a big-picture kind of thinker, and small details like scheduling aren't her forte. She's also aware that this is a part of her personality that might piss people off. She certainly isn't late intentionally, and she's trying very, very hard to improve, but if she messes up, she owns it. And if someone brings it up, she tries to keep in mind that this person isn't out to insult her but is probably trying to deal with her hurting them.

Sometimes it's hard to get called out on our bullshit. It can be embarrassing. But taking it in stride and embracing that you're an imperfect human can make for smoother relationships. As you admit your own mistakes, you'll actually get closer to your truth, because you're quickly recognizing your faults (versus ignoring them) and working to improve them. And as you begin to accept the imperfect parts of yourself, you actually start letting other people off the hook more easily, too. You lower your expectations, begin to be a little more forgiving, and let go of their faults and your own more easily.

Be kind to yourself in the moment, and be sure to extend the same sweetness to others. When you do this, you'll be better able to understand where others are coming from, and then address (the issue someone has with you), accept (this isn't your strength), apologize (especially if you hurt someone), and move on.

Know That Someone Shot Gandhi

In 2010, Nina, her hubby, Mike, and her mom, Rita, took a sabbatical and went to northern California for a year-long course in classical spiritual philosophy and meditation. This was a big decision for Nina and Mike. They left their established careers, sold their dream home, and pushed off the family planning. Nina truly unplugged: she had no access to TV, movies, the internet, phones, or friends. She even told her friends that if they wanted to get ahold of her, they would have to write a letter. She sent and received 150 handwritten letters that year.

It's interesting what happens when you completely remove yourself from distractions. When big stuff comes up—stuff you might have been avoiding or subconsciously suppressing—there is nothing around you to distract yourself. You have no choice but to turn inward. You can't scroll through your phone, turn on the tele, call a friend, or go grab a coffee . . . you have to just deal. Here's another thing to note: you can run off to the Himalayas (or wherever), but your mind will be right there with you, whirling with the same old shit. Where you are physically makes no difference at all, so why not just stare your mind down and figure out what's going on?

During that year in California, many things came up for Nina. And when they did, it was just her, the majestic mountains, the seemingly never-ending Eel River, and the towering redwood trees. She had no choice but to face all that was swirling within.

One of Nina's biggest struggles was (and still is) people pleasing. She has a hard time when she gets the vibe that someone doesn't like her or disapproves of a decision she's made. If she needs to do something that someone else might not be a huge fan of, the guilt sets in and her heart starts to pound out of her chest. Knowing this, she tends to put others before herself, always making sure she gives off the best, most-pleasing impression.

It was a beautiful sunny morning in Cali. Nina and Mike had just gotten out of class and were starting off on a long walk. Nina expressed her frustration over why she thought a certain person didn't like her. She claimed to have tried everything, but nothing seemed to be working—being nice, helping that person, being emotionally supportive. Nothing made a difference.

Finally, Mike turned to her and said, "Nina, someone shot Gandhi." Huh? She wondered if Mike was even listening.

Mike was totally listening.

"Someone shot Gandhi," he repeated. He went on to remind Nina that Gandhi was a remarkable soul. He fought for peace through non-violence and is revered to this day. He drove the independence of an entire nation through love. He gifted the world with profound wisdom. But guess what? Someone didn't like him. In fact, they disliked him enough to shoot him. The same holds true for Abraham Lincoln, Malala Yousafzai, Martin Luther King Jr., and John F. Kennedy. These people were and are great leaders who inspired great political change. Who actively stood up against what wasn't right and risked their lives for the greater good. But no matter their achievements, someone wasn't happy about it.

So, if someone couldn't like these exceptional people or what they stood for, then there would definitely be people out there who weren't big fans of Nina. She was very lucky to be surrounded by incredible people, many of whom loved her dearly. But she had to realize that she couldn't possibly please everyone. She had to understand that she would never get to a place where everyone she came into contact with would adore her. For Nina, this was a huge aha moment. Suddenly, it was so clear: she needed to stop putting effort and energy into making sure everyone approved of her—especially at the expense of her own integrity. Instead, she had to simply be who she was and let the rest go. In time, she also realized that when she pulled back on those people-pleasing tendencies, she had so much more mental energy—and love—to put toward the people who did count.

Know this: There will be people in this world who just aren't fans of you. Who judge you, for whatever reason, just for being you. It's important to simply be cool with that. Nina's wise sister-in-law Susan once told her of the saying "What people think of you is none of your business." Keep that one in mind. People will have their opinions about you, and that's fine. If someone doesn't like you for who you are, that's fine, too. Let them. You just be the best person you can be and let the rest of that shit go.

Be Unfuckwithable

According to Urban Dictionary, the most popular definition of *unfuckwithable* is "When you are truly at peace and in touch with yourself, and nothing anyone says or does bothers you, and no negativity or drama can touch you." What a liberating place to be. For some, being unfuckwithable is easy, but if you're a natural people pleaser or care about how others perceive you, becoming unfuckwithable can be hard. But it's so worth it, because it's also super-empowering.

It starts by really understanding whether you're allowing people to fuck with you—maybe through subtle control or manipulation. They create drama or make you feel guilty. If this sounds familiar, it's time to wake up and honour yourself. As Will Smith once said, "Stop letting people who do so little for you control so much of your mind, feelings and emotions." Unfortunately, it's sometimes exactly those challenging people who have the most control over what's going on in that chatty mind of yours. Maybe they make you feel angry or upset, and then you replay certain situations in your head. They might not directly be saying or doing anything to you, but you're letting them mess with you, nonetheless. Why is this happening? It's because you haven't upped the unfuckwithable ante.

It's liberating to realize that it's up to you to teach others how you want to be treated. You can't be upset about the way someone treats you if you *let them* treat you that way. No one can make you do anything. We all have a choice in this matter. The more comfortable you are in your own skin, the more you will be able to stand up for what is right for you and not be affected by what other people say or do.

Also, just because you are nice to people doesn't mean that they have to be nice back. They don't owe you anything. Sure, we're all taught to treat others the way we want to be treated, but it's important to remember that some people just don't have the capacity to do that. And that has absolutely nothing to do with you, so let it go. If you stand in your unfuckwithable roots, situations will have less power over you—and there may even be consequences for those who cross your line, like you might not be willing to do as much for them. The more you protect the integrity of who you are, the less it will matter whether people accept you or not. And over time, you'll feel less and less guilty about being true to who you are.

It's Not about Being Nice

*And then I learned the spiritual journey had nothing to
do with being nice. It was about being real, authentic.
Having boundaries. Honouring my space first, others
second. And in this place of self-care being nice just happened, it flowed not motivated by fear but by love.*
—Michelle Olak

Life. Changing. Quote.

When you feel as if you're on a path of goodness, it's
possible to slip into a space where you think you always
have to have a smile on your face and be nice to everyone,
no matter the circumstance.

Being nice is tricky. If someone ever says to you "Well,
you're doing all this work on being a better human—*you*
should be the bigger person," bolt as fast as you can. Just
because you're working hard to be and perceive yourself as
a better person doesn't mean you have to put up with being
mistreated, or be "nice" all the time. You should *never ever*
feel like you have to take shit from others.

When Nina's mom, Rita, was sick, she took on a secret
mission with one of Nina's dearest friends, Tracey. A year
before Rita's passing, sweet Tracey would bring Rita, wheel-
chair bound and all, beautiful stationery and cards. Rita used
them to write numerous letters and notes for Nina to have
as a keepsake after she passed. Nina had no idea this was
going on until after her mom's death, and she still doesn't
know how many letters and cards are left in this vault that
incredible Tracey keeps so safe. On the day of Rita's funeral,

Tracey handed Nina and Mike a card each. The front of the envelope read "For Nina/Mike, Upon Death." This was just the beginning. Nina got one at the hospital the day her daughter was born and one on her thirty-fifth birthday. And she got a letter for Rita's grandchild when the little thing turned two. Nina wasn't even pregnant when Rita wrote these letters! It was unbelievable. Imagine, staring death in the face with such confidence that you can write to your loved ones knowing you won't be here.

One of Nina's favourite cards was labelled "For when times are tough and you need some motherly advice." Pretty much every line in there is a nugget of sweet wisdom, but here is one of the paragraphs that resonated most: "Maintain your self-respect, never feel pressured into compromising yourself. Your core being full of life, love, and freedom should be protected. Remember—do not do injustice, but do not let it be done to you—Cardinal Rule. I learnt the hard way—you must not."

Why are we always taught how to treat others but not taught how to treat ourselves?

Being a good person does not mean allowing yourself to be taken advantage of. Be strong. Stand for what you believe in. You don't have to be a jerk and stoop to other people's level—you can stand strong with class and integrity—but it might mean not being nice to everyone all the time.

Stop Trying to "Fix" People

SOMETIMES WHEN YOU find something that works for you, you get so excited about it that you want to help others. This impulse comes from a well-intentioned place, no doubt, but it's really not your job. Trust us, we've been there. You see all this great change in yourself as a result of pursuing your passions, reading mind-blowing books, starting a new diet, or working out more often, and you want the same for those around you. It's a very sweet thought, but some people are comfortable sitting right where they are. Perhaps they're not ready to take those steps. When you try to get people to jump onto your bandwagon, you become the person who is doing the "should-ing" on their end.

As you ride along your journey, simply *stay in your lane*. Of course you can share what you've learned, but don't do it with the expectation that the person you're sharing with is going to change. Stay focused on the road ahead of you. Continue to do things that make you feel good or that continue to peel back your own layers. If someone is curious about what you're up to or wants to be on the same high, they'll simply ask. It will sound something like "Hey, you seemed a lot calmer in the last few board meetings. What are you doing these days?" Or "Your skin looks great. What have you been doing differently?" When they do ask, by all means put your indicator on, switch lanes, and lend them a helping hand. If they don't, it's okay to let them be.

When you try to *fix* other people, it's often you who ends up frustrated. Sometimes you can even internalize that and start to see yourself as a failure in this totally unnecessary mission you set for yourself. This dynamic could potentially go on for years, until your relationship comes to a head because the person didn't change the way *you* wanted them to, or they got tired of not being able to live up to your expectations. It's a mess, and can be avoided. Why expect the change in the first place? What they do is up to them, and as we keep saying, *you can't control other people.*

The only person you can change or fix is you. If people don't want to be on the same path that you're on, don't take it personally; they are just fine where they are. In fact, they might even get defensive or be insulted if they feel you are trying to change them. If you find yourself wondering how you can help someone through their childhood issues, familial concerns, or ongoing sadness, help them in a way that *they* want to be supported. Maybe they need a shoulder to cry on, someone to vent to, or a simple act of kindness. Maybe they have no interest, at this point in time, in "solving" whatever is going on in their world. So, unless someone sends a clear signal of interest, stay in your lane and focus on the amazing transformations within you.

Remove the Rock in Your Shoe

WHEN YOU BEGIN to adhere to what you really want inside—by standing up for what you believe in, saying no to shit, and focusing on you—the path that's right for you starts to become super-clear. Say you've been following *that path* since high school: You get your high-school diploma and then your undergraduate degree. Maybe you even pursue a graduate degree. You find a decent-paying job, land your first promotion, and before you know it you're well into your career. Suddenly, you might have a *how did I get here?* moment. You might realize that while you're pretty happy with where you are, you're not doing what you really want to do. You're not wholeheartedly passionate about your career. Maybe there are certain aspects about it that excite you and keep you motivated, but deep down, something doesn't feel quite right. You wonder if this is really what you're meant to do.

Have you ever asked yourself this question: *If money weren't an object, what would I do?* One of Nina's teachers from California told her that as long as you're not doing what you're meant to do, you'll feel like you're walking around with a tiny rock inside your shoe. That shit's kind of uncomfortable—even worse than when your sock slides partway down your foot and into your shoe.

We get it: you have responsibilities, accountabilities, a family to feed, a career to pursue. How could you possibly leave it all and follow your heart? Well . . . there's more than one way to pursue your passion. Sure, you could make a drastic change and completely switch paths, or you could do it gradually. Perhaps you keep your full-time job and pursue your passion on the side, and see where it goes. Our friend Arti aced her commerce degree and entered the workforce as an accountant, without really knowing what that meant. She went from audit management to consulting, and while it started off ballin' and exciting, it slowly became lacklustre. Arti had struggled with her weight as a child and had dealt with depression and anxiety, and the concept of well-being was something that had always intrigued her. She started exploring hobbies and got into health and fitness. As she kept at her day job, Arti began to acquire certifications in things like personal training and fitness instructing on the side. In time, this ignited a passion she never knew she had. She started feeling antsy in her role as a finance consultant, so she pitched her company on the idea of creating a well-ness role that she could fill. Given current trends, it agreed. She also started her own wellness business on the side, which she plans to pursue full-time one day.

If following your passion full-time means you're mak-ing less money, there are tons of ways to curb your spend-ing (check out the *Mr. Money Mustache* blog for ideas). Maybe you take fewer vacations, cook more at home, buy stuff in bulk. Or if you like your lifestyle the way it is and need to remain steadfast in your career, that's totally cool, too. Just try to do things outside of work to remove that rock from your shoe. If you're passionate about art, take some classes on the side. If you've always wanted to be a firefighter instead of an engineer, be a volunteer firefighter every other weekend. Make sure you're fulfilling that spark within. It's an integral part of you.

And if you find yourself wanting to switch gears one day, you don't have to figure out *exactly* what this passion of yours looks like in the professional sense, with a five-year financial plan and all. You can if it makes you feel better—there definitely is some planning involved, like knowing how much you need to sustain yourself (obvs)—but remember that things don't often go as planned. Sometimes, in fact, what you envision completely flips on its head, and that can be okay. Just start dipping your toe in, see how it feels, and go from there. As we said in chapter 3, don't get too attached to your plan or think you're a failure if it doesn't go exactly that way.

This pursuit could take time and patience, and there needs to be a certain element of implicit trust that everything will work itself out. The funny thing is that sometimes the moment you let go—let go of expectations, let go of planning every step, let go of the P&L—is exactly the moment when things fall into place. Maybe when you're not looking for it, you'll get that big break.

When you start to shake out that rock in your shoe, you are getting closer to your core. And that means you can do a better job of removing the clouds and being exactly who you are meant to be.

Just Ask for It

INTENTION SETTING is a fantastic way to get closer to living your truth. Put out there what you want for yourself, and see what manifests. When you start visualizing what you want in your life, you'll get a better idea of what your authentic self looks like.

Your brain doesn't know the difference between an actual experience and an imagined situation, so constantly visualizing failure isn't going to put you in a good place. On the other hand, if you visualize your future the way you want it, you might get there. It just takes time and patience.

Bestselling author Louise Hay has inspired millions with her teachings on self-love and intention setting. She is also a huge proponent of creating one's future through thoughts. She details how to do this in her book *You Can Heal Your Life* (which has been a life-changing read for both of us). If you've dabbled in intention setting, you know this shit can work wonders. We have so much to thank her for. She says setting intentions is just like growing vegetables. When you plant a tomato seed, you don't expect to see a tomato the very next day. You have to plant that seed in the right soil, expose it to sunlight, and give it water. After a bit of time passes, you'll see the first sprout, and then some stems and leaves, and finally what might look like a tomato. Even then, the tomato is green and you have to wait for it to ripen. And we're talking about a tomato here, not your entire future, so you can only imagine the amount of love and energy required for that to take shape.

Louise also says that asking for what you want is akin to ordering something at a restaurant. You don't keep troubling the waiter every five minutes, inquiring if the kitchen is working on your order and wondering when it's going to come. You have implicit trust that once you place your order, you will get exactly that. It's just a matter of time. So, have that same trust in your intentions for your future. This is a tough one for most of us. In fact, sometimes when opportunities present themselves, we're so shocked that we don't even see what's falling into place right before our eyes.

So, let's give this a whirl. You know the drill. Close your eyes and take a deep belly breath. Visualize your ideal future in detail. Who do you want to be, emotionally, intellectually, personally, professionally? Don't put limitations on this vision in the practical sense. Don't think about time, money, or any obstacles in your way. What does this future look like? See yourself one year from now, five years from now, and ten years from now. Make sure that in your vision, everyone around you succeeds. Put it out there and begin to create the life you are meant to live. Become authentic to the person you are meant to be.

CHAPTER 6

Forgiveness

It's Time to Use the F-word

FORGIVENESS IS HARD AF. Depending on who or what you're trying to forgive, it can take months, years, or decades—or even be a process that lasts a lifetime. But there's a reason forgiveness can play such a key role in finding your calm: it's that when you start the process, you can finally begin to let go of all the stuff you were holding on to, which opens the door to a more peaceful you.

So many things can be brewing within us, and sometimes we don't realize that forgiveness is the golden ticket out of the storm. It can start with forgiving that jackass who stole your parking spot during the holiday mall rush, or Aunt Kelly for making a snide comment about your fashion sense when you were fourteen, or mean Mrs. Smith who always put down your math skills, or a parent for mistreating you. Or how about those horrifying, unexpected cards you're dealt: a loved one who was taken away or your own unexpected illness.

Forgiveness can be the uphill battle of all uphill battles, but also the most rewarding. When you forgive, you start to let shit go. The shackles of emotion that are holding you back no longer have the same strength. The anger, bitterness, sadness, and resentment, as well as the subtler emotions associated with the very thing that needs forgiving, can be thrown in the trash. Forgiveness doesn't mean things won't hurt anymore or that you'll suddenly, magically, never remember Aunt Kelly's comment or Mrs. Smith's degrading remarks; it just means you're able to let go a little. You're able to sit in the eye of the hurricane instead of getting pulled in and triggered every time those memories seep back into your subconscious mind.

Nina's journey to forgive her dad started during her "I'm doing me" commitment. It was twenty years in the making. She didn't even realize how much she was holding on to until she dug deep and looked the past square in the face. The early years of her parents' marriage were steeped in abuse toward Nina's mom. It started off as physical abuse but later gave way to verbal abuse, using control and manipulation. Divorce was taboo in Indian culture, so her mom fought through it. Her parents went on to have Nina and, five years later, Nina's brother, Vijay. Nina's mom told herself that if the abuse was still happening when her son turned ten, she would leave the marriage. And she did. In December 1996, she courageously served her husband with divorce papers and told him to vacate the house. For Nina's dad, this came completely out of the blue; it shocked him and shook him to the core. After twenty-two years of sheer and utter control over this woman, she had pulled the rug from under him.

The next six months were emotionally trying and unstable for everyone. Nina's dad's behaviour was unpredictable and slightly deranged. Even though he was no longer living at home, he would come by in the morning and evening. Some days he would be doing the dishes (a task he'd never performed) and begging for forgiveness, promising all kinds of change, and the next day he would be standing behind her mom's car, blocking her from going to work, and yelling, "You stupid bitch! You aren't going to get away with this!"

Nina and Vijay didn't leave each other's sides. They'd always been very close, but the divorce took their sibling bond to a whole new level. They were young, scared at times, and frustrated by their dad's behaviour. They leaned into each other and tried to keep things light with silly jokes and sleepovers in each other's rooms. One night, Nina's mom had a meeting with her VP, which was scheduled to run until 8 p.m. She left spaghetti in the fridge and told them to have dinner and get themselves to bed. Their dad had taken the day off and was subtly hovering around them all evening. They were hanging out, doing homework and watching TV, when their mom surprisingly walked in around 4:30 p.m. Her meeting had been rescheduled, and she'd decided to take Nina to her optometrist appointment, which, though she had cancelled it earlier, was luckily still available. "Can I come, too, Mom?" Vijay asked. Nina's dad jumped in and promised he would take Vijay to the mall to buy him a pair of jeans, instead. As Nina and her mom were leaving, Vijay looked down from the second-floor landing and asked,

"How about two jeans?" Nina's mom laughed. "Whatever you want, Vi!" she said.

What happened next was something no one anticipated or could ever even have imagined. While Nina and her mom were out, Nina's dad killed Vijay and took his own life in a gut-wrenching murder-suicide. The brutal act was premeditated. The detectives involved in the case told Nina that had her mom's meeting not been cancelled, Nina would have suffered the same fate as her brother.

Nina was sixteen at the time, and the years after were excruciatingly painful. She tried to process all that had transpired. She struggled with survivor's guilt and PTSD—post-traumatic stress disorder—from witnessing the crime scene, and had many sleepless nights trying to piece together her brother's last, struggling moments. She didn't realize it at the time, but she likely fell in and out of depressive states. For the first two years, she couldn't even grieve Vijay because she was so angry with her dad. *Why couldn't he just have taken his own life?*

Vi was a kind and gentle soul. He had excelled in every sport and was the acclaimed fifth-grade class DJ. But everyone loved him for his soft heart and his sparkling almond-shaped eyes, along with his ear-to-ear smile. He was the one who convinced the boys to let girls join their soccer match at recess, would give his last snack away if someone told him they were hungry, or remind us to look up at the full moon. He was immensely loved by all, and the loss was unimaginable.

Nina got professional help, but she also followed in her mom's footsteps with spirituality and meditation. And that is where she was finally able to find some peace. They truly saved her. Which is why she's now so passionate about sharing them with others.

You never really come to terms with or "get over" the loss of loved ones: you just somehow learn to live a new normal without them. Nina eventually pushed her dad out of her mind and just went on as if he'd never existed, so that she could finally get on with honouring Vijay. It wasn't until twenty years later that she realized something important: the decision to push him out just meant he'd been swirling around in her subconscious somewhere, along with all the emotions he'd triggered in her. During her journey to find her authentic self, Nina read a lot about forgiveness, and she realized that the only way to truly let go of her anger and resentment was to forgive her dad. This was less about him than it was about her. Although forgiveness is something she's still working through, the initial push helped her kickstart the process of letting go. She's not sure if you ever get to a place of complete forgiveness with this kind of hurt, but she's come a long way and doesn't get triggered as much as she used to. While she continues to have bouts of anger and resentment, she's definitely in a more peaceful place.

As part of her very pragmatic approach to authenticity, Nina started to research how to forgive. She found that there are many different ways. There is absolutely no set path, since everyone's experience is different, so it's about leaning into what works for you.

Forgiveness isn't condoning what happened, or making excuses for the person who caused pain, or righting their wrong. This isn't about *them*—it's about *you*. It's making a choice to release yourself from the stuff you're holding on to. When you release, you feel so liberated, and so much lighter.

Shedding the Weight

Have you ever done some deep breathing or had a session with a great therapist and walked out thinking, *I actually feel lighter*. Or perhaps you've solved an issue with a friend or a family member and you get off the phone or walk away from the conversation and say to yourself, *It feels as if a weight is off my shoulders*. Why is that, and what is it that you're letting go? It's not physical weight—it's emotional weight, and you know for certain because you can *feel* it.

Imagine if there were a scale that could measure your emotional weight. You might be walking around with what your doc deems a healthy physical weight, but what do you weigh emotionally? How much mental and emotional weight are you carrying in the form of guilt, anger, sadness, jealousy, resentment, anxiousness, and so on? Fifty pounds? One hundred and fifty pounds? Three hundred pounds? Maybe someday we'll have technology that can actually measure that. Of course, all these emotions are natural and will be felt at some point, but it doesn't hurt to have a sense of everything that is weighing you down. In other words, take care of your mind like you do your body and start to let that shit go. By making yourself aware of this emotional weight, you can dig into it and start shedding those emo pounds.

In the sun-and-clouds analogy we discussed earlier,

there are different types of clouds. There are wispy ones that just cover the sun and still let you soak up all that you need. There are sparse, grey rain clouds that zip past for a quick shower. And then there are the dark, thunderous, "my power might go out" clouds. The emo counterparts of these clouds might be preventing you from accessing your inner happiness. But some of the weight that comes with the thunderous ones is so deep inside you that you might not even know it's there.

Going through the process of shedding that weight is not something you think to do daily. You're running around, meeting friends, making sure you drink enough water, getting in your workout. But when you take the time to sift through the shit you're holding on to and try to release it, it can have a positive effect on your day-to-day mood.

What's interesting is that it's not just a lack of time that can cause you to put off the work required to forgive. Turns out there's a reason you might *intentionally* avoid adding this task to your to-do list: it can be super-painful to look at the things people have done to you in the past, or the things you need to forgive yourself for. Maybe you'd rather not. Maybe you just don't want to feel those feelings.

But resisting that impulse and actually *going there* can have serious benefits. Harvard Medical School psychologist Susan David, PhD, says that "radical acceptance of all our emotions, even the messy, difficult ones, is the cornerstone to resilience, thriving and true authentic happiness." She also says that when emotions are pushed down, they can get stronger. Remember, *what you resist persists*.

In her TED Talk "The Gift and Power of Emotional

Courage," Susan explains that you wouldn't be human if you never got stressed, or sad, or had your heart broken, or failed. These emotions are part of what it is to be alive and have a meaningful life. As we learned in our discussion about perspective, the crappy stuff can help us to notice and enjoy all the sweet goodness in life. When we go through the hard bouts, we appreciate the good even more.

Don't shy away from digging deep into your anger toward others, your guilt surrounding your own actions, or any shame you might be feeling around events that happened in the past. We know—*yuck, yuck, yuck!*—this doesn't sound like fun, but looking at these feelings, acknowledging them, and moving through them can help you take the weight off.

As you look at these hurts, treat them like the most delicate piece of china. Be there for the pain, but don't pressure it by saying things like "You need to have healed this much by this time post-breakup." Or "It's been thirty years and it's time to get over this already." Be true to your emotions and honour them. Maybe something happened ten years ago, but you're only looking at it and healing now. That's totally okay. Just like Nina. There's no time limit to the process, or instructions on the exact way to feel or handle situations that have put you through gut-wrenching pain. The key is to simply be there for yourself, and to be kind and gentle as you work through things.

In this chapter we focus on different ways to let go, through forgiveness, of the emotional weight you're carrying. This is a very personal process, so be kind AF with yourself and do what works for you. At first, you might not know exactly how to forgive, and that's okay. Being open to it is a great first step, so trust both the process and that things will all fall into place. Before you know it, you'll be wondering why you feel lighter or calmer. What used to trigger you won't affect you as much as it once did, and you can start living without as much shit holding you back.

Forgiveness = Freedom

ECKHART TOLLE is a *New York Times* bestselling author and spiritual teacher. He spent much of his life under the age of thirty struggling with depression, anxiety, and fear. He is now a huge proponent of acing that present-moment stuff we've been talking about and has written remarkable books on how to do just that, such as *The Power of Now* and *A New Earth*. He says, "Forgiveness happens naturally as soon as you realize that the past cannot prevail against the power of presence."

In chapter 3 we talked about how thoughts of the past take you away from the present. The reason forgiveness can have such an impact on you is that when you keep going back to what hurt you, you are holding on to the past. And, of course, when you're in the past, it's impossible to access the happiness and serenity that are right under your nose.

No one is suggesting you negate the past or what transpired there, but the present is where you can find that calm you've been looking for everywhere else. It's also where you can create a positive future. The process of forgiving others and also yourself is freeing. You go from being caged by your past to freely spreading your wings and letting that shit go. It's liberating to even visualize.

Think about how good a spring cleaning feels. You remove all the crap from your closet, and you feel like you've got a brand-new space. Same goes for a mental spring cleaning. Removing the old stuff that's been there for a while feels amazing, and once it's gone, you can make room for the new. It's hard to experience true freedom when things are holding you back. You're too bogged down.

There are many ways to forgive and . . . not necessarily forget, but move forward. You can't ever really forget all the things that hurt you—they are a part of you and your memory. But you can become much less attached to those things when you're focused on the present.

Anger Is like a Ball of Fire

THIS MAY SOUND counterintuitive, but when you are angry at someone or something, the person you are hurting the most is yourself. Anger is like a ball of fire—go ahead and throw it, but know that you'll burn your hand in the process. Of course anger will bubble up now and again—you can't help it sometimes—but holding on to it just burns you. By all means, look at those emotions. Acknowledge them and then let them go. Allow them to move through you.

Like we said, forgiveness is not as much about the other person as it is about you. Forgiving is hard at first, and it might make you feel as if you're handing someone a "get out of jail free" card, but it's not about that. Sometimes it's not even about telling someone you forgive them, but simply forgiving them in your own mind. You're the one carrying this shit around, not them. Aunt Kelly might not even remember that comment about your poor fashion sense, and Nina's dad had been dead and gone for twenty years while she held on to the whole mess. For what?

Of course, you have to be ready to forgive. As we said earlier, it might take months or years to start the process, so be patient with yourself. If you're still processing the emotion around the issue, that's okay. But perhaps put the thought out there that you won't carry around this extra weight for your entire life.

When you finally do enter the realm of forgiveness, you'll notice a big change. Any time the thought of that person or incident bubbles up to your conscious mind, it won't affect you in the same way it used to. Sure, maybe you'll get a ping of pain or a pounding heart for a few seconds, but then you can breathe and get back to calm mode, because that ball of fire is no longer a ball; it's a little spark of residual stuff that you can more easily work through.

Use Forgiveness to Go

YOU'RE OUT AT A PARTY and your girlfriend makes a comment in the midst of a conversation with some friends that mildly embarrasses you. Momentarily, it ruins your groove, but you brush it off so you can enjoy the rest of your night. The next morning, though, you're mulling it over and getting more and more steamed. You bring it up, and she gives you a decent excuse: she didn't mean to, she thought it was funny, and she gets nervous at parties. She confesses that what she said was stupid and apologizes.

Now, if this is a common thing and you're pissed more often than not, you know the drill: set boundaries for yourself and show how you want to be treated. But if you understand where she's coming from, it truly is uncommon, and you want to get to a place of mental peace, it's time to use the F-word.

Think of why you should forgive her. Think of the reasons she might have said what she did. Think of the times *you've* done or said unintentionally hurtful things and she forgave you.

This is not about formally saying "I forgive you," like something out of a romantic English period piece. By all means do that if it feels right. But this process is more about helping *you* get peace of mind so you can get on with being your badass self. And the benefits it will have for your relationship can be tenfold. Instead of spending the day annoyed at each other, you can move on and enjoy it.

Disclaimer: none of this means that you don't give yourself space to get angry, upset, or sad, and to understand why the comment hurt you so much. Feel those feelings!

The more you can better understand why something hurt you, the more you can move past it, because you're being accountable and responsible for your own emotions.

Forgiveness is simply a mental muscle you can use to let things go more easily as they come up, and feeling your feels is part of that process. You can use the F-word with close friends, even strangers. Think about that time you called customer service regarding an erroneous charge on your statement. After an hour on hold you finally get in touch with a customer service rep. They are anything but helpful and giving you heaping spoonfuls of 'tude to boot.

You're fuming as you think, *How can this company get away with robbing people? Why is this person not listening to me? WTF?* Sometimes the squeaky wheel really does get the grease, but there's a difference between being assertive and losing your wits. You start to lose your cool and become unnecessarily mad and frustrated. Then maybe you even regret your behaviour afterward.

Cue forgiveness mentality. Try to remind yourself that this person is doing their best with the tools they have in life. Maybe they hate their job. Maybe they're having a bad day. Or maybe this is just their personality. But the less time you spend trying to figure that out before you move into forgiveness, the faster you can wave frustrations goodbye. Most often, people are doing the best they can.

You may also need to forgive yourself for losing your cool. You had the right be mad, but you didn't mean to lose your marbles. Be gentle with yourself and others.

So, when daily annoyances pop up, use "forgiveness to go" to help you get to calm more easily.

Walk a Mile in Their Shoes

AN EFFECTIVE WAY to kickstart the forgiveness process is to try to walk a mile in the other person's shoes. This is not about making excuses for them or even acknowledging that the way they behaved was okay. This is about better understanding where they were coming from. It's an exercise that takes a boatload of courage, so if you're not comfortable with it, no need to go there. That said, it can be very a powerful tool when it comes to letting go.

Sometimes we are hurt by the people closest to us, and we can't understand why they would treat us a certain way. Let's take that snide comment from Aunt Kelly about your fashion sense. Who knows why she said what she said? It obviously had nothing to do with you. Doesn't mean it didn't hurt, but what was going on with her? Maybe she saw you in that dress and it triggered a memory from when she was young. Or maybe she had a bout of anger looking at the innocent you, because she was robbed of her own childhood in some way. Knowing the comment had nothing to do with you can help you let it go.

To take this a little deeper, let's look at your parents. Maybe they didn't let you pursue your dream in acting and pushed you into law because they felt it would be better for you. Perhaps they did this because they had always struggled to stay afloat financially, and felt that a law degree would guarantee you a certain level of income, whereas an acting career is not as defined a path and can take years to establish. What they didn't realize is that you could very well be the next multi-talented Viola Davis. They were blinded by their own path—their own struggles and worries throughout life—and they didn't want you to suffer the same fate. It may not have felt like it, but maybe they did what they did out of love, not because they didn't want what you wanted for yourself. In fact, in their minds, they might have thought they were doing what was best for you.

Next up? The really nasty stuff—abuse and other inexcusable acts. Where does *that* come from? We are lucky to live in an era where mental health is not just acknowledged but cultivated. There are so many preventive initiatives and ways to address what's going on in our heads. Gone are the days when struggles were pushed under the rug (*phew*). The celebrities—actors, musicians, and athletes alike—who have been open about their mental-health struggles have been huge inspirations to others: Kristen Bell, Dwayne Johnson, Lena Dunham, Zayn Malik, DeMar DeRozan, Clara Hughes, Chrissy Teigen, and so many more. By being vulnerable and sharing their stories, they help to prevent others from feeling as if they're alone in this battle or that it's not normal to feel a certain way. A huge "Thank you" is owed to them.

When our parents and grandparents were growing up, mental health wasn't talked about so openly or even understood. It was often chalked up to bad or "odd" behaviour. People didn't generally share or discuss the bad stuff that was going on; back then, it was viewed as airing your dirty laundry. Many things were not dealt with emotionally, and if people suppressed enough shit growing up, it could manifest at some point—sometimes in horrific ways. The more Nina researched, the more she realized that her dad likely

Talk It Out

WE'VE SAID IT BEFORE and we'll say it one last time: you need to let that shit out before you can let that shit go. It is so important not to suppress your emotions and, in fact, express them in every way. Not letting them out may lead them to come out in other ways—emotionally, maybe even physically.

So often, boys in our culture are told "Don't cry," or "Toughen up," or "Man up." Of course men want to be strong, but according to the research we've seen, the thing that makes men—and all humans!—resilient is actually *feeling* those emotions and moving through them, not pushing them down.

Jay-Z called this out recently in an interview where he talked about how ridiculous the social stigma is around men not showing emotion and having to be macho. He's been open about the therapy he's undergone, and how it's helped him process his own emotions and better understand others.

Crying is sexy and strong, and being vulnerable is even sexier. If you can be aware of your emotions and be open to expressing them, good or bad, you're shovelling less crap under the rug. When you end up not addressing shit and sweeping it all under the rug, you'll eventually find yourself trying to get through life by walking on wobbly ground, where it's easier to trip, fall, and slip.

You know all the ways to talk it out: make a call to your friend, cousin, partner, or parents, or see an awesome therapist (48 percent of American households have seen one, and you'd better believe we have therapists who have helped us address some rough goes and process our emotions). You can go to a workshop or to group sessions— knowing other people are going through something similar can make things that much easier to tackle. You don't even have to be formal about it. When you feel something start to bubble up, just grab someone and talk it out.

Talking out any emotion—including anger and frustration—is a good idea. Sometimes it's only when you talk things out that you realize something subconscious is bubbling to the surface. Talking things out is a great first step to forgiveness.

It's Not Just about Others

YOU MIGHT ASSOCIATE forgiveness with others, but it's also critical to learn to forgive yourself. Sounds cheesy, but it's extremely impactful.

Self-forgiveness can apply to things big and small: Like *Why did I stay in the relationship for seven years, when I knew on day two that they might not be the one?* Or forgiving yourself for the typo in that email you sent to the entire office.

Stuff you've been holding on to about yourself builds anger, resentment, and a whole slew of other emotions. All that heavy baggage can put blockades up in your next relationship, or make you feel a bit more nervous than necessary when writing your next mass email.

Self-forgiveness is perfect for those moments you feel anxious about being worried, then angry that you are worried, and then sad about that. When you can catch yourself going there, take a few deep breaths and say some gentle and forgiving AF things like *I know I'm not perfect. I allow myself to make mistakes and I forgive myself.* Just saying the words "I forgive myself" can unleash a wave of good feelings. Remind yourself that you are human and are trying your best.

And if you're having a hard time forgiving yourself, you can even forgive yourself for *that.* By doing so, you'll be able to better slip out of the emotional windstorm you've been caught in and let go of the things you've been using to beat yourself up.

Let the Tiger Be

JUST TO REITERATE, when you're on the path to forgive, it doesn't mean you need to become besties with the person you're working to forgive. The entire process might happen within and require no external conversation. Sometimes we can fall into the trap of thinking that forgiving means fixing a relationship and solving it to the point where things are fantastic again. If you can get there, great, but forgiveness doesn't always have to look this way. You can forgive someone you're not talking to anymore, or someone who is no longer here.

If the person in question *is* still here and will always be a part of your life, it's healthy and okay to give yourself same space. If creating space is something you struggle with because you feel it's rude or that you should treat everyone equally, then know it's not about how you treat *each person* but how you treat *yourself* and honour your own boundaries. Are you allowing this person to play an active role in your life at the expense of your own peace? If someone is not healthy for your well-being, give yourself some breathing room.

Nina asked one of the Swamis from Cali how to deal with challenging people. She strongly felt that everyone in her life should be treated equally and didn't know what do with those who were not so nice. "Aren't we supposed to love everyone just the same and not have judgments about who gets our love and who doesn't?" she asked. Nina's teacher confirmed her instincts. "Yes," he replied, "you're right." She was relieved but still confused, so he offered a brilliant analogy.

He said that when you enter a jungle, you love all the animals equally. You love the little ant, the sleepy sloth, the cheeky monkey, and the beautiful birds. You even love the ferocious tigers. *But*—you wouldn't try to play with the tiger. You know better than that because you know he's going to attack you. So, go on loving him, just love him from a distance. *Boom!* That was it. You still treat everyone equally, but you create some distance around the tigers in your life.

This could mean people in your family, friends you've had for decades, or a co-worker you've known for almost your entire career. If the relationship isn't good for you, it's okay to take some steps back. You can still love that person, but you can do it from afar. This helps foster positive emotions as opposed to letting yourself be negatively triggered all the time and having to go through the anger-and-forgiveness cycle on Repeat.

Stop the Blame Game

SOMETIMES IT FEELS GOOD to grab a drink with a few friends and vent about the person who is getting on your last nerve. Let's take Jen, who is a high-school teacher. She has always been passionate about being a teacher, and she was lucky enough to find a gig at her local school teaching her specialty, math.

Well, teaching isn't quite the same as it used to be. Kids are now all over their phones, and you need to find creative ways to teach, since everyone's attention span seems to be a tad shorter. Jen's approached her principal with several recommendations for shifts in the teaching system that would help engage this new generation, but the principal isn't really taking her suggestions into account. Every day Jen comes into work hoping there will be some change. But when the final bell rings, she leaves frustrated, feeling as if her work struggles are playing out like Groundhog Day.

Jen is quick to blame the principal for inaction, and this creates even more frustration. Every time a student acts out or Jen loses control of the classroom she mentally chides the principal for not letting her use the tactics she thinks will help.

The brilliant Dr. Brené Brown—a research professor at the University of Houston and the author of four books that topped the *New York Times* bestseller list—is a huge advocate of vulnerability. One of the things she says about blame is that it's "simply the discharging of discomfort and pain and has an inverse relationship with accountability." In a way, blame deflects what's going on with you and gives you a false sense of control. The problem is that you hold on to that negativity, so instead of doing something productive about the situation and how the situation is making you feel (for Jen, it might mean having a serious and honest conversation with the principal), you continue to fume. You might think that the problem is out of your hands when you blame, but it's not. To her friends, Jen would say things like "That principal is such an idiot—the entire school is going down," or "I've tried so many times to get it into her thick skull that something needs to change, but she's not budging." Jen thinks the situation is no longer in her hands, yet it nevertheless continues to affect her.

Jen is a fantastic teacher. Her students love her. And of course it is frustrating that her principal is not taking her seriously. What she *can* do, if talking to the principal is not working, is make small changes in her own classroom and perhaps inspire other teachers to do the same. Blaming the principal is not going to propel her forward in any way. In fact, it's holding her back, since she's always overcome by the emotions associated with making these classroom issues someone else's fault.

When things go awry, it's so easy to point the finger and blame someone else. Maybe it's something small, like blaming the friend you got buzzed with last night for you not finding your keys in the morning, or blaming your partner for choosing the "wrong" vacation destination because it rained the entire time. Or maybe it's bigger stuff, like blaming people in your life for bad things that have happened to you. When you blame, you are handing the reins to someone else and giving up control of your own life. On

Make Time for Tea and Stress

WORKING THROUGH STUFF and walking your path toward letting go can be exhausting at times. It can feel all encompassing. You're bringing up emotions you haven't dealt with in some time or maybe didn't even know were sucking up space in your subconscious.

Sometimes it's not even about working through shit; life can just feel stressful in general. That chatty mind of yours is owning you, day in and day out.

It happens. We're all there from time to time. One way to work through it is to actually allocate time for stress. So, you come home from work and give yourself thirty minutes to just bitch. Set an actual timer and then bitch to your heart's content. Call a friend or talk to your partner about the fact that Andrew is getting on your last fucking nerve at work, how you're annoyed at the friend who didn't invite you to their wedding, how you're pissed that your favourite team got swept in the playoffs again, how you're stressed that your kid is acting out at school, or how you're not sure how you're going to make the mortgage payment and pay for that new roof in the same month. Let it *all* out!

Then, once you're done your bitch fest, take a few deep breaths and let that shit go for the evening and into the next day. We get that sometimes stuff comes up when you're not expecting it, and you could be triggered by a whole slew of things outside of this half-hour stretch, so don't suppress stuff. But it might be an effective tool to allocate time in your day for your internal pressure cooker to steam. For some, it beats having a shit-cloud hanging over their head the entire day. So, when your chatty mind starts poking you about this or that, use your observing mind to say, *Hold that thought until 7 p.m.* Park it and go on with your sunny day, and then, when you have the chance, address all that you need to address.

But when that timer goes off, remember to go back to enjoying life. Focus on the macro perspective, be grateful for what's around you, enjoy an ice cream cone, laugh at a random YouTube video, cook a fantastic meal. We know it's not possible to always box your challenges, and we're not encouraging that; we're just sharing a technique that works for some, because, yeah, life isn't perfect.

Dig Up the Shitty Stuff

SO MANY OF US don't even realize what we're holding on to. There's a reason for that: Why would you want to go and revisit all the times you were made to feel shitty? It sounds like it would be a perfect game of "Would You Rather." *Would you rather revisit all the times in your life you were humiliated and hurt by someone, or have the same song stuck in your head for six months straight?* Tough decision.

It sounds like no fun at all, and truthfully, it isn't, but it *is* extremely liberating and healing. No pain, no gain. Think about a workout. You physically put your body through torture sometimes just so you can look good at the beach. Same thing goes for your mind. It's painful to go to those places, but putting in the work can help you lift a massive amount of emotional weight.

Take a moment to think about shitty things that people did to you. When you think of the word *forgiveness*, who pops into that noggin of yours? Go back—like *way* back. List 'em all, and be uber-nice to yourself in the process. Think of the person who said that *thing* in middle school. Think of the time your parents said your marks weren't good enough, or your partner made you doubt yourself, or your boss belittled you. Write down the incident in great detail if you want, or express it out loud, as recommended by Louise Hay, and then say the words "I forgive _____ for _____."

Remember that forgiving *them* is really about *you*, and being able to finally let that shit go. Maybe what they said or did is still not cool or okay, especially if it was repeated. But this is about letting go of all of the emotion that resulted from that incident—emotion you may be holding on to in some way.

This exercise is about forgiving others, but you can use the same approach to forgive yourself. Are you still holding on to mistakes you made in the past? Write them out or say them, and try repeating, "I forgive myself for _____."

Turn Fumes into Fondness

ONE OF THE KEYS to a happy mind is intentionally wishing happiness for others—even those who have massively let us down. Sounds counterintuitive, but it works. The Dalai Lama says, "If you want others to be happy, practice compassion. If you want to be happy, practice compassion." When you are in a conflict with someone, the faster you can understand their pain and relate to it, the faster you can resolve the conflict and mosey into forgiveness territory.

One way to get even closer to forgiveness is actually wishing for the person you're mad at to be happy. Doing this will help you to separate from the pain this person caused. Lovely feelings will be evoked, making you feel good all-around and quelling the potential vengeful gremlin that lurks inside, just waiting for an opportunity to come out.

Think of someone you don't like very much: that dude who cut in front of you in line at the convenience store, the head chef at the restaurant you work at who can be a real dick, or the person who stole your girlfriend in high school—anyone, as long as they are in your "kind of hate you" bucket.

Take a few deep breaths and try to centre yourself. Think about this person laughing and enjoying themselves. Think about everything going swimmingly for them in life. You can't help but smile and enjoy it a little. And if not, that's okay, too. Just the fact that you tried to cultivate a smidgen of happiness and compassion for this person is a great first step.

Try this any time your mind is swirling about someone you're PO'd with. It can be a helpful tool in getting past it.

You're Not the Only One

As you go through the process of forgiveness, it's worth remembering that you're not alone. This can be a comforting thought after a hurtful rejection that has you curled up in a ball on your couch asking, *Why me?*

The proof around you is endless. Look at what your friends have gone through. Look to movies, art, film, and what people around the world are going through. We're all human and we all feel the same emotions. This includes rejection, shame, sadness, jealousy, et cetera.

The singer Adele once said, "In order for me to feel confident with one of my songs, it has to really move me. That's how I know that I've written a good song for myself—it's when I start crying." She knew that when she expressed her own emotions, other people would relate, because they must have felt those things, too. Her instincts proved correct; the reason her songs are so powerful (beyond her exceptional voice and musical talent) is that so many of us can relate to the joy and pain in her music.

On some level we all know that we're not alone in what we feel, but we don't often take the time to meditate on it. Sometimes when we feel rejected, hurt, or anxious, or that we've been taken advantage of, we feel like we're the only ones. But so many people feel the exact same things you do.

The rise of memes on the internet (bless them) capture in just a few words and a low-res image the essence and awkwardness of being human. Look at all the likes and regrams these get. Remember that life isn't perfect, but at least we can go through this stuff knowing we're not alone.

The Thorns Get You to the Rose

THE REASON YOU'RE in a position where you need to forgive someone is, obviously, that they hurt you in the first
place. Or maybe it's not *someone* who's hurt you but rather
life itself that just hasn't gone the way you'd anticipated.
Anger can also lead to a loss in faith, and leave you questioning why the fuck something is happening to you and wondering how it's fair. Which is completely normal and okay.

Maybe there are some deep-rooted things you need
to work through. You're taking the necessary steps to get
there, but along the way you still can't figure out why things
transpired the way they did. Perhaps you'll never know, but
where you can find peace is knowing that . . . sometimes
you have to go through the thorns to get to the rose.

Imagine if life were always simple and easy. There are
two things to consider. The first is that you wouldn't appreciate the good times in the way that you do if you hadn't
endured the bad. But the second and more important thing
is that you wouldn't be *who you are* today without your challenges. Enduring those thorns is what made you strong. It's
what built your character. It's what made you value life the
way you do. It wasn't okay for those people to do those
shitty things to you, or maybe it wasn't fair that you had to
go through the crap you did, but you are a different person
because of what you experienced.

In Japan, Kintsugi, or "golden joinery," is a long-standing
tradition in which broken bowls are repaired with gold. So
instead of seeing a bowl riddled with cracks, you see a stunning piece of art, where the cracks are filled with gold. The

point is to emphasize the beauty in what once was broken. The Japanese believe that when you have suffered, it makes you more beautiful.

Challenges are not pretty. They can be downright brutal at times. But you come out of them with wisdom, and they shape who you are. On your path to forgiveness remember this: you are a stronger and better person for what you've endured. Give yourself a pat on the back for making it through. Knowing that you got to that rose is a powerful way to let go of the thorns.

CHAPTER 7

Behind the Screen

Finding Your Tech Zen

LILLY SINGH—A.K.A. IISuperwomanII—is a hilarious AF YouTube personality. She's also an author, vlogger, actress, and UNICEF's newest goodwill ambassador. In one of her videos she talks about how we are basically in a relationship with our phone. We interact with it more than with any living person in our life, and we get pissed at it when it's not doing what we want it to. We swear at it, roll our eyes at it, even throw it on the couch when we're fed up. We laugh or cry over the messages we receive through it, and we feel sad when we can't find it. We buy it new cases or change the hardware when we're not feeling it anymore.

We couldn't live without our phones, laptops, tablets, et cetera. They give us the ability to stay in touch with loved ones, keep up-to-date on what's happening, share incredible moments, virtually see people halfway across the world, and connect with humans we've never met. Devices have helped us overcome our fears and allowed us to reach out when we maybe wouldn't have otherwise. They help us be our authentic selves and enable us to create a world we feel good about and are comfortable in. We are very lucky to be living in this connected era.

Social media in particular have enhanced our relationships. Facebook, Instagram, Snapchat, Twitter, LinkedIn—you name it: we are now able to be part of one another's lives in ways we never imagined. You can see wedding photos, babies, trips, work updates—all the great moments that make up a beautiful life. Sharing these precious times with others can be even more meaningful when a ton of people are liking your shit. There's no longer a need to invite the family over to go through a slideshow of your favourite vacation pics (this actually used to happen, back in the day).

Social media can help you convey your points of view and give you a platform to address things you're passionate about in life. Not only does this drive self-expression, but it also helps local businesses and can inspire social change. Look at what the online world has done for the women's rights movement with #metoo. In the thick of the movement there were 1.7 million tweets across eighty-five countries. Social media also helped to spark a conversation around gun violence and gun control that drew hundreds of thousands of people out for the March for Our Lives protest. It's been used for so much positive change in this world.

Kate can attest to the benefits of Facebook for her own business, Mind Matters. She launched it in 2016 to help create a shift in the way we discuss and approach mental health. The goal was to get people to think about improving their mind in the same way they do their body. With psychotherapists, productivity gurus, art therapists, and mindfulness instructors, she launched workshops with cheeky titles like "How Not to Give a Sh*t: A Workshop on Stress" and "Mindful AF." Thanks to those "share" and "like" buttons on Facebook, they garnered thousands of responses resulting in most of the events selling out—without any money spent on advertising. Which was extremely helpful, as Kate did not have advertising money to spend.

But while these social platforms can have huge benefits, they can also sometimes make us feel as if we're not up to snuff. Sometimes *you know* when you've had too much—maybe after spending longer than you anticipated scrolling through your feeds. It can feel like you have a social media hangover. You're angry or upset but not sure why. You just can't seem to pinpoint it. Perhaps it's the result of a deep creep that led you to a random person's profile—like your cousin's best friend's brother, with his spectacular wedding in Italy. Often, in the moment, it feels great, and you want to keep scrolling, but it can potentially leave you feeling crummy—like finishing a big bag of chips you didn't intend to polish off.

What's important to understand is that these posts are, in many cases, everyone's highlight reel of life. Their best moments: Kygo's crazy set at Coachella; the family pic in front of one of the Seven Wonders of the World; the new, innocent, beyond-gorgeous baby in a tutu ten times her size. You love sharing these moments because they make you feel good; and others genuinely do want to hear about your crazy music fest, or trip of a lifetime, or latest addition.

But know that these are the "icing on the cake" moments. What you don't often see are the shit moments: the depressing comedown after the concert high; the pics of how pissed that family was when their flight got cancelled and they had to pay $4,000 to get on the next flight; the sleep deprivation or colicky baby who doesn't stop wailing for five hours straight that sends the parent into an emotional tailspin. These days more and more people *are* posting about life's shitty moments, too—and kudos to them for doing that, because it's not easy to put the tough stuff out there on display. But sometimes it's that rawness and realness that leads to true connections.

As long as you know that what you're seeing on social media is a somewhat false take on reality (meaning, those pictures likely don't represent the entirety of that person's life), you're all good. But if you think that people's lives are actually that amazing all the time and you wonder why yours is so shitty, don't be fooled. All those perfect selfies are snapped by humans who cry and get angry and feel alone and have shit moments—just like you.

Nina took a Facebook break a few years ago. She loved the platform, but it had started making her feel anxious about her own life. An acquaintance went on a crazy-amazing trip around the world and posted pictures of her family with comments about how blessed she felt and how much she loved life. It made Nina feel that this was the trip she'd been yearning for and had never gotten to take. But when the family returned home, Nina found out her acquaintance and her husband had decided to get divorced on that very trip. WTF? You'd never guess that behind all that perfection were long, melancholy conversations about what was truly going on. Nina realized that what she was seeing wasn't a representation of real life, and that the way she was digesting it wasn't healthy. Take relationships: you see fun moments and selfies, chill nights, sexy dress-up dates, cute kisses—the whole gamut. Then, suddenly, there's a breakup and . . . nada. With no warning, this perfect love story you've been following abruptly ends. Sometimes, all the couple-y pictures are even deleted. Do you see pictures of the intense fights, the uncontrollable crying, the accusations and anger? Nope. But those things had to have happened. Maybe you were so invested in this couple and their social media journey that you even want an explanation now that it's over!

No one has to post the shitty. Most people have the freedom to post what they want, but it's important to use a realistic lens while scrolling. Next time you're thinking about how perfect someone's life looks and it makes you feel a bit off, just know that behind the screens they're a lot more like you than you might at first think.

The other thing to consider is that social media can give you a rush of dopamine, the feel-good chemical that's released in your brain and that makes you feel happy. This reaction occurs when you eat a piece of chocolate or receive a sweet kiss from a new crush. That's what can make being online feel so addictive—your brain is thinking, *I want another hit of that, please.* It also explains why it's so easy to continually scroll. Subconsciously, you crave the hit. This is why it's helpful to lean into your observing mind when you're mindlessly on your device. Notice how it is making you feel before, during, and after. What are your motivations when you're jumping on? When you're honest with yourself about how you use tech, it can help you to find that right balance. Only you know the answer to what feels good and what feels icky, but the key is to be aware of your feelings and convince yourself to stop when you're not into being on social media anymore.

It's ironic that in this day and age when we're more connected than ever, we sometimes still feel disconnected. In the midst of this powerful and often amazing shift in tech, we don't want to forget or lose good old in-person human connection. A phone can't replace a warm hug from a close family member, a hot date night, dinner out with friends, or bonding time with your kids or nieces and nephews. In this chapter we'll go through some tips that will help you find a proper balance between digital and human connection.

It's good to be aware of those social media hangovers and to make sure that all this tech isn't sending us into an emo slump. Remember that happiness can be accessed within, and make a mental note when you find yourself searching for it a little too far out there.

The Instant Gratification Era

It's all just a sweet click away. In chapter 4, when we explored perspective, we talked about how easy it is these days to get what you want faster than ever before. Now you can immediately stream a flick you've been meaning to see (versus schlepping down to the video rental store and hoping it's available), download your new fave tune instantly (versus scouring stores for the record), and see a picture the moment after you take it (versus waiting a week for your film to be developed).

Even the dating scene is fast. You can swipe right and—*boom!*—you've got a date Friday night. Or you can DM that crush and spark a flirty chat. Back in the day, when you had a crush on someone and you wanted to get in touch outside of school, it was an entire production. First, you had to muster up the strength to use your land line, which everyone in the house shared. Next, you had to warn everyone in the house that you were making a call. (This was so that they wouldn't use the phone—or get on the internet, if you want to go back to the mid '90s.) Then, you'd pick up the phone and dial your crush's land line, heart racing and all.

Typically, your crush's parent would answer, "Hello?"

Oh fuck. You'd clear your throat and put on your best voice. "Hello, Mrs. Chan, can I please speak to Carol?"

"Sure, may I know who's calling?"

Gulp, heart racing even faster. "It's Eric."

If the parent was nice, they would pass the phone to your hottie, but some parents would actually ask *why* you were calling. It was awful! No one could get in touch with anyone without the entire house knowing. And, hopefully, you didn't have a sneaky sibling who would pick up the extension line while you were using the phone, just to taunt you.

Things are *so much* easier now. You have your very own totally personalized phone. You can ping whomever you want whenever you want. You can instantly send messages back and forth versus passing a handwritten note to your bestie in math class. You can make calls without having to alert the entire world. It's incredible, and it's given you the ability to have your own private life.

With all these great advancements in tech, we've gotten used to the notion of instant gratification. Simon Sinek is an author, motivational speaker, and marketing consultant. He has some key insights into the impact of the digital age and how instant gratification has affected us. The challenge, he says, is that some things in life cannot be achieved instantly, but because we're so used to instant, we get frustrated when we have to be patient.

Make the distinction between what can be gained instantly and what cannot. Sure, music, shows and movies, food, and dates can satisfy your craving for instant gratification, but what are some things that can't be so easily attained? With the click of a button you can swipe right to go on a first date, but it might take months to establish a good relationship. You can apply for a job instantly, but the interview process will require time, and once you land that gig don't expect to work your way up to CEO in six months—getting to a senior position can take years. If you're learning a new skill, like how to play the guitar or how to knit a sweater, that shit's gonna need some time, so don't lose your cool if you're not getting it right away. And when you do bump up against something you can't access immediately, know that this is a time to exude some good ol' patience.

Our need for instant gratification can also get in the way of getting shit done. If you're a natural procrastinator, this era doesn't help, since it's filled with easily accessible, juicy distractions. Tim Urban, the popular blogger from

Wait But Why, believes that inside a procrastinator's brain lurks something he calls the "instant gratification monkey." This guy prefers play over work, and tends to take the wheel in the midst of getting shit done. Tim, a confessed procrastinator, says the instant gratification monkey is responsible for taking him off task. One minute he's hard at something productive and the next he's diving deep into what happened in the Tonya Harding and Nancy Kerrigan case, then checking to see what's in the fridge from ten minutes ago, then following that up by watching videos on magnets and Justin Bieber's mom. Tim calls this zone the "Dark Playground." The problem with this place is that it doesn't feel so good. It's like you're half enjoying it but also half worried because you know you need to be focused on the task at hand. If you can push through the feeling of "let me google my name and see what photos come up again because I forgot," you might be able to get into a state of flow or, more importantly, get your work done sooner so you can watch that YouTube clip without the anxiety. The more you do it, the easier it will get. You'll feel in control more often and be able to cross shit off your to-do list.

Remember that the subtle things in life take time and patience, so stay committed and keep your eye on the prize. It will pay off.

Close All Tabs

IT'S MONDAY MORNING and you're at work, sitting in front of your computer. You have a huge PowerPoint deck to get done by the end of the day and you're about half-way through. You'd meant to finish it over the weekend, but that Saturday night out combined with a gluttonous Sunday brunch, complete with mimosas, made you feel as if you couldn't possibly open your laptop and be any kind of productive.

So here you are. You have the perfectly made coffee to support you. You get started and are ten minutes in, feeling great, when out of the corner of your eye you see that cutie from finance walk over.

"How was the weekend?" she asks.

You channel your inner Kit Harington and smoothly roll your chair back to chat. Fifteen minutes go by and your chatty mind is reminding you of that unfinished deck. The conversation ends and you get back to work. Ten minutes later and, *shit*, in comes an email from your VP, Amran, wanting an update on another project. You respond to him in a timely fashion and then you're back to your deck. You're in a good groove, when your buddy Xavier messages you about dinner tonight. You forgot to make reservations at this sick new Thai place, so you quickly do that . . . and back to your deck.

This is a pretty common workplace scenario these days. Constant interruption. While multi-tasking can serve you well at times, there's something to be said for staying focused. Sometimes it's not even a colleague, boss, or friend who's distracting; it's having PowerPoint, Word, Apple Music, Skype, and email open all at once, not to mention all kinds of other things we keep switching to while we're trying to accomplish one thing.

Neil Pasricha, the *New York Times* bestselling author of *The Book of Awesome* and *The Happiness Equation*, is a huge proponent of finding your life's happy. In one of his articles he talks about David Meyer, a mathematical psychologist and cognitive scientist, who says that all this switching back and forth between things is costing you. He says that not being able to focus for even ten-minute intervals can result in a 20 percent to 40 percent loss in potential efficiency. Essentially, you get a bout of writer's block every time you come back from a distraction. You've experienced this. You're in a good flow, but then you get interrupted and lose your train of thought. Gloria Mark, of the University of California, Irvine, discovered that "a typical office worker gets only 11 minutes between each interruption, while it takes an average of 25 minutes to return to the original task after an interruption." If you're stopping every 11 minutes, you're never getting to a place of clear focus. How is this impacting your efficiency and quality of work?

Next time you're working through something, try turning your phone over or closing all tabs except the one you're working on—or do both. Sometimes the thought of turning off email notifications can cause anxiety, because you want to always be available. Perhaps this is something to discuss with your manager and team. Of course you have to be accountable within your role, but you also want to produce your best work. If you're a leader, perhaps you can encourage your team to close email notifications so they're not so easily distracted every time they hear a *ping*. This should result in increased productivity. Is it really imperative that they (or you) answer every single email right away? Chances are it's not, and if you do find you really need people for something urgent, try walking up to their desks or calling them in order to avoid online distractions that might take you off-task. When we stay focused on the task at hand, it gets done faster and our output is often stronger.

Try Not to Fucking Miss It

HAVE YOU EVER BEEN to a concert where everyone's really amped to see the band? It's five minutes until the show starts, you're drinking a beer, and the whole room is buzzing. Your friend thinks the band is going to blow the lid off the place by opening with their hit song, but you know they're going to save it for the encore. Then, as the lights dim and the band rushes the stage, with everyone screaming, 75 percent of the people in the room whip out their phones. If you've got your phone in front of your face for the majority of the show, are you really experiencing the concert in its absolute amazingness?

Was it worth it to pay $80 for those tickets just to watch the whole thing through that tiny little screen? Living in the moment isn't snapping a pic of everything you do in a day. Don't get us wrong here: we love it when you get that perfect grammable moment. But once you get it, maybe it's time to just enjoy the band. You spent money for this, and time scheduling the whole thing, so take the two or three hours you're there to really experience it. Not for anyone but you.

A good way to get into the moment is to lean into your senses. Focus on one thing at a time—the sound of the bass, the way the crowd is going wild, the joy of your friend jamming out next to you, the feeling the music gives you. This can shut down any chatty thoughts you might be having about sharing that video or picture (like what cute message and emoji you're going to post it with, and whom you're going to share it with). Staying in the moment this way will help you really get the best out of the concert. You might find that you enjoy it even more.

If you do plan to take a vid, try to make that intentional, too. Remind yourself why you want to share it and how sharing it will enhance your experience. This goes for any event that's worth sharing. And once you get that perfect pic or video, share it, and then go back to experiencing life in the moment.

You Can't Fool the Kiddos

IF YOU HAVE kids, have they ever asked you to put down your phone? You're not alone. (We've been there, done that.) How many times do you pretend to pay attention to them while scrolling or harmlessly sending that last quick message? Kids are way more intuitive than adults; they know exactly what's going on. They know when they're being ignored and when you're choosing your phone over them. When that happens, they either shut down and continue to play quietly on their own or they scream louder for your attention. Neither is optimal. Say it's the former, and you continue looking at your phone, taking the quiet as a sign that the kids no longer need you. You've miscalculated. They've just internalized that—once again—the phone won.

There's a public service announcement featuring Will Ferrell that's all about encouraging a device-free dinner. It starts with a mom and three kids around the dinner table. The kids, almost in tears, are talking about how much they miss their dad, and Mom is empathizing. You're thinking the dad has passed away, but then the shot pans out and there he is, sitting at the head of the table on his phone, telling them to be quiet because he's trying out a filter that makes him look like a cat. At one point they all start sharing things with him to see if he's paying attention:

"I got implants."

"I started smoking."

"I'm selling bongs out of our minivan."

His wife says, "I'm dating your brother."

The youngest daughter tells him she's cooking meth in the basement, and he's so preoccupied with his phone that he responds with "Great idea, kiddo! That's why you're so popular at school!"

It's all a hilarious exaggeration, obviously, but it calls attention to a very real issue. Sometimes, as parents, it's hard to enforce phone rules for yourself.

During the week, how much time do you get with your kids? If it's a small percentage of your day compared with work, then make that time count. It will mean the world to them. Fast-forward twenty years and imagine that you had spent all of that small amount of time on your phone instead of sharing real moments. What would you have missed out on? Your kids would be off at college or living in their own homes. How would your relationship with them differ if you'd chosen quality time, instead? Oh, and you'd better believe that when they're old enough to get their own phones, they'll mirror whatever tech protocol is in place at home. Before you know it, *you* might be seeking their attention, not the other way around.

One approach when your kids are there is to make your phone into a "we" activity instead of a "me" thing. There are fun ways to use your phone with your kid—making funny Snapchat filter faces together, watching a quick video of their last soccer match (and high-fiving them for that killer goal), or FaceTiming Auntie Shahina across the pond. You can play music on it together and get lit around the house. Okay, maybe not get lit, but you know what we mean.

We've all had moments where we think it's no big deal to get that one last email out or quickly text the WhatsApp group back about weekend plans, but those moments add up. So just be aware of them. Ask yourself if you really need to be responding or scrolling in this moment or if it can wait. Perhaps set some boundaries and tell yourself that for two of the three hours you get to spend with your kids after work, you won't look at your phone. It's next to impossible to hear the phone buzz and not look, so put it on airplane mode or keep it out of earshot.

The thing is, young kids are almost always in the moment—that place where you, too, can find your peace and happiness. They're happy collecting rocks outside, creating their next Picasso knock-off, or building a train set. They can teach you a lot about life in the here and now; they are wise little things that way. When they want your attention, take the opportunity to be present. You might actually notice that *they* are the ones calming *you* down after a stressful day.

Make Time for Real FaceTime

IT'S NOT JUST KIDS who crave your attention. It's your partner, parents, siblings, friends, and co-workers. Have you ever been to a restaurant and noticed an entire table of fellow diners on their phones? What about witnessing a meal getting cold because people are trying to craft the best foodie shot? (Guilty over here!) We all do it, because it's fun to share those delicious moments, but maybe set some limits for yourself. In its *Mindfulness* special edition issue that came out in 2016, *TIME* magazine suggests phone stacking. It's a game people play when they're out with family, friends, or colleagues. Everyone stacks their phones in the centre of the table, and the first person to pick theirs up pays the bill. The writers also suggest putting your phone in airplane mode more often, doing a digital Sabbath, or simply not carrying your phone everywhere.

And when you've actually scheduled time to be with someone, make an effort to do just that. Of course your phone is a great way to keep in touch regularly. You see each other's Insta posts, you share YouTube videos, you like each other's Facebook updates—it's actually your device that keeps your friendships so strong. But when you finally do decide to grab dinner or a drink, try to honour that time.

When it comes to your partner, this "time honouring" practice can be a little tougher. You see them every day, and the time you spend together isn't as much of a novelty as it can be with someone you don't see often. Still, try to create some space where neither of you is on your phone.

Maybe it's right before bed. Many of us use this time to scroll while simultaneously giving each other the day's update, but putting the device down will heighten that all-important human connection, especially with the people you love the most.

Ice Storms Make Babies

Ever wonder what might happen if you *didn't* spend a good chunk of your evening checking your phone on and off, or if your last few moments in bed were spent snuggling with your partner instead of scrolling Instagram?

Neil Pasricha has some very effective tools for how to strike that perfect balance between phone life and real life, and how that balance can help mitigate stress. He suggests things like not looking at your phone for an hour after you wake up and an hour before bed, or leaving your phone in the car after work so you can't instinctively check your work email every time you hear it buzz, or even charging your phone in the basement of your home (or at least another room) so you create a bit of a barrier between it and you. He believes steps like these provide a little space and breathing room so you can experience more of life in the flesh.

Technology is a great tool, but when we pull back a little and make room for more of the cozy stuff, miraculous shit can happen.

In December 2013, a massive ice storm made its way across North America. Once things settled, it was truly a beautiful sight: ice coated anything and everything—tree branches sparkled and glistened in the sun, and icicles hung from benches, garbage bins, bikes, even litter. People turned their driveways into ice rinks and played hockey. Cars were completely frozen over, which prevented people from going out. The hydro towers were affected, too, and eventually the power went out. More than a million residences were in the dark, some for days.

Fast-forward nine months. Mike and Nina are entering the labour and delivery unit at their local hospital, ready to have their sweet pumpkin. The hospital is packed with preggo patients ready to pop. Although it's uncommon for this particular unit to run out of space, that's exactly what's happening. The nurses are giggly about it, and Nina asks what the unforeseen influx of people in L&D is all about. One of the nurses finally explains with a wink: "It's been nine months since that ice storm, and I guess, without power, couples were spending *a little extra* time with each other."

It was too funny—babies were popping up everywhere! Toronto hospitals actually reported a mini baby boom due to the ice storm. It kind of made sense. Nine months earlier, people had been homebound. On top of that, cooking, watching TV, or using their phones or computers weren't really options . . . so people made a whole heck of a lot of cute babies, instead!

Have you ever had your internet down or lost your phone and thought, *Wow, I have so much time on my hands.* Or *Things seem eerily quiet and calm.* When we shut off the stimuli that's buzzing at us from all directions, something happens. Not only does our mind slow down, but there's also a calming effect on our physical body. Studies have found that silence can actually stimulate brain growth. A 2013 study found that at least two hours of silence can create new cells in the hippocampus (an area linked to memory and emotions). Try bringing a bit of silence and calm into your day or week, even if it's just for ten minutes. If it's intentional, it can have a great effect on your mood and expand your already brilliant brain.

Unplug on Vacay

BACK IN THE DAY when there were no such things as laptops or smartphones, the feeling you had on the last day of work before your vacation was *the best*. You would record a new voicemail message, telling everyone the dates you'd be gone and whom to contact if it was urgent, and you'd craft the perfect email OOO alert (out-of-office alert). You'd switch the OOO on and log off for the last time *ever* . . . well, until you got back, but it felt like ever.

When was the last time you did that? Now when you go on vacation, you might pack work right along with your new bumpin' swimsuit and vintage shades. You might check an email from the beach, maybe even call in to meetings if you're "just" up at a cottage. *Why?* This is *your* time off! If this is the norm in your workplace, why not think about starting a new trend—unplugging for, *gasp*, an entire week. *But how will the company go on?* you're asking. *How will the universe run in perfect order without me?* Trust us, it will. Even if you own your own business, you deserve some down time, and customers are more understanding than you think. Who knows? You might even be more respected for your decision, as unplugging is a *thing* now.

Nina noticed a trend with the teams she managed. On the one hand, employees who were checking in on vacation came back just as exhausted and burned out as when they left, and were maybe even pissed off about checking in while they were supposed to be in relax mode. On the other hand, those who unplugged came back refreshed and recharged, and even brought new, innovative ideas to the table. Of course work was on their mind while they were away, but thinking about it with a clear head (versus amid the usual day-to-day clutter) allowed them to think *way* outside the box. When you think with a clear mind, your creativity can skyrocket. Nina knew she had to do two things: first, make it a mandate that people were not allowed to check in while they were on vacation; and second, lead by example. Huge bonus for her. So, she started getting officially pissed whenever someone checked in while they were supposed to be soaking in some me time, and it worked. The employees were happier and more engaged, and they wanted to work even harder when they got back.

Obviously, you have to be accountable in your role and to your company. If this is something you struggle with, we're not saying you should turn into an ass and just disappear without notice, but perhaps you could talk to your manager or team and see if it's feasible to completely unplug. If it's not, then set boundaries for yourself. Maybe check in only in the morning and evening, or have a "no phones at the beach" rule. Being on vacation is a recharge for your body, mind, and soul, so honour that. Your company might actually thank you for it when you come up with the next huge profit-driving idea.

Your Presence Is a Present

WHEN YOU'RE GOING THROUGH a hard time—maybe you have health issues, a family member passed away, you're experiencing a breakup—social media can actually be a great place to find support. Receiving messages from good friends or old acquaintances can really help lift you up.

So often in these moments people are not sure what to say or do. It's comforting to get those social media messages, but a person's presence can mean so much more. When someone comes to your house, makes a date, even mucks up and says the "wrong" things, it counts! There is nothing like physical human connection.

It's cheesy, but your presence is a present. Having a warm body show up for your birthday party means more than just a post on your wall. Same thing goes for a breakup. It's the friends who check in on you, or come over for a glass of wine and a good cry, who make it easier to get through all the ups and downs life throws at you.

If you're the one doing the supporting, be aware that at times like this that chatty part of your mind can get all wrapped up in anxiety-producing thoughts: *Am I saying the right thing? Hopefully, this advice sounds right. Maybe I should send a text instead of calling.* Friendships aren't perfect, and just like romantic relationships, we stumble our way through. At the end of day what's important is that you are there for each other. And simply being present can be powerful.

Own Your Story

BELIEVE IT OR NOT, your flaws and imperfections can help you connect with others.

Think about every story written since the dawn of time. There's always an arc where the main character gets into some serious shit, which then leads them to another path. This is true whether we're talking about the two-thousand-year-old *Odyssey* or the latest Spider-Man movie. There are always things that go wrong: the movie isn't just about Spider-Man saving the world from evil, The End. It's the ups and downs that make stories so interesting. Same goes for you and your life. If Spider-Man isn't perfect, why do you have to be? When we open up and share with others our own heroic journey—filled with rejections, sadness, jealousy, hatred, and massive bumps in the road—magical things happen. First, you are being open about who you really are. Second, you're connecting with another human being. Being open can help to build deeper connections, and it can remind others that they aren't the only ones who have low lows to go along with the high highs.

Remind *yourself* of this when you're sharing in person or online. Your own fear of rejection and judgment can stop you from sharing your whole self, and you might miss out on an opportunity for a deeper connection. It's your flaws and hardships—and your ability to move through them—that help to continually push you toward a better path and turn you into the human you are today. It's these moments that build character and make you strong.

Have you ever come across a post in which someone was honest about a breakup, a death, or a traumatic event, and your heart breaks for them? You automatically feel an immediate connection with this elementary-school acquaintance you haven't spoken to in years. It can be so powerful and healing. When you share the rough patches, you're doing the world some good. It helps others feel as if they're not alone in this life that ain't always a pretty picnic.

As you begin to share a bit more of yourself, you are opening a window to connections that can lift you and others. Of course, sharing is a highly personal choice. Only share what you're ready to and want to; this shouldn't feel like another *should* on your list. Do it in your own time, and only when or if it feels right.

As *Love Warrior* author and one of our faves Glennon Doyle Melton once said, "We can choose to be perfect and admired, or to be real and loved."

Do It for the JOMO

So, you decided that you didn't want to go to that bachelorette party in Miami. You made the decision to (a) save money, and (b) focus on work. You're good with that, and give yourself a big pat on the back for being such a responsible adult. Then, all of sudden, the pictures start flowing in. The ladies post a hilarious Insta story that has you in stitches and texting *Wish I was there!* ☹ You get this pang of *Ugh, should I have gone?* FOMO (fear of missing out) quickly ensues.

FOMO can creep up over the wedding you decided not to attend, the vacation you didn't book, the birthday bash you opted out of—really anything you were tempted to take part in but ultimately decided against. One reaction is to spend the coming days kicking yourself—of course you're going to get those feels, and that's okay. But another approach is to really take the time to remind yourself of why you didn't want to go, and then to give yourself kudos for being the authentic you and setting boundaries.

And remember, social media is a highlight reel. Ever been at a so-so party, but then someone grabs their phone and says, "Smile!" and everyone puts on their best party face? If you've said no to an event, keep this type of experience in mind as your scroll through your feeds. You have no idea what the party was like: maybe it was the jam of the century, or maybe it was the dud of the year. All you can do is focus on what's in front of you and applaud yourself for making choices that align with your needs.

By constantly making these little choices—like saying yes to the things you really want to do and no to things that might be temporarily fun but not necessarily good in the long term—you are building the blocks needed to make a great life. Future-you will thank past-you for making these wise decisions. While it might mean having to contend with FOMO now and again, you'll feel more like yourself and closer to your goals when you can confidently stand in those decisions. It makes no difference whether that goal is to be generally happier by giving yourself space, or finding time to work on the side hustle you've been dreaming about. Focusing on that can allow you to actually experience JOMO—the *joy* of missing out.

Kate knew a guy in high school who was one of those hockey kids. We probably all knew someone like this—the person who had dance rehearsals every weekend, or the friend who competitively swam. This crowd spent all their free time immersed in the passion of their choosing. From the outside, it often looked painful. The hockey kid practised so much, Kate never saw him at the school dances, at the park on weekends, or at after-school hangs. While she was out enjoying the days that many call the "best time of your life," he was on the ice, winter and summer. It didn't seem like much fun. Then, in university, she found out he'd been drafted to the National Hockey League and was kicking ass professionally. He had a great career. In high school, he'd been focused on his goal of playing hockey at a high level, and was okay saying no to all he missed out on. And it paid off for him in a huge way.

Not all stories finish this way. Many of "those kids" don't end up playing in a professional league or going to the Olympics, but the lessons these kids were taught were invaluable: commitment, hard work, and dedication. Even if you don't "make it big," those values carry through, enabling you to experience JOMO for the sake of your own good. One of our friends, Robyn, was a competitive gymnast when she was younger, and the perseverance and the tenacity this lady has to this day are remarkable. While she hasn't done a back flip in fifteen years, she learned that short-term sacrifices for the benefit of your passion pay off in the end. She now runs her own education company, has started a non-profit to teach literacy to inmates, and also manages to work out six days a week. (Like, how?) Her commitment to the things she puts her mind to is inspiring.

So, when you say no to stuff and then see what you're missing all over social media, focus on what it is you want. Whether that's building your start-up, becoming closer with certain friends, or giving yourself more time to Zen out, know that you are growing, piece by piece, into the very human you imagined you'd be on that vision board you created back in grade eight. Rejoice in your decision, and bring more of what it is you desire into your life.

Here's What to Do with
That Peanut Butter and Jealousy

A DEEP CREEP on someone you admire—someone who also happens to have a perfectly crafted feed—can leave you with an Instagram hangover. This includes feelings of happiness, anger, love, enjoyment, and hate. How it is even possible to feel all those emotions at once? Some believe that all those emotions really lead to one biggie: jealousy. The whole experience can be really confusing. As you scroll, your brain is convinced you like the activity, but once you're done you don't feel so good. You've already comforted yourself by thinking, *These pictures are posed—they are well crafted—this person's life isn't perfect*, but you still find yourself sitting with an unwanted feeling.

Kate's guilty pleasure is keeping up with the royals. She has a fascination with the monarchy, and totally admires Meghan Markle. She found herself getting pangs of jealousy after the epic royal wedding in May 2018. She was so happy for this union—even woke up to watch it and got all teary—and so excited for all that Meghan will bring to this role. So, what left her feeling these icky emotions?

The first thing to do when jealousy comes on is to acknowledge it. Next, explore what it is you like about the person. This might tell what you're craving and feeling less than satisfied about in your own life. Jealousy is not an easy pill to swallow, but we promise that looking at it can help you move past it. Kate noted what she loved about Meghan: She's sweet, charming, kind-hearted, and smart (all characteristics Kate admires). She's self-sufficient, thanks to a great acting career, and is a feminist and humanitarian who's done work with a number of NGOs and the United Nations.

As Kate took inventory of all this great stuff, it hit her: first, she herself really wanted to make more of a social impact, beyond her work in mental health. Second, weddings can definitely trigger Kate, given her single status. Make that one of the weddings of the decade and, well, it's no surprise it triggered her even more. Third, and last, while totally unrealistic (remember, we told you we weren't perfect), she felt jealous about the money Meghan had earned during her acting career—a jealousy sparked by lovely decor pics of the Toronto home Meghan sold prior to the wedding. Kate knows it's the internal stuff that makes you happy, and she reminded herself that all the pretty objects in the world won't bring permanent happiness. Digging deeper, Kate realized the trigger was more around financial stability. She'd been working in the start-up world for the past two years, and the cash flow can be up and down.

Everything Kate felt in the wake of the wedding was normal; it was okay to want to bump up her social impact or desire more financial stability. And, in fact, her reaction actually helped her to pinpoint the areas in her life that she wanted to keep improving. But she also tried to be realistic in terms of what was possible. Doing more non-profit work was feasible, and pushing to drive more revenues with the start-up was another actionable step. On the romance side of things, Kate spent time thinking about how grateful she is for the relationships she has had, and worked to accept where she is at.

She also started to embrace and celebrate how great Meghan is. We're lucky to have someone like her on the planet, especially in a global role that will allow her to make a real impact. When Kate thought about the new royal this way, it made her happy, and reminded her of how much she wanted to continue to cultivate the characteristics she admires in Meghan.

You can do this with anyone who inspires feelings of peanut butter and jealousy. All those characteristics that make you jealous? Celebrate them—especially if you actually know the person. Instead of focusing on the *Ugh, wish I was more like that,* enjoy their presence and the things they bring to the world. Sounds hard, but it becomes easier as you work on it.

Be as nice and gentle with yourself as Yoda is to the Jedi. It's normal for feelings of envy to arise now and again, so don't judge yourself. Be self-compassionate. Find that calm, nice voice inside you that can navigate this prickly and confusing emotion. Leverage your observing mind and lean into the feelings jealousy is prompting. You can write them down or go over them in your head. And then you can decide this shit is not worth holding on to and let it go. Or you can take a look at the things the person you're jealous of has that you would like and see how you can work to achieve them. If it's not entirely possible (like, say, becoming the next Duchess of Sussex), work to accept that. Use gratitude to focus on all the great stuff you've got going on.

One final piece of advice: if you know that someone is a trigger for you, maybe don't creep them as often. Give yourself some healthy space. Sometimes that's what you need to move past the ugh. But sometimes jealousy can actually provide clarity about the things you want in your own life and help you find reasons why you're happy for the other person instead.

Spread the Likes

IT FEELS GREAT when you get a virtual thumbs-up, or a like, or a comment, or a message that's flattering. It reminds you of why you're on these social media platforms in the first place. And when you spread the love to others, it actually makes you feel good, too. We often talk about the high we get from other people liking our stuff. Though there can be jealous thoughts and a lot of comparisons, there's also a joy that comes from throwing down a like for someone else.

Hold that feeling if you can. Remind yourself why you are happy that the other person is succeeding at something or experiencing something wonderful. Maybe you have a friend who's been on countless hopeless dates that really brought down their self-esteem. But then they swipe right, find the love of their life, and update their relationship status. You literally couldn't be happier for this person. Stay focused on that feeling, because wishing happiness for others is a way to access good feels for yourself. Science has shown that practising compassion can help us relieve stress and better face difficult situations. A study of US soldiers who took compassion-based training found that, afterward, they were better able to recoup following stressful situations.

If mustering up feelings of happiness for all doesn't come naturally to you, that's okay. But maybe give it an honest try. You might have heard that forcing a smile can actually make you feel happier. Same goes for compassion; you kind of feel happier even if your heart's not yet totally in it. And as you start to more often feel and wish good things for others, you'll find it lifts you up while you're it.

Get More Than Twenty-Four Hours

ONCE, KATE and her fellow social-media-addicted friend Molly decided to take a social media break for two weeks. They let another friend change their passwords so they couldn't cheat. At the start Kate felt like she'd quit coffee, and was agitated every other moment, but after a few days things began to look up. A number of things happened during this experiment. First, Kate began to notice how often she was checking Facebook while working away on her laptop. She hadn't even realized it, but her fingers would immediately go to the Facebook URL whenever her mind hit a roadblock. This social media break forced her to focus on her task instead of heading into the feed spiral.

The second thing Kate noticed was that she had a shit-ton more time in her day. She was emailing old friends, cleaning up her desktop and files, and getting tasks done way faster. Of course she missed her feeds, and regrettably ended up developing a new habit of googling celebrities, but that didn't feel as bad, for some reason. Regardless, the two-week break definitely had an effect on how she used social media. She realized she didn't need as much of it in her life, and felt like she had better self-control around it. She now spends less time than she used to monitoring Facebook and the gram; she still checks in daily, but less often. And when she does, she's more aware of it.

Try experimenting with a break—whether it's a day or week—just to notice how you feel and how it impacts your day. Play around with it: it might change the way you use the platform for the better.

Keep a Mood Diary

REAL FRIENDS ARE THOSE with whom you have human connections. You have sleepovers and coffee dates. You hit the bar together or tag each other in memes. They will be there when you need a shoulder to cry on, or you fail your exam, or you call it off with the certain someone you thought would be your life partner. They hold more weight in your life because they're not just there to see your highlight reel but are there for you when things are shitty.

This may seem obvious, but when you look back on the past year or even the past month and someone asks you what the highlight was, would your answer be "That post I put up and got two hundred likes for"? Or would it be something you did with an actual human, in person?

Social media can be a great place for self-expression, finding new friends, and catching up with the old ones. It's awesome, but just like the fries we talked about in chapter 1, social media also has a peak enjoyment.

As you continue to use your observing mind, take notice of how your feel during and after a hit of the gram. Maybe even write it down—sort of like a food diary, but a mood diary, instead. You might find that social media is the culprit behind your 3 p.m. mood slump. Only you know how it's affecting you, if at all. If you find it's upsetting you more often than not, it may be time for a little detox, or just some downtime to set boundaries. Maybe you decide on specific times of the day in which you engage with social media, as opposed to hitting a dose of each app every time you look at your phone.

Human Connection Is
More Important Than Ya Think

PRETTY SERIOUS BUMMER ALERT: a recent study showed that young people are far lonelier than senior citizens.

The study showcased that this situation wasn't just about social media; it also reported feelings of loneliness in those who barely use it. David Cordani, CEO of Cigna, the company that sponsored the study, said that meaningful social interaction was what was needed to reduce the feeling of isolation. In other words, more of that real face time. Social media takes us away from human-to-human interaction, but so does bingeing on Netflix, too many hours of video games, and watching one-too-many YouTube videos of dogs acting like humans.

Jagdish Khubchandani, a health professor at Ball State University, says that social media's screen-time type of conversation provides "a false sense of relief" with respect to connection. Even though we think we've spent a crap-ton of time interacting with people, we are actually doing it alone.

Another study showed that a lack of true connections can be a great detriment to our health—akin to obesity, smoking cigs, and high blood pressure. Who knew? But if we turn this around and begin to have more face-to-face connections, it can lead to a 50 percent increase in longevity, strengthen our immune system, and help us recover from disease faster. And, of course, it works to mitigate anxiety and depression.

In a *Harvard Business Review* essay, Vivek Murthy, a former US surgeon general, called loneliness a growing health epidemic. But the great thing about all this research is that we are now acutely aware of the issue and finally starting to turn this ship around. Britain recently announced the appointment of the world's first minister for loneliness. Tracey Crouch will lead a governmental group dedicated to tackling the issue. Speaking on her newly created role, Tracey says, "I could be the minister for happiness, because that's exactly what I'm trying to achieve." Even the government is focused on helping people find their happy!

It's not just young people who experience loneliness. It's an issue across the board, and human connection is a powerful way to address it.

Next time you think about calling Granny or texting your tablet-obsessed nephew, why not go over with their favourite whisky or juice box for a hug, instead. We get that everyone's schedules are packed, but setting aside time for meaningful connection can make all the difference in their day and boost your mood to boot.

CHAPTER 8

The Reveal

What the Fuck Did You Just Do?

WE WOULD NOW like to invite you to stand up, take a badass bow, and give yourself a massive pat on the back! The mountain you've climbed as you've worked your way through this book to find moments of peace is *mindfulness*. You've probably heard this buzzword recently. Mindfulness is having a moment, similar to the one yoga had in the early 2010s. Celebrities are touting it as a way to stay calm, and top corporations such as Google and Microsoft are using it to improve productivity and focus. Science is also proving that this stuff really works. And surprise—you just learned the essence of it!

So, what does the word mean? There are many different definitions, but at its most basic, *mindfulness* is "the art of being fully present." Let's go back to the simple example we used in chapter 1: During your commute to work are you ever really just walking, riding a bus, biking, or driving? Are you noticing the trees, being aware of what's popping up around you, and being grateful for your breath? Or are you feeling anxious about the day ahead, wondering what to make for dinner, or harbouring guilt over something you feel bad about saying? These thoughts will always come and go, but mindfulness is about relating to them differently. It's creating some space between you and your thoughts so you're less triggered by them and can steal moments of peace here and there. Creating some distance between the thoughts that are swirling in that mind of yours allows you to think about yourself differently. You stop identifying quite so much with the clouds that are obstructing the real you and start identifying more with the happiness within: love, joy, bliss, and peace—*this* is your essence, not that swirling hurricane.

All the tools we've talked about—awareness, self-love, acceptance, perspective, authenticity, and forgiveness—are ways to help you let that shit go and access the present moment, which is the crux of mindfulness, and the place where you can find your calm. Mindfulness is also about remembering that happiness isn't *out there*. It's right under your nose, and can be cultivated in nature, in your current relationships, in the everyday. It's not in the external things you can't control but right there within you. To quote one of our favourite Buddhist monks, Thich Nhat Hanh: "Mindfulness is the energy that helps us recognize the conditions of happiness that are already present in our lives."

The benefits to the practice of mindfulness are endless. Research has proven that it can help you be happier and less stressed, sleep better, become less emotionally reactive, and improve your productivity (to name just a few).

It's about using that "awareness" you've been cultivating with your observing mind to identify less with the thoughts that come from your chatty mind. *This practice of being conscious of the present moment* is *being mindful.* When you are aware of your thoughts and the multitude of feelings that go along with them, you are leaning into yourself—and only yourself—to access the serenity within. Serenity doesn't have to come from the number of likes on your Instagram post or the delicious brownie you downed in a few minutes (although these things can certainly spark bouts of happiness). It can come from yourself, which makes it so much more powerful, and sustainable. You might be thinking, *Well, how do I know when I'm actually present?* Eckhart Tolle says, "The moment you realize you're not present, you are present. Whenever you are able to observe your mind, you are not trapped *in* it." You now know how to do this, and it's something you can do anytime: at work, hanging with your partner, or simply standing in line at the grocery store.

All these things ladder up to a more mindful you. Noticing your feelings and being compassionate with your best friend even as you get into a fight. Combatting the small stuff that stresses you out at work with gratitude and perspective. Cultivating some serious self-love after a date rejects you. That's all part of it. Mindfulness is not just about sitting in lotus position in the corner of your room, or venturing to a remote village perched on a mountain. It's about being conscious of your mind and thoughts and moving them to the present moment, which leads you to a calmer, kinder, less agitated state in the everyday.

We have found mindfulness immensely helpful. We would even go as far as to say that it's changed our lives—so much so that it sparked us to start our own businesses focused on just that. It can be such a powerful tool, especially helpful when the big shit-storms roll in. When you know you can lean into yourself, you've created a strong anchor that will prevent you from getting picked up and blown away with the winds.

Mindfulness doesn't mean that the crappy feelings will all magically go away. Even the Dalai Lama admits he sweats the small stuff: "You never stop getting angry about small things. In my case, it's when my staff do something carelessly, then my voice goes high. But after a few minutes, it passes," he graciously admitted. But when you practise mindfulness—using the tools we've introduced here—it can help you let that shit go so you're not holding on to it for longer than needed.

We've been practising mindfulness for some time (twenty-five years, combined), and believe us when we tell you there's still a bunch of stupid-shit we hold on to, get worked up about, or pout over. We're human! Mindfulness is not about accessing calm via the absence of thoughts or feelings—it's about acknowledging them and helping us accept and move past them. It's about lessening our fear around the icky thoughts we sometimes don't want to admit we have. But when we do look at them, and hold them gently using our observing mind, we're taking the steps necessary to work through them in order to let them go.

Now that you have the tools you need to weave more moments of calm into your existence, this chapter will help you apply mindfulness in specific facets of your life, relationships, work, sports, et cetera. The more aware you are of your thoughts and emotions while being rooted in love and compassion, the easier it will be to access that happiness within. Remember: as we mentioned earlier, we didn't come up with this genius stuff; it's the core philosophy of many Eastern religions that have been around for millenniums.

Bonding with Bae

The best relationship advice Nina ever received was from Martin, an ex-colleague. He said, "Don't let years of being together turn *What can I do for you?* into *What can you do for me?*" When you're at the beginning of a relationship (a.k.a. the honeymoon stage), it's all about making the other person happy. You do little things for them, like pick up their favourite take-out meal, shave your legs, get tickets to see a new band they're into, and maybe even randomly offer a shoulder massage. Your initial thought pattern is *What can I do for you?* Sometimes, after things get oh-so-comfortable (to the point where you're popping each other's back pimples and "dressing up" means wearing your favourite sweats), that thought process can slowly change to *What can you do for me?* The domestic task counter is switched on: *I did the dishes, cleaned the toilets, and took the garbage out, so you need to mow the lawn, make dinner, and do the laundry.* I mean, we're all for an even task load, but how many thoughts about your partner are rooted in what you want and need from them versus what you can *do* for them? This is where compassion and letting go of expectations can come in handy.

It's so easy to keep tally. We all do it. We move to "me" mode and focus only on our wants, as opposed to putting ourselves in our partner's shoes and thinking about what could help them out. When you can, why not move into

"What can I do for you?" mode and try doing little things that make them happy. It can have a great effect. Relationships are *hard*, and there's tons of behind-the-scenes administrative stuff you don't see in Instagram posts. When we shift gears and approach the mundane tasks with a helpful 'tude, it can make things a little easier. Studies have found that bringing in compassion and kindness can help with long-term success.

In 1986, psychological researcher and clinician John Gottman and his colleague Robert Levenson at the University of Washington created something called the "Love Lab," where they set out to discover what helped couples stay together and have lasting, loving relationships. In their experiment they interviewed newlyweds and then caught up with them again six years later to explore the differences between those who stayed together and those who either divorced or had a strained relationship. They found that the couples who had stayed together had built a foundation of trust, intimacy, and comfort.

Gottman wanted to dig deeper into exactly how they built this foundation, so in another study he monitored couples on a weekend retreat in 1990. He found the key to strong relationships was kindness, appreciation, and generosity. "There's a habit of mind," Gottman said of the strong relationships, "which is this: they are scanning the social environment for things they can appreciate and say thank-you for. They are building this culture of respect and appreciation very purposefully." The strained-relationship or divorced couples, on the other hand, "scanned the social environment for partners' mistakes."

What they found in the research was that kindness doesn't just derive from doing the small things—like arriving home with chocolate, or offering a back rub. It's also about understanding where your partner is coming from and recognizing that the intent of what they are doing is positive. Your partner might not get each action right, but if you can see the positive motivations behind it, you're immediately more grateful and appreciative, as opposed to angry and contemptful.

We touched on this earlier, but when it comes to your expectations of your partner, be realistic. You can't expect your partner to be exactly like you, so try to accept the things that aren't and let go of trying to make the person something they're not. It's not fair to think that they can fulfill all your dreams and wishes like the characters in Disney films.

Remember, you can only change yourself. Your partner shouldn't be seen as a project for you to work on. This will frustrate the shit out of you—and, let's face it, them, too. Of course you want to love and help each other be better people, and encourage each other to do certain things, but be aware of whether you are pushing too far or making your partner uncomfortable. They have to want to be in your lane. As we discussed in previous chapters, finding the balance between encouraging and *should*ing is key.

It wasn't until Nina and Mike were in Cali for the year that they realized how different they are. When they met, they had so many similarities. Their friends used to say they were the opposite-sex versions of each other. At the core, though, they're totally different; it just took years to discover this. Mike is super-responsible and practical, and Nina is more of a "fly by the seat of her pants" kinda gal. The fact that they have such different approaches to life meant that Nina and Mike would argue (and still do) over things.

They came to two helpful conclusions:

1. It's important to see each other's differences as a positive and lean into them like a strength. So, for example, Mike is stellar at finances, while Nina is known for having amazing relationships. If they need to decide about something, they discuss it at length, but the person who is stronger on the topic will have the final say. The other person might not agree with it but would totally respect it.

2. You can't *convince* another person to think the way you do, which means there is no right or wrong in arguments. Being mindful of why your partner reaches the conclusion they do will save time and effort versus wasting too much energy in the "how could you even think that" department. Combining this with accepting the fact that they don't think the way you do can alleviate a lot of frustration. So instead of conversations devolving into a fight, they more often than not now go like "Oh-h-h-h, okay, I get why you think we shouldn't splurge on that weekend away; it's because we just went on vacation and it would be wise not to spend again so soon." Or "Oh-h-h-h, okay, I get why you think we *should* splurge on a weekend away; it's because you live for each moment." Nina and Mike resolve this

by leaning into conclusion 1—knowing where each other's strengths lie. In this case, it comes down to finances (because they had just gone on vacation), so it's Mike's call. Once the decision is made, they shift to acceptance mode and move on, versus continuing to ruminate.

While it's important to think about your partner, it's also important to remember that self-love is key. You need to make sure your own cup is full, or you won't have water to pour into your partner's. Relationships are very much like a Venn diagram: two circles that overlap a little. You are still very much your own person. You need your space, and you need to do things that fulfill you. Your partner can't be absolutely everything to you, nor can you expect them to be. Maybe you've got an issue that you need to talk through. Your cousin has been through the exact experience, while your partner has not. Who does it make sense to have an in-depth talk with? Or maybe your partner wants to go golfing every month, but you're not a fan; so, do your own thing, like go to yoga classes, and let them do theirs. It's healthy to have your own life. If you embrace that part of the Venn diagram that is just you, you'll be fulfilled and better able to enjoy the places where you and bae overlap.

Have you ever seen the movie *Meet the Patels*? The father has some incredible insight. He says that after thirty-plus years he is still learning things about his wife. You are never going to get to a point where you're 100 percent in sync and the relationship is all good all the time. Relationships take work and compromise and are far from perfect, but if you can come from a place of love and understanding, it will make all the difference along the way.

Mums and Paps

Who hasn't had a moment where they're PO'd with a parent? Relationships are complicated, and we can't expect things with Mums and Paps to be all *Leave It to Beaver* all the time (just like we can't expect our friendships or romantic relationships to be all rainbows and unicorns, either). It's helpful to realize that your parents are human beings and, just like you, they aren't perfect. They make mistakes. They couldn't possibly have anticipated what it would be like to be parents, or have known exactly how to do the job right. Like everyone else, they are just doing their best. They were messy, imperfect adults before you were born, and they didn't magically turn into different, more perfect versions of themselves just because they had a child. They looked to their parents and cultures for guidance. Some chose to do exactly what their parents did, while others tried to shift things around, acknowledging that perhaps their parents didn't have the most effective strategies. The point is, if they hurt you, they didn't mean to, they likely just didn't know any better.

There are, of course, more severe cases. As we discussed in chapter 6, some of our parents struggled with undiagnosed mental-health issues. Back in the day, it was taboo to see a psychiatrist or therapist, whereas now it's becoming as common as going to the dentist. Many parents thought that as long as they put food on the table and had a secure job, things were golden. Maybe they were hurt by their parents and subconsciously continued on in the same way. Or maybe they didn't even know the extent of their hurt and ran on autopilot to survive. Now there are millions of books, articles, and studies on how to raise children. But even with all these resources, most parents know they're not perfect. They are, however, trying their best.

Here's where you can be more mindful via compassion: you can put yourself in your parents' shoes and try to understand why they think the way they do or treated you a certain way. There's likely a reason, and there's a good chance it has to do with how they grew up. If you are holding on to hurt or anger toward your parents, work toward letting that shit go. Letting go of the anger or blame can lead you to a deeper understanding, maybe even forgiveness. That could mean enhancing your bond, mending a challenged relationship, or healing your own heart while still keeping your distance—or anything in between. Only you will know what feels right. But what letting go (via acceptance, perspective, maybe even forgiveness) will do is help *you* move forward. It will allow you to no longer identify or focus on the shitty stuff, and instead embrace your unique relationship with them.

Focus on all the things they *have* done for you: the sacrifices they had to make, the food they provided, all the cartoon-themed birthday parties they held for you, and the countless times they schlepped you back and forth from school and your part-time job. Try to focus on the good they've brought into your lives. If you're a parent, you can only hope your kids will one day do the same for you.

The Bambinos

Dr. Shefali Tsabary is a psychologist, author, and speaker who lectures extensively on mindful living and conscious parenting. She flips parenting on its head by making it less of an authoritarian relationship and more of a mutual one. In her book *The Conscious Parent*, she talks about how our children are gateways to our own evolution and how they can "awaken us." It's interesting to really home in on how you parent and explore how much of that is a result of how *you* were parented. Are you subconsciously passing emotional stuff you endured during childhood onto your children? Tsabary helps us address these patterns and change them, instead of carrying them forward into the next generation.

She says, "When you parent, it's crucial you realize you aren't raising a mini-me but a spirit throbbing with its own signature." She talks about the danger of putting pressure on your children to be all the things you couldn't be. Maybe you never had the chance or prowess to become a professional athlete, so you shape your kid to reach places you couldn't. Or you push them to be a doctor or engineer, when it's the furthest thing from what they want. Children come with their own essence and dreams, and we need to honour who they are.

She also talks about the power of being present with your children. When you're in the presence of a child, you can sneakily steal tips on how to be present. Watch them joyfully do up a zipper or enjoy an ice cream cone without another thought or care in the world. You can even home in on their tiny little hands and toes or feel their rapid heartbeat, and be in awe of how magical it is that they exist.

Ever had one of those moments where you feel like you're being pulled in a million directions? You're getting everyone in the car and your infant is crying while your toddler's asking if she can wear her favourite headband, which is back in the house, and then you realize you forgot to take your four-year-old to the washroom and your coat gets stuck in the car door as you're getting her out, and suddenly all that goes through your mind is *Fuck me!* It's in crazy moments just like this that we lose our cool and feel totally overwhelmed, but the funny thing about these moments is that they're also opportunities to hit Pause and just breathe, slow down, and be present.

If you find yourself in a situation like this, take a dee-e-e-e-e-e-e-p breath and just focus on one task at a time. You can't possibly do two things at once, like calm the infant *and* get the headband. You can only do one thing at a time, so just do that thing and let go of the rest. Remember the incredibly mindful grocery-shopping trip we explored in chapter 1? Switch to that mode and talk yourself through being present: *Okay, now I'm unbuckling her seat belt and getting her out. Oops, my coat got stuck in the door, let me just unhook it. Now I'm taking her inside to put her on the toilet. Now I'm going upstairs to grab the headband. Now I'm helping her wash her hands. Now I'm getting a toy for the infant. Now I'm giving that toy to the infant. Now I'm putting my toddler back in her chair. Now I'm buckling her seat belt.* Your chatty mind will try to stress you out even more. It will go on about how you're probably going to be late for that meeting, or make you worry about your infant, who's still wailing his eyes out. That's okay. Do your best to acknowledge those thoughts, and use your observing mind to notice what you are doing. This will help you stay present and avoid getting caught up in the hurricane, which can lead to a whole whack of intense emotions.

Parenting infants and toddlers can be challenging, no doubt, but let's not forget the teenage years. As we all know from personal experience, being a teenager ain't a piece of cake. So, what makes us think that parenting one is going to be any easier? It's hard to find a balance between guiding (*Honey, I'm not sure that girl is the best influence on you*) and ordering (*You're not allowed to hang out with that girl anymore*), but at the crux of it, every child just wants to feel loved and embraced for who they are. The best thing you can do, especially at this stage of your child's life, is to assist them in cultivating their authentic selves. It's a scary time for them, too: their bodies are changing; they're learning more about who they are; they're getting their hearts broken, and taking on academic pressures, and finding their social groove. Nina's sister-in-law Dusty (one of the most amazing moms she knows), says, at the end of the day, if they feel unconditionally loved, it's really all you can ask for.

You know the saying "It takes a village"? Back in the day, an entire community of people would help raise kids—from birth up to young adulthood. Now we're all in our own little units, tackling this monumental task without nearly as much help. How amazing is it when your parents, in-laws, siblings, friends, or aunts and uncles come over to lend a helping hand for even a night? People used to have that support 24/7, so remember that and go easy on yourself. Make sure you're giving yourself a meaningful pat on the back every so often for doing a kick-ass job.

your aunt, sibling, or good friend—try to understand why you're getting hung up. If it's because you treat them a certain way—with kindness, for example—and expect the same, then be aware of this and know that just because you treat them kindly, it doesn't mean you will receive that same TLC back. The first thing to do in this situation is accept it. Accept that this person is not like you. Keep things fact based as opposed to emotional. Once you accept the person for who they are, you will naturally stop having unrealistic expectations. You will no longer get upset at the things they do because you now know better. After you accept the situation, you can either create some healthy distance between the two of you, or you can continue to have them be a big part of your life, imperfections and all. You will know what works for you. If you do choose to continue having that person in your life, you'll likely notice a shift in your relationship. There will be less frustration and anger about them not doing certain things, and much more room for love.

Let's say you find yourself always having to take charge of the social calendar and plan fun things, but you have a family member or friend who never reciprocates. If you can learn to accept this about them and remind yourself that social planning isn't naturally part of their makeup, it won't piss you off anymore. Then, when you meet up at some gathering you initiated, you won't find yourself thinking, *You're so freakin' annoying. Why is it always me who has to plan this shit?* Instead, you can just enjoy your time with them, knowing that when you do get together, it rocks. Instead of wasting mental energy on who you want them to be, you're embracing them for who they are and letting go of the rest.

The more you practise mindfulness, the more in tune you will be with people. It won't make you the perfect friend or relative, but it will give you really good insight into what the people in your life need. It's kind of like leading a team at work: each person is driven by different things. Some friends may look to you for emotional support, while others just want to hit the bar and have a blast. Mindful listening is also a powerful way to connect. Sometimes people just need to feel heard. They don't need advice or an action plan, just a shoulder and a hug.

As we keep reiterating, these tactics work well with a big scoop of self-love. Make sure what you're doing feels right to you and that you're setting the right boundaries for you to feel happy. When you take care of yourself—and your cup is nice and full with cucumber, mint, and lemon water—your capacity to be there for others will skyrocket. So, do your thang, and watch the effects ripple out to everyone around you.

Our Furry Children

Bless these furry miracles. How is it possible for such small creatures to bring so much joy into our lives? Their love is utterly boundless. No matter what mood you're in, whether you did a good job at work or not, or paid them as much attention as they would have liked, they love you. There's so much we can learn from them about mindfulness. They *always* live in the present, easily forgive and forget, and love unconditionally.

Kate's dog, Harry, lifts her up every time she sees him. He can do no wrong, even if he doesn't always respond to "come," barks when she's in a store, and takes everyone's socks. His personality is totally charming, and he's an endless source of comfort. It's actually a known fact that pets relieve stress. One study found that 74 percent of pet owners reported a mental-health improvement as a result of pet ownership.

Next time you're spending time with your precious pet, use it as an exercise for mindfulness. Take a few breaths and think about how grateful you are that they exist and how they're always there for you, no matter what. Learn from how present they are. They always seem to be in the here and now. Everything is exciting: the ball, your undies, another furry friend. Notice how they easily forget their own wrongdoings, and yours. Last, really observe your pet by using your senses (like you did that piece of chocolate back in chapter 1) to calm your chatty mind. Observe their fur, paws, eyes, how they slurp water. You'll start to appreciate their sheer amazingness even more, and your swirling troubles and worries will slowly quiet down.

Did You Get the Memo?

With over 80 percent of Americans feeling stressed on the job, organizations are looking for ways to help their employees regain their calm and find more focus. To address these issues, companies have been putting big bucks toward mindfulness initiatives. The trend originated in Silicon Valley, with Google being one of the first to implement mindfulness and meditation practices in their offices. In 2007, they kickstarted Search Inside Yourself. One of their engineers, Chade-Meng Tan, had a dream to change the world. He developed an internal course with leading experts in mindfulness, neuroscience, and emotional intelligence, and it's now Google's most highly rated training course and is offered to organizations globally.

Companies are starting to see tangible benefits of mindfulness. In fact, SAP—a multinational software company whose products allow businesses to track customer and business interactions—states that a "one percentage point increase in employee engagement translates to a rise of 50 to 60 million euros in operating profit, while a one percentage point increase in its business health culture index can add 85 to 95 million euros." It also claims to have seen a 200 percent return on investment in mindfulness, with the training leading to a rise in employee engagement and a fall in absenteeism.

There are numerous ways companies can implement mindfulness on their own. Here are some to consider:

- Start and close meetings by having everyone take a few deep breaths.
- Ask everyone to keep phones at their desks during meetings and only look at their laptops when they need to, so attendees are present and mindfully listening.
- Launch a gratitude wall, which can be personal or professional (or both), to harvest a positive environment.
- Encourage random acts of kindness, like leaving positive handwritten sticky notes on someone's desk or grabbing someone a coffee.

- Plan social events to increase team cohesiveness and camaraderie.
- Implement a Monday Meditation, where everyone in the company takes ten minutes to gather themselves so they can disconnect and get into the work zone.
- Allow for a good sense of balance by implementing a few guidelines (these have all been proven to drive efficiency and creativity):
  » Nix emailing about work outside of office hours (this allows employees time to recharge).
  » Allow for a decent lunch break, along with mini-breaks, so employees can mentally refresh. Encourage employees not to ruminate about work during this time but to socialize, listen to a podcast, or go for nature walk, instead.
  » Institute a "unplug on vacation" policy. Employees will come back with an increased sense of motivation as opposed to with continued mental exhaustion from checking in.

It's no secret that when employees are less stressed, they will perform better; they beat the sleep-deprived, irritated, "constant bags under the eyes" crowd hands down. If you want the best out of your people, put them first. The company will naturally prevail.

Be the Boss You Want

Being a leader is a huge responsibility—not just to the company P&L but also to the peeps you manage. It's kind of like having two jobs: you have to adhere to your role's responsibilities, but you also have to lead people. And sometimes the latter takes a good deal more effort, energy, and focus. Ever heard the quote "Your manager is the lens through which you view the organization"? It comes down to this: an employee can love their job, feel great about their co-workers, and be really passionate about their company, but if their boss is a self-absorbed jackass, they're not going to feel like coming in to work every day. Conversely, if their boss kicks ass, they'll likely feel motivated to do what they need to do to stay the course—even if the company is restructuring and they've been waiting on a promotion for months.

If you happen to *be* the manager, this can be a heavy load to bear, as everyone looks to you for answers, guidance, and inspiration. So, it's important to not just set the tone professionally but to just downright be a good person and lead by example. Be tuned in to the members of your team by being fully present when you interact with them. If your mind is wandering as they're talking or you're preoccupied with reading an email or deck, use your observing mind to veer back to the conversation. Listen attentively by prioritizing eye contact over screen time. People feel good about themselves when they feel heard, and will naturally be more passionate about working for you.

You can also work hard to avoid multi-tasking when you're in meetings and stay focused on the job at hand. This will yield stronger outcomes and make meetings much more worthwhile.

Keep in mind that each of your team members is motivated by a different thing. Some might want to be the next VP, while others might crave balance and never want to go past the manager level. Build connections with your team by cultivating authenticity and knowing what makes each individual tick. By encouraging your staff to stay true to their authentic selves, you'll get a lot more out of them. You don't want a group of yes-robots or mini-yous, anyway. Once you get a sense of each member's capability, empower them through the right mix of autonomy and guidance.

You likely spend more time with the people you work with than with your family during the week. Work is already stressful, so it's critical that everyone feels good about being there. You want your team to get things done not because they fear you but because they're inspired by you. So, try to exude compassion and lead with genuity, and have the right balance between confidence and humility. A great way to display humility is to hire people you think are smarter than you and be open to learning from them.

This one's obvious, but worth including: it's important to be approachable. To achieve this, you want to demonstrate one of the cornerstones of mindfulness: compassion. Cultivate bottom-up conversations by scheduling check-ins and one-on-ones that focus on the employee rather than the ongoing project list. In this way, you'll be offering them your full presence. Ask whether they are motivated by what they're working on, where they see themselves going next, and if there's anything on their mind that they want to discuss.

What if there are massive changes happening in your organization? With all the resizing and restructuring going on these days, this is certainly common, but that doesn't make it any less stressful. When times are turbulent, leading with acceptance ("This is what it is and we will get through it") and focusing on where you *can* have an impact might play a key role in keeping everyone calm.

If you're planning to implement all the amazing mindfulness tools you've learned, know that it's up to company leaders to set the example. If your employees organize a Friday Meditation or a speaker to come in for a Mindfulness 101 talk and the managers are too busy to attend, it sends the wrong message. Employees will likely feel they, as well, should be too busy to attend, and the initiative may fall to the wayside. If you're really passionate about putting people first, make it a priority—and make sure it comes from the top down. It won't be long before you see the results (as so many companies already have).

Moving Past the Mondays

Mindfulness is a great way to push through those Monday feels and 3 p.m. slumps. Even if your whole team isn't on board yet, here are some tips you can use to find some peace:

If you're happy with your gig, then go back to that place of perspective and gratitude when the going gets tough. Think about how you once only wished you could make the salary you're making right now. Find gratitude in knowing that your employer picked you out of so many.

To stay authentic and help find your voice, have work mentors. These could be people you admire and aspire to be. That VP who isn't afraid to speak up and go against the grain, the cook who maintains her calm in the kitchen, or the small shop owner who runs community workshops. The more you can learn from those who inspire you, the more you will be able to lead in a way that feels right for you.

When it comes to our jobs, it's natural to get frustrated here and there. Be cognizant of what you can and can't control. Work hard to change what you have influence over, and let go of what you don't. Going home and stressing about the unknown or that jerk who's never going to leave is only going to drain your energy.

Try bringing in some mindfulness to your workplace. You spend a great deal of time at work, so finding peace while you're there can make all the difference.

How *Not* to Get Schooled

The pressure to have the perfect grades, a good social life, and a killer Instagram profile as you balance a part-time job outside school is a fucking heavy weight. Students trying to do it all are *fried*. It can be a tough go. You feel very much like an adult with all your responsibilities, but at this age you're likely still under a parent's wing.

The key to making it through these years without carrying a big ball of stress around inside you all the time is to really try to lean into your authentic self. Figure out whether the expectations you're feeling come from you or from someone else. Maybe they're coming from your parents, profs, friends, or other students. If that's the case, remember what's important to *you*. Bring in some serious self-love to help keep you grounded while you try to figure this out. It's easy to get caught up in a degree you think you *should* be pursuing instead of following what's true to you, or to go out for the fifth night in a row just because all your friends are.

You've heard the story tons of times: someone goes to college for advertising, finishes, and then realizes they really wanted to pursue their passion for music. Or maybe they switch majors partway through. That's okay. People switch gears in their adult lives all the time (note: this insight is coming from two marketing junkies turned mindfulness advocates in their thirties, well past the completion of our business degrees). Don't feel guilty about changing direction. There's so much pressure to pick a degree and stay the course for the rest of your life. If getting a degree is important to you, then do it. Just don't look too far ahead and worry about what it could mean for the rest of your life.

Keep perspective in mind. An incident that you feel extremely embarrassed about now—whether "now" is college or high school—won't be a big deal later on. We promise. We did many embarrassing things (which shall not be mentioned here) that are no longer top of mind. Trust us when we tell you that what might feel like a big deal at the moment might be something you laugh about with your friends in the future.

Also try not to get wrapped up in what others are doing. Let go of the comparison game and keep in mind that you've got a long life ahead of you. Gary who got accepted to Stanford might have a rough start to his career. Joanna who dropped out of college might become a famous entrepreneur. Who knows what happens after that? All humans have ups and downs, and it's best not to focus on what others are doing and to simply try your best. That's really all you can do.

Technology has made it easier than ever to shame or bully people. Some of the great tools you have against this are cultivating self-love and speaking up, confiding in your close friends, and talking to the people you trust. Also know that your bully might have hidden wounds. While their behaviour may be inexcusable, this might be why they are acting out.

Finally, remember that school, just like work, can leave you running on empty. So, in the midst of all your hard work, make time for yourself to relax, do things you love, and treat yo' self.

Create Way Outside the Box

Leveraging mindfulness is a great way to recharge and get creative AF. So often, obstacles at work or school are dealt with using the same dusty methodology. It's easy to be rooted in habitual thought patterns and lean into solutions based on what historically worked or didn't. But doing this really puts a damper on your ability to be creative. Once in a while, pause, take a step back, and think outside the box. Like, *way* outside the box. How can you unlock a way to approach things differently?

In the *Mindfulness Pocketbook*, Gill Hasson addresses how to problem-solve with creative thinking. She says that "while mindfulness is about focusing on the present moment, there's an important place for mind wandering." We know we've emphasized the importance of not getting caught up in the chatty mind, but we're talking about something different here. When you let your mind wander intentionally, you're tapped into your observing mind.

The distinction is that a directionless wandering mind is unproductive, but a deliberate and intentional wandering mind is actually a really powerful tool for creative thinking, and you can develop awesome stuff.

As Hasson says, mind wandering "enables you to . . . transcend fixed ideas, rules and ways of doing things . . . [to find] original, unconventional and innovative ways." You can more easily put aside beliefs about what has or hasn't worked in the past and open up to new ways of thinking. As Albert Einstein once said, "You can't solve a problem with the thinking that created it."

Hasson suggests that when you use this method of intentional mind wandering, you want to be rooted in a beginner's-mind approach. Having a beginner's mind simply means that you engage with things as if you were doing them for the first time, almost like you're a child. You can test your beginner's mind with something as simple as a book. Think of ten ways you can use a book, other than reading it: as a paperweight, gluing and stacking several as a base of a coffee table, utilizing the pages as wrapping paper, et cetera.

Then close your eyes and take a few deep breaths. Reflect on all the possibilities of what you are creating: a piece of art, a school project, a work deliverable. It's important to not focus on any constraints (Hasson gives examples like time, size, money, and resources). She says that it might feel like a stretch to think without limitations, but the important thing at this point is to simply imagine the possibilities. Being non-judgmental is also key. Don't think about an idea as good or bad, or big or small. Don't limit your thinking in these ways.

Nina uses this exercise with her corporate clients. It gives them a moment to think non-traditionally, and it's incredible the ideas they come up with. After being with the same company for years, someone will find that a totally new concept suddenly surfaces. As you go through this exercise, write your ideas down when they're fresh. Then flesh them out on your own or with someone you trust, and play with different ways to implement them.

Win-Win

Negotiation is a bit of a stiff word, but really, we're always doing it in one way or another: from getting your kids to wear pants instead of shorts on a cold day, to convincing your partner to splurge on a dinner, to driving conversations around a boardroom table. Changing the way you think about negotiation to make it more inclusive can be a powerful thing for both you and the person you're negotiating with.

Mindful negotiating is far from hard bargaining. With hard bargaining, the sides come from an opposing position and work their way to a mutual consensus; keeping a poker face about the range of things you can offer on your end of the table is encouraged. Mindful negotiating is about showing your cards, and being true and honest from the get-go about what you have to offer so the conclusion you reach is optimal for both parties.

Essentially, it's a one-love approach. You aim for a win-win outcome, where both parties gain as much as possible out of the situation. In *Happiness the Mindful Way*, Ken A. Verni talks about how negotiations go from "dividing the pie" to "expanding the pie." Instead of each party walking away with half of the whole, both sides end up broadening the scope of what they're negotiating for, and walk away with more.

Let's break it down. Say you're looking for a perfect place to call home. You've got a budget, and you're aware that you're in "end of the month" crunch time. The landlord of the place you're eyeing is in a tight squeeze. There haven't been many bites, and she's eager to rent. In a traditional negotiating setting, she'd come at you with a certain amount, and then you'd come back with a counteroffer. The conversations would end with you finding some middle ground, but both losing out a bit. If you negotiate mindfully, with the intent of everyone winning, you come from a different place. At the risk of sounding cheesy, you come from a place of heart, not head. So, you might say to this potential landlord, "Look, I'm pursuing my side hustle and working part-time. All I have is X amount to allocate for rent." In other words, you show your cards. If the landlord says that's too low, fine. It's all good: you save some time and move on. But it's possible that she might hear you out and say, "Okay, I really wanted $50 more, but that's fine. I get your position." She might just appreciate your honesty and "no bullshit but authentic" approach. And she might think, *This is someone I would like to rent to, someone I can trust, and I'm happy to help them catch a break.* Then—*boom!*—you have your place *and* you met someone really nice along the way. Your relationship moves beyond that of landlord and renter because there's mutual respect and genuine care for each other at play. As a result, the relationship is a lot smoother throughout your stay.

When you negotiate mindfully, it concludes with trust. This makes the other person want to continue to work with you in the future. We've seen this strategy work at the most senior levels of organizations, too. If you apply this to work—say you're an agency—your clients will thank you for it, and it just might generate more business. They might even trust you with information they don't tell other agencies or give you insights on how to succeed. Same goes for restaurant owner and server, gallery owner and artist, coach and athlete.

Of course, we're not saying you should be fooled by someone who is trying to take advantage of you, so feel them out. If your intuition says this person is able to come from a good place while negotiating, then give it a go.

Sweat It Out

We all know exercise can have a great effect on our mood and can help to nix stress. However, sometimes going to the gym or doing a group class can foster some not-so-mindful thinking: *Am I doing this right? How come my legs are shaking and no one else's are? Is this shirt appropriate gym attire?*

If you have those thoughts, that's totally cool. Think about it: you're in a room with people you don't know, in clothing that's attached to your body, doing moves you may never have done before. It can all make you feel like you're in a Cirque de Soleil group you didn't train to be in. It's normal to have these thoughts. But to mitigate this kind of thinking, you'll want to lean into your observing mind to get back to the present moment, even bring in some self-love and gratitude.

You can do this by focusing—like *really* focusing—on your body and what it's doing for you: the way your legs feel, the way your arms lift, the way your glutes tighten, et cetera. As you notice your body and muscles, and how they're doing what you ask of them, your chatty mind will slow down. If you're in a class, you can use your observing mind to focus on what the instructor is saying or doing. You can also listen to the wheels of the bikes in a spin class or the sound of everyone's shoes hitting the ground in an exercise class. If you're going for a run, you can observe what's around you. You can even get as pragmatic as listing items in your head as you go by—*there's a tree, recycling bin, dog walker, purple flowers,* et cetera—or notice the sound of your feet hitting the gravel or your arms swishing against your shirt.

Give yourself massive kudos as you work out. You're taking the time to treat your body and do something good for it. You can also foster gratitude for how your body can move, lift, twist, and run. Treating your bod to a workout is like giving it a sweet gift, and saying thanks for all the work it's been doing.

Mindfulness can help you focus on what you've set out to do and enjoy your workout, rather than getting caught up with chatty-mind thoughts.

Head in the Game

Succeeding in sports certainly requires athletic ability, but having a good game also comes down to what's going on in that noggin of yours. The more you're in your own head, the less focused you are on the task at hand. A multitude of thoughts can be swirling around: feeling anxious about whether you're going to win, beating yourself up about the shots you missed last time out, getting worked up over that jerk on the opposing team who loves to talk shit. Your chatty mind might also be yelling things at you from the self-hate zone: *You suck! You're not good enough for this team!* There are so many ways you can be subtly distracted, and suddenly, you're off your game. When thoughts of the past or anxieties about the future arise, being mindful can help you get into a state of acceptance. Instead of seeing a losing game as a failure and dwelling on it, or being anxious about whether your knee is going to act up, you can more easily stay focused on the here and now.

Mindfulness will allow you to use your observing mind to catch yourself when you're not in the flow of the game. Maybe you suddenly notice a defeatist attitude creeping in, or that you're increasingly distracted by an unfair ref. When you become aware of these things, use your observing mind to bring you back to the present and you'll easily get into your flow again.

Some psychologists and mindfulness coaches also use visualization, which is a great intention-setting technique. They'll have players visualize themselves up on the podium receiving a medal, or holding that championship trophy.

When you're playing, stay focused on the present—on passing that ball, serving with intent, swinging your bat. Another way to bring mindfulness into your game is to do body scans as a part of your training and every time you are warming up. Work your way from head to toe, making yourself aware of the different feelings and sensations in your body. This keeps you in the moment and makes you aware of anything your body might want to nudge you about.

Many athletes are leaning into mindfulness and meditation to improve performance. One of the founders of mindfulness in sport is Zen master Phil Jackson, former head coach of the Chicago Bulls and Los Angeles Lakers. He leveraged mindfulness to inspire some of the greatest athletes in history, including Michael Jordan, Shaquille O'Neal, and Kobe Bryant. He went on to win eleven championships—more than any coach in the history of American pro sports. George Mumford, who is often referred to as Phil Jackson's secret weapon, has taught mindfulness and meditation to athletes for decades. He's authored the book *The Mindful Athlete*, in which he details the techniques he leveraged to take athletes to the next level. On the back cover you'll find this quote from Kobe Bryant: "George helped me understand the art of mindfulness: to be neither distracted or focused, rigid or flexible, passive or aggressive. I learned to just be."

Sleepy Time

Mindfulness can be a great way to help you sleep better. It can calm and clear your head, leaving you feeling all relaxed and ready for deep sleep. There are a few things you can do before bedtime to get you to a blissful state:

- *Think about what you are grateful for.* What amazing things happened today that you didn't expect? Who are the people in your life you are thankful for? Is there something you are proud of that you can give yourself a pat on the back about? Take a moment to be downright happy to be alive.

- *Send some compassion to someone else.* Maybe there's someone in your life who's going through a really crappy time. Think about them getting through this and being in a happy state.
- *Use perspective.* Think about the moon hovering over you, how you are on this planet floating in the middle of space, and how bright the stars are. Think about the galaxies that are far away. Zoom out to see the big picture.
- *Remind yourself that you are worthy.* You are loved, and you are enough just as you are.

Take deep belly breaths and be gentle on yourself while you use your observing mind in these ways. Cap your thoughts by homing in on your breath and focusing on it, as we laid out in chapter 1. And remember that this stuff really works. A University of Utah study found that "people who reported higher levels of mindfulness described better control over their emotions and behaviors during the day. In addition, higher mindfulness was associated with lower activation at bedtime, which could have benefits for sleep quality and future ability to manage stress," according to Holly Rau, a researcher.

Try the above before bed or throughout the day. It can have a great effect on your sleep.

Bringing Home the Bacon

There's a story about a fisherman. He makes enough money to comfortably feed himself and his family. Each day he fishes off the shore of a beautiful beach and spends time with his friends and family.

A business-savvy man approaches him one day and says, "I'll sell you a net, and with this net you can catch more fish and make more money."

"Well," the fisherman queries, "what would I do with more money?"

"You could buy a bigger boat and catch more fish!" replies the businessman.

"Oh, okay," the fisherman says. "And what would I do then?"

"You could launch a company and eventually get so big you'd have someone to do all your fishing for you!"

"Okay, and then what?" the fisherman asks.

"You could *triple* your size and begin exporting all your fish."

"Hmm, okay. And after that?" the fisherman inquires.

"Then you'll have so much money you can just sit here and enjoy the beautiful beach," the businessman says.

The fisherman ponders for a few seconds and replies, "But that's exactly what I'm doing right now."

Money wasn't going to make the fisherman any happier—and he knew it. His story reminds us to not get caught up in the race that everyone's running just for the sake of it. Lean into what you want in life, and how you want to spend your dough.

Mindfulness can help you be aware of your relationship with money and how you feel when you buy things. Of course, remember that *things* aren't what lead to permanent happiness—it's what's inside. Sometimes, on a whim, you might buy something to perk yourself up. Kate's done this (with shoes, lattes, you name it), only to eventually notice there's still something she's not addressing. Look inside, not outside. Also, be conscious of whether you are buying for yourself or because of some external pressure. The more you can observe your feelings, the better able you'll be to focus on buying things that truly suit you, not to mention being more satisfied with what you already have.

A Buddhist theory holds that one of the causes of suffering is our desire to continually want more, be it a bigger house, a higher-paying job, a solid relationship, or a cookie at 3 p.m. When we can recognize this feeling of wanting and realize that it's only ourselves (and not things) that can satisfy it, we can step off the desire treadmill.

Sometimes we live hand-to-mouth. We make $100—we spend it. We make $1,000—we spend it. We get a big promotion, and our lifestyle changes. What do we do with that extra money? Dinners out, movies, weekends away, more vacations, ante up the wardrobe, buy a nicer car, a bigger house—it doesn't end. Of course having money and nice things can make us happy up to a point, but take the time to notice your feelings around it and when that happiness starts to dissipate. Sometimes it's when you let go and don't stress about money that things start to fall into place.

You can also use mindfulness when you're feeling stressed about money and thinking too far into the future.

Wield some of the perspective we talked about in chapter 4. There are millions of people in the world who survive on much less than we have, and at the end of the day, they're okay. We make choices in life, and we can always scale back. The important thing is to go back to knowing that big picture: you'll be okay.

Ever played the "So what?" game? This was one of Nina's mom's favourites. With every challenge in life she would say, "So what?" She always did it with the small stuff—like, *So what that our favourite restaurant is closed. We'll go to another one.* Or *So what that it's rainy on vacation. We'll still have a blast.* She was such a tough cookie, and she had an incredible ability to do this with the big things, too: *So what that my legs don't work anymore. I can still use my hands and talk.* Of course there was emotion, but this attitude kept her grounded and rooted in gratitude, which meant that nothing would faze her. After she lost her son, everything else paled in comparison, so she always had a big-picture perspective. Playing the "So what?" game can help you put your finances into perspective, too.

Tim Ferriss, an entrepreneur, motivational author, and speaker, recommends practising poverty when you can in order to eliminate your fear of it (he was inspired by the philosopher Seneca, who did this). He says he'll spend a week living extremely frugally, and realize it's not that bad. This approach helps him get rid of the "fear" of losing it all, and makes him enjoy what he has.

If money made us happy, then every millionaire or billionaire would be ecstatic all the time, but that's not the case. As one of the greatest rappers ever, The Notorious

B.I.G., once said, "Mo' money, mo' problems." If finances are stressing you out, try flipping to gratitude for all you have going on.

Slow Mo'

While it's true that using mindfulness in your day-to-day, crazy-busy life can help you be less reactive, more clear-headed, et cetera, there is also a big benefit to pressing the Pause button and taking things slowly. Remember, relaxing is productive. It helps to boost your immune system and recoup from the stress you've been facing. A way to sneak some relaxation into your day, regardless of what you're doing, is to take things slowly. This can get you out of your head and into the sensory world (an effective trick to calm your mind).

Say you're having a crazy day at work. You haven't had a moment to catch your breath. It's 3 p.m., and you've decided to run to the local coffee shop to grab a pick-me-up. Instead of walking as quickly as possible, try holding yourself back and walking at a slower pace than usual. You'll notice your whole body and mind slowing down a little. Take some deep breaths and use your senses to notice what's around you: the smells, the pavement, the markings on the wall. This will help get you out of a stressful, swirling mind and focus on the present. Doing this can act as a Reset button, so when you get back to your place of work, you're feeling more in control and ready to take on any task.

You can do this at home while you're cooking dinner, or on the weekend as you're walking to meet a friend. You can even pause and do this in the midst of a stressful day at work, while you're sitting at your desk. If you feel yourself rushing unnecessarily, intentionally slow your pace. You'll notice the calming effect it can have as it brings you right into the present.

Little Prompts

When you're always on the go, it's not easy to remember to pause, take a breath, and slow down. It doesn't hurt to have reminders around to nudge you into peace mode now and again.

You can choose something like the *ding* from a text to remind you to take a few deep breaths. Or use things that are already part of your daily routine—brushing your teeth, for example, or opening a door—to remind you to do them mindfully and with intention. You can also add items to your living space that help to wipe away the day's bullshit, like natural oil diffusers, incense, and candles. Scent can have a powerful effect on helping your mind and body wind down.

We've mentioned this before, but music is another way to quiet the mind and change your state from fritzed to blissed. YouTube, SoundCloud, even Apple and Google Music have ways to get you to Zen out. You can listen to calming music on your way home or as you're doing the dishes.

You can also wear certain things that remind you of that place of peace, like a necklace, bracelet, or ring that has a deeper meaning. Catch a moment of Zen as you touch the item while riding the subway, or when you look down at your wrist as you type. Some people even get tattoos as friendly reminders.

There are mindfulness and meditation apps, too—like Headspace; Stop, Breathe & Think; Calm; Aura; and Buddhify. Remember that it's important to lean into what works for you as opposed to jumping on whatever is popular, so play around with each and see which ones stick.

The more little reminders you have around you—in your living space, on your phone, on that body of yours—the more you'll automatically weave calm into your life. And before you know it, taking a breath and letting shit go will naturally become a part of your daily routine.

CHAPTER 9

Next Level

The Mind Workout

THERE'S A TOOL we haven't talked about yet, one that can help immensely in letting that shit go and finding your inner Zen: *meditation*. If you're interested in taking things to the next level, this chapter will help. And if you're not ready to dive into meditation just yet, don't judge yourself for stopping here. Maybe you'll come back to it a month or a year from now, or maybe not. Either way, you do you.

We know. Meditation can sound intimidating if you've never tried it before. Just *sitting there*, listening to the inner workings of your mind. There are many different ways people interpret meditation, but essentially, it's *a means of transforming the mind*, and it has some massive benefits.

Meditation originated in the Hindu tradition and is also at the core of Buddhism and Taoism. This ancient wisdom was established centuries ago by enlightened souls who were in tune with life itself. It's now popular around the world and has been a great tool to help people get peaceful. Science is also now proving its benefits: turns out that physical changes to brain structure can be seen during meditation.

Meditation is such a powerful tool because it helps you better manage your chatty mind. It's a gateway to serenity. Meditating also heightens your ability to practise mindfulness. It will bring out the best parts of you and allow you to catch more moments of calm amid your crazy days—whether at work, at home, or at the gym.

We said this earlier, but the point is kind of worth repeating: you put a ton of great effort into that precious body of yours—cleaning it, feeding it, dressing it, working it—but don't forget about that melon. Mindfulness is a sweet way to cultivate your ability to access peace, but meditation homes in on developing that awareness muscle. As you meditate, you are dedicating a chuck of time—even if it's just five minutes—to actively work out your mind. During that time, you are laser focused on leaning into your observing mind and addressing those swirling chatty-mind thoughts. As a result, it's easier to do the same when your noggin or situations get the best of you in the everyday.

Like any form of workout, meditation takes time and patience, but before you know it, you'll start to see the effects. If you look in the mirror before and after your gym workout, you won't notice a difference in your body. But what happens if you consistently work out for a sustained period of time, let's say four weeks? Try the mirror thing again and you might think, *Hot-diggity-damn!* Same goes for meditation. You might not notice a difference or feel like you're getting anything out of your practice after a day, a week, or a month, but suddenly, you'll find you just feel lighter, you're smiling more often, and you are just genuinely happier. You'll also find that you're not as affected by the crappy stuff going on around you or by the thoughts of that chatty asshole inside your head. Essentially, it becomes easier to just let that shit go.

Speak to any meditator about how the practice has affected their day-to-day, and they will confirm this. Some will even say that their days are different when they start with a meditation as opposed to when they don't. Meditation can be easier to integrate into your day once you make it part of your routine, just like showering, eating healthy foods, and getting in your workouts. It really helps to have a moment with yourself—either without so many clouds or just to observe those clouds—and find out what's going on in your mind.

Meditation is also another way to listen to the person inside who is the most qualified to answer your questions. Yes, we're talking about you. That's intuition. Have you ever heard someone suggest, "If you're not sure what to do, meditate on it"? There's a saying: "In prayer you speak and in meditation you listen." It's not like you hear the voice of a godly saint giving you answers (or maybe you will). It's more like an inherent *knowing* of which path to take at the fork in the road. If there's a situation you've been contemplating for some time, the answer may be clearer after meditating. When you struggle with what to do in certain situations, deep down you always know the answer that feels right to you. Meditation will cultivate your intuition. Not only does this give you more clarity but it also helps you live your most authentic life. What rings true for you becomes more and more obvious and can be accessed right within you.

Another plus? It won't cost you a fortune! Remember, you just need one ingredient: you. One study found that practising mindfulness and meditation might have more of a lasting effect on reducing stress than a vacation does—and you don't even have to dish out airline points for it.

There is also much to be said about the societal benefits of meditation. It can bring people together in subtle ways. It reminds you of the *oneness* of everything as opposed to the things that separate us. It can stop you from constantly comparing yourself with others—be it that "too well put together" person who walked past you today; or your friends; or those picture-perfect influencers online. It's driven company growth, helped teams win championships, and changed relationships at the core.

Remember how in chapter 1 we talked about how the journey to find happiness is not about searching "out there" but unravelling who you really are? You know that image we have in popular culture of the "happy monk"? He's got no savings account and no possessions beyond the robe on his back, but he's happy. Why? Because of what's right there within him, not what's outside of him. Through meditation, you—like the monk—will be able to access the serenity that comes from being more present.

In this chapter you'll find twelve tips that cover some helpful things to know about meditation. We'll address many of the questions we get asked about common myths, talk about the scientific benefits, and offer advice on the hows, wheres, and whens, along with some general guidelines. Meditation is a very personal practice: it's not a clear, straightforward path by any means. It's not even a practice that can be taught to the nth degree, like law or science; it's very subtle. Use your intuition, find your groove, and pick the pieces that make sense for you. Unlike in many areas in life—where you get gold stars for being "the best" (Top Salesperson, Most Valuable Player, or Best Actor in a Drama, et cetera)—there is no such thing as a top meditator. Put that out of your head and don't worry about focusing on a goal. There is no goal. Meditation is just about helping you find more moments of peace throughout your day and remember who you are at the core, which can ladder up to a happier you.

There Is No Good and Bad

NO ONE HAS HAD the same life experiences as you or is moved or triggered by the same things. It's up to you to find your own path. In school we were taught that teachers have all the answers, or that the experts know all, but meditation doesn't work that way. You can take guidance from friends, or teachers, or books. There are so many tools and techniques to leverage, and we can't stress enough how important it is to lean into your intuition. If you learn a technique that's not sitting well, it's all good. It just means that technique is not for you at this point in your life. If you learn something that makes you feel super-empowered, go for it. It really is that simple. You might have to download five mindfulness or meditation apps before you find one that works for you. And you might go back to the first one two years later and get something out of it that you couldn't the first time around.

The thing is, your practice will change over time; it's like the relationship you have with your job, people, or the food you eat. During the first year you might find great peace in guided meditations. In the next year you might only want to meditate in silence. It could be different month to month, week to week, even day to day.

The most important thing is not to have expectations of your practice, because that is a distraction in itself. Meditation is the process of simply *be*ing. The moment you label your meditation as good or bad, or right or wrong, you are judging it. Focus on the fact that you've actually made time to do it. That in itself is absolutely magnificent.

The Magic Happens in and out
of Your Experience

THE BEAUTIFUL PART about meditation is that you can feel the effects in and out of your practice. While meditating you might experience a state of pure bliss or a running mind, but either way you'll start to feel better in everyday life. Meditation teachers often refer to your practice as planting seeds: you won't see the effects immediately, but you are setting yourself up for positive results.

This works because you have a better understanding and awareness of your mind and thoughts. You might feel calmer in those stressful work situations. You could start becoming less fazed by people who used to bother the crap out of you. You might even start appreciating all the good stuff in your life that you hadn't noticed before. You will essentially start to morph into a better and calmer version of yourself. *That's* why meditation is magical.

It Changes Yo' Brain

STUDIES HAVE FOUND that the brains of people who've practised meditation for just eight weeks start showing physical changes. It's groundbreaking, as science is now able to measure the positive benefits of meditation and validate what the ancients have known for centuries.

Sara Lazar is an associate researcher in psychiatry at Massachusetts General Hospital and an assistant professor in psychology at Harvard Medical School. She is one of many neuroscientists who have been studying the impacts of meditation on various cognitive and behavioural functions. She and her team have used magnetic resonance imaging (MRI) to look at brain activity before and after meditation.

One study found that long-term meditators had more grey matter in the prefrontal cortex—the part of the brain associated with working memory and executive decision making. Although the cortex typically shrinks with age, the researchers found that in one region of the prefrontal cortex, fifty-year-old meditators had the same amount of grey matter as twenty-five-year-olds.

Another study took people who had never meditated through an eight-week meditation program. Following the program, the researchers discovered a shift in brain volume in five different areas:

1. The *amygdala*—the part of the brain associated with the fight-or-flight response, and emotions like anxiety, fear, and stress—had shrunk, which

suggests there is a biological mechanism that correlates meditation and stress reduction.

2. There was thickening to the *posterior cingulate*, which is related to mind wandering and self-relevance.

3. There was increased grey matter in the *left hippocampus*, which is the main area of your brain associated with learning and memory. It's also heavily affected by depression and PTSD.

4. There was increased activity in the *temporoparietal junction* (TPJ), which is the key region for creativity, empathy, and compassion.

5. There was a thickening in the *pons*, an area of the brain stem where many regulatory neurotransmitters are produced.

All this scientific stuff is super-compelling, and you can't really argue facts.

It's Not a Race

WHEN KATE FIRST started meditating, she had thoughts like *I'm doing this incorrectly. I've been practising for a few months now, I should be better at this.* There were a few things wrong with this mentality. The most important is that meditation is "non-striving." This kind of goes against everything you've been taught in school—to *be the best, win the game,* and *try harder.* Of course you want to try to make time for your practice, but when you're in it, you just have to *be.* The key to doing this is to let go of any judgments about yourself and your meditation.

According to Jon Kabat-Zinn, a leader in the North American mindfulness movement and the founder of the well-known MBSR (mindfulness-based stress reduction) program, "meditation has no goal other than for you to be yourself. The irony is that you already are. This sounds paradoxical and a little crazy. Yet this paradox and craziness may be pointing you toward a new way of seeing yourself, one in which you are trying less and being more."

Given that we live in a hypercompetitive world, it can be strange at first to try not to "achieve" something. It's counterintuitive, but the way to get closer to a Zenful mind is not to push yourself or focus so much on the results—in other words, to be gentle and non-judgmental.

Each One Is Different

No two ocean waves are the same. Some are large, some small. Some crash with a few bubbles, some with many. Some are crystal clear and some drag in shitloads of seaweed.

Just like ocean waves, no two sittings are the same. Don't expect them to be. You might have what you feel is a "fantastic meditation" one day—you walk away feeling as if you've slept for hours, or maybe you've got a body buzz or natural high. The next day, though, the waves are six feet high: your mind and heart are racing, the thoughts are end-less, you can't shake your to-do list, and that issue that's been bothering you keeps bubbling up.

This is totally okay.

When your mind is racing during meditation, it could be that your subconscious is bringing something forward that you need to address. This is a good thing, and part of the process of letting things go. Sometimes the sittings that don't feel as comfortable can lead to a greater feeling of calm for the rest of day because you brought something up, addressed it, and let it go.

Be gentle with yourself, and enjoy the process. If you do find yourself judging, just acknowledge and accept it, and know it's just a thought that will pass.

How to Sit

THERE'S NO RIGHT WAY to sit for a meditation. Yes, there are formal, traditional positions, but the most important thing is to be comfortable while being alert; that's really the intent of those traditional positions. Take the following as a guide, but lean into what works for you.

You can sit on the floor or on a chair. Try to keep your back long and straight; lean back too much and you could get comfy enough to fall asleep!

If you're sitting on the floor, cross-legged is the most common position. If that doesn't feel right, don't give up until you get a firm meditation cushion; it helps keep your butt elevated so the bottom of your spine doesn't curl. Find one that works for you and fits your body structure. Some cushions or mini-chairs allow you to straddle a seat or have a little back rest if you need a touch of support. There are many, many options out there.

If you're sitting on a chair, make sure your feet are flat on the floor. If your legs are crossed, you'll have a harder time sitting straight. Having your legs at a ninety-degree angle also helps with your posture. It's also optimal to sit closer to the edge of the chair and not lean on the backrest.

Meditation can put you in a relaxed state, but you want to be alert-relaxed, not sleepy-relaxed. One way to tell the difference is if you feel your eyes getting heavy. If you do, try opening them just a smidge.

The key thing with your position is not to be falling asleep or focusing on your body during your meditation. For example, you don't want to be meditating on a sore back or knee. You want to be comfortable so you can focus on your meditation, not on your body. If your body is troublesome and you *really* need to, you can lie down. The trick here is to not get so comfy that you fall asleep.

Where to Sit

IT'S YOUR CALL. Some people like to have a spot in their living space for yoga or meditative practices, and that's great. But really, you can do it anywhere—in your work chair, on your bed, in the park. As you go through different exercises, you'll see that some can be done in a casual setting. Meditation doesn't always have to be formal.

Many teachers recommend practising in the same place each time. This can help you make meditation a habit as well as bring good vibes to a particular zone. Charles Duhigg, author of *The Power of Habit*, says that the building blocks for a habit contain three things: cue, routine, and reward. The cue is anything that triggers your brain to perform the habit, the routine is performing the habit itself, and the reward is what you get from it.

When you're building a new habit, the brain's reward response hits once you've completed the routine. What's interesting about habits is that once they are ingrained, as soon as you see the cue, your brain experiences the reward response even before you've done the routine. Essentially, you're kind of getting rewarded for something before you actually do it, like having dessert first—yes, please!

Sitting your keister in the same spot every day can really help to kickstart your practice and make it a habit. You can even get uber-spiritual and make a little altar for yourself. Kate has a collection of gemstones, a little sculpture of the Buddha, incense, and mala beads. Just looking at the altar invokes peaceful feelings and makes her want to get into that spot. Nina's had the same meditation cushion for fifteen years—she brings it to the weekly classes she takes and to the workshops she conducts. She typically sits in the same place in her home, a spot where there's lots of sunlight, which helps her get into her Zen mode.

But if you can't get to your spot, that's totally cool, too. Sometimes Nina sits up in her bed and meditates. When she wants to get right into it and doesn't want to wake up anyone in the house by creaking her way down the stairs, she just sits up and away she goes. And sometimes she sits in her backyard, amid the breeze and the sounds of rustling leaves and chirping birds.

If you're travelling for work or away on vacation, you can absolutely continue to meditate. And if you missed your morning meditation at home, no problem. You can do it on the subway. You can meditate *anywhere*. It's great to have a spot in your living space, but don't depend on it.

When to Sit

EXPERTS SAY THAT meditating in the morning is best, and our own experience supports this. Your mind is fresh, and you're more alert than later in the day. More importantly, your chatty mind is also waking up and hasn't yet gone from zero to sixty with its swirling thoughts of the day. When Nina was in Cali, one of her teachers used to say, "Meditate before you enter the world." Before you look at your phone, before you talk to anyone, before you watch anything—essentially, before that lovely mind of yours feeds itself goodies—meditate!

Once again, what's most important here is that you're doing it, so if meditating in the morning is not possible, don't let that stop you. Do it in between classes, after you drop your kids off at school, once you get home from work, even before bed.

The reason for doing it at the same time each day is to create a cue to help you build your habit, but there's absolutely no judgment over when. Just do it. Remember, focus on the fact that you're taking the time to practise.

How Often and for How Long

THIS IS ANOTHER ONE that's totally at your discretion. Some people have a practice that is a set amount of time, and some sit for however long suits them on a given day. You can have a meditation minute, sit for thirty minutes a day, or go to a retreat and sit in silence for hours.

Some mornings you'll get up super-early and feel like you want to dedicate that time to meditate, and you might sit for longer than you had anticipated. Other mornings you'll feel rushed and spend less time. That's okay. Just go with the flow. There will also be certain phases in your life where you'll get into a good routine, just like with the gym, and meditate every day; and some phases where you do it on and off because work or another aspect of life is taking up more of your time.

The point is, don't be hard on yourself. If you get to it one day and not the next, it's all good. It's great to have a routine and different ways to lean into your practice—like how, where, and when you sit—but if you don't meet all those self-made requirements, that's totally fine. The fact that you're taking time for your mind when you can is sweet, so give yourself some kudos for that in itself.

Find Your Fury

THE IDEA OF *sitting there* with your thoughts can initially feel intimidating; after all, you're opening a drawer of thoughts that may not have seen the light of day for some time. It's like that junk drawer in your house you've been meaning to clean out. There's some stuff in there you might not like and want to toss. But there might also be little things that spark joy, à la Marie Kondo—and those you want to hold on to and cherish. There may be yucky stuff (jealousy, anger, or resentment) swirling in your mind that you weren't even aware of, but that's okay. It's important to embrace all the thoughts, even if it might not initially feel good to do so. Don't get all Judge Judy on what you are feeling. These are just thoughts, and as humans we experience the full gamut of them—that's what makes life! The more you can observe them and lean into them, especially the prickly ones, the more you'll be able to gently and softly move *past* them, and the lighter you'll feel. As for the good thoughts, you'll want to continue to cultivate them.

As we noted earlier, science shows that meditation can change the neural networks in your brain. So even if you have a bad day, or month, or quarter, or, heck, year, you can shift gears by putting in the mental work. Remember that progress is not linear. Meditation isn't like an escalator to enlightenment. It's more like a hiking trail. You'll climb jagged mountains, reach awesome peaks, and then head into valleys; tramp through muddy paths and then catch breathtaking views where the whole world makes sense. When you look back at the entire path, you can see that it's beautiful—the hard stuff is what makes the journey worthwhile and the nice bits that much more enjoyable. Think about the people who climb Everest. Moving past the difficulty and facing it is what makes reaching the top so sweet. But remember that there's no goal or destination; this is about *being* and remembering who you already are—that sunshine-y goodness.

The negative thoughts we have are similar to the parts of the trail we didn't enjoy but are sure as hell happy we got through. So, when you open the drawer to your mind and find the potentially ugly stuff in there, remember that this isn't all of you, just as the shitty and difficult parts of a hiking trail don't compose the entire trail.

You might even get to a point where you're happy you've found those less-than-pleasant parts of yourself. Louise Hay thinks you should treat them like a treasure. Finding them is half the battle, and equipped with your mindfulness tools (like self-love and acceptance), you'll be better able to handle them.

#squadgoals

ONE WAY TO really keep up the habit of mindfulness and meditation is to find a group that practises in your 'hood. Ever notice that you can be motivated by others when you attend a class at the gym? That's because being surrounded by those who are on a similar path can make you feel supported. With a meditation group, you'll also learn new meditations and be able to share any of the challenges or bumps you've experienced—the highs, too.

You'll find new friends, and a sense of community. Just knowing that there are others out there dealing with the same stuff that you are—like stress at work or how to handle anger—can be a relief in itself. A group can also remind you of concepts you might have forgotten, or things that you needed to be reminded of. When Kate listens to Nina's teachings in our mindfulness and meditation workshops, she usually learns something new, even though she's heard them countless times.

No one around you? Go online. If you want to learn about what others are doing to meditate, there are tons of blogs, YouTube videos, and social media accounts to follow. Somewhere between your friend's announcement that she's expecting and your ex's post from an out-of-town baseball game you can find nuggets of wisdom. It might help with that inner Zen you're trying to find in your online life. That said, there's great benefit to getting out there in person and actually *practising* with others.

The Sanskrit term for this is *satsang*, which means to "gather together for truth" or to "be in the company of the truth." *Sat* means "true" and *sanga* means "community." Hindus believe that sitting in *satsang* is essential to your practice. When they refer to the truth, they are speaking of that happiness within, as they believe this is your true nature and the nature of everyone else. One love. It's the principle of surrounding yourself with good people, since the people around you influence who you are. If you gather with others who want to learn and meditate, it makes your practice even stronger.

We Are All Connected

THAT SUNSHINE you can access within yourself—that permanent happiness, unconditional love, and sheer bliss—is the same sweet sunshine for everyone, as the ancients say. Gender, race, nationality, profession, political leaning—beyond these labels, we all have access to the same powerful stuff that can make us happy. It's not as if each person has their own individual sun beaming down on them; we all feel the warmth of the same sun that connects us.

You might have heard the term *namaste* and seen people fold their hands together and bow their heads as they say it. *Namah* means "bow" and *te* means "to you." The ancients believed that the divinity in you is the same as the divinity in everyone, so when you bow, you are acknowledging the divinity or sun in each other. The hands coming together is also a symbol of bringing that oneness in you and oneness in me together.

If you can, remind yourself of this oneness. *You get angry sometimes—I get angry sometimes. You breathe air—I breathe air. I poop—Barack Obama poops.* We are all human, and so similar. Imagine if we just focused on our similarities and not our differences, and how it could impact our outlook and day-to-day mood. Next time you go for a stroll down the street, think about how you're connected to the sweet old lady, the cute kindergartener, or the person in a suit.

Meditation cultivates this connection—not just to people but to nature and everything around us. There is so much joy and happiness to be experienced. When you start to let that shit go, the goodness starts to trickle in.

WHAT FOLLOWS are a few basic meditations to kickstart your practice. If you've been following through on each tip throughout the book, then congratulations—you've already started to meditate! Some of the tips—like "Talk to the Little You" or "Picture the Shit Drifting Away and Visualize the Good"—are meditations in themselves. Basically, if we asked you to start with taking some deep breaths, we cheekily snuck in a mini-meditation. Feel free to go back to those tips at any point and leverage them as a meditation technique if it helped you find some peace.

One point we want to reiterate from chapter 1 is that *the thoughts don't stop*. Don't expect to get to a thoughtless state the entire time you sit in meditation. You will absolutely have moments of peace and stillness—in between the ebb and flow of random thoughts. Whether you're having a stressful day or sitting in meditation, the chatty mind keeps chatting. You may have some meditations where your thoughts are fewer and farther between, but they will always be there. This is why sitting in meditation and focusing on observing your thoughts is such a great practice—because you learn how to do that in everyday life.

We've laid out three common meditation techniques for you to try.

Work That Nostril Magic

FOCUSING ON BREATH is the most common and universal meditation technique. You now know how to take big belly breaths with your tummy ballooning in and out, and this is a great tool to use in meditation.

Here's how it works: As you sit, close your eyes and take those deep breaths. Use your observing mind to go back to focusing on those breaths every time your mind wanders. Remember to inhale and exhale through your nostrils as opposed to your mouth. There are varying techniques around this, but if you breathe through your nostrils, you will have more control over the breath that goes in and out.

You can focus on one of many elements of your breath that we discussed in chapter 1: your belly inflating and deflating, the count of the inhale and exhale (however many seconds works for you), the air going in and out of your nostrils. You might even start to notice things like how the air coming in is always cool, while the air going out is always warm.

Don't overthink it: *Shoot—that breath was shorter than the last. How long should I count for? Am I doing this right?* Just do it without judgment. In between the oscillation of the mind and the focus on the breath, you'll get little bouts of peace. And don't *look* for these peaceful moments, either—they will come naturally.

Your chatty mind will start to run off, thinking thought after thought. That's all good, and it happens to the most experienced meditators. Don't judge yourself. As you notice it run, use your observing mind to acknowledge that, and then bring your focus back to your breath.

There, you did it! That's meditation. Start by doing this for two minutes and work your way up in duration.

Relax That Sexy Bod

DOING A BODY SCAN is another way to shift focus from your chatty mind. You can go from head to toe or vice versa, focusing on each body part.

Here's how it works: As your chatty mind wanders, bring it back to the body part you are homing in on. Let's say you start with the top of your head. Picture a glow there and continue that glow all the way down your body as you focus on each spot. Go from your head to your shoulders, arms, hands, fingers, chest, back, stomach, pelvis, butt, thighs, knees, calves, feet, and toes. You can get as specific as you want, by focusing right down to your fingernails and toenails. And you can even go internal and reflect on the inner workings of your body as you move down it.

As you're scanning down your body, make a conscious effort to relax your muscles and ease any tension. If a part of your body bothers you, like your shoulders or knees, give it some extra love and attention. Once you've gone through your body, look at yourself from a bird's-eye view. See that glow you've just created around yourself. See how peaceful and calm you look; notice how relaxed you feel. Take a few deep breaths before you end your practice and open your eyes.

You can spend as much time as you want on each area. In our workshops we take five minutes to do this scan, but Nina's mom used to take her class through this for thirty minutes. Do what feels right for you.

Let the Thought Drift

A GREAT WAY to create more distance between you and your thoughts is to acknowledge them and then watch them float the eff away. This creates the sensation that they are not continuously swirling in your mind but that they come and go.

Here's how it works: As you sit in meditation, breathing deeply, take notice when your chatty mind starts swinging from branch to branch. Observe the thoughts. Instead of focusing on your breath or body scan, watch the thoughts come and go. Simultaneously, focus on what is still there: the beautiful, peaceful you; that sunshine. This helps you to not identify with your thoughts and remain in the eye of the hurricane.

You can use many different visualizations for this. Here are a few ideas to get you started:

- You can see each thought as an ocean wave, coming and going, all different shapes and sizes, and watch those thoughts merge back into the ocean, which represents you. You are the depths of the ocean, calm and still.
- Each thought can be a cloud drifting away. You watch each pass by, and know you are the permanent blue sky, vast and endless. Clear of any bullshit.
- Your thoughts can be like snowflakes, each one unique. Observe them hitting a mountain peak and melting into the snow. Know that you are the permanent mountain, strong and solid. You got this.

- Each thought can be a channel on the television and you are the ever-present screen, unfazed no matter what show is playing.

Boom! You've got a whole tool kit to kickstart your meditation practice and ante up your calm.

Conclusion

RAMANA MAHARSHI, a great saint who spent much of his life in meditation and cultivating mindfulness, said, "If one's mind has peace, the whole world will appear peaceful." If we continue to cultivate that magic within, our outlook will change and everything will feel that much more Zen. Not to mention we'll be putting some of that same goodness out into the world.

The tips in this book helped us overcome some seriously dark moments in our lives. If not for the wisdom of the ancients, we're not quite sure how things would have panned out. We're far from perfect, and we're nowhere near reaching the point of guru-like enlightenment, but we've definitely been able to live calmer, more content lives. We hope these tips bring the same peace and happiness to your lives by helping to calm your mysterious, beautiful, and powerful mind.

As you start to apply these tools, lean into yourself and do what works for you. You have the blueprint to your own mind. Remember, also, that progress is not linear: you'll have ups and downs, but giving it an honest shot is the first step. Every day, every moment, every interaction is an opportunity to practise what you've learned; to plant that seed, find peace, and watch it grow.

Only you have the key to unlock that inner happy—and to let that shit go.

Sources and Acknowledgements

IF YOU WANT to dig deeper into the stats, facts and quotes we referenced in this book, you can find them on our website at www.letthatshitgothebook.com.

Nina

When you lose your entire nuclear family, all your relationships start to hold more importance. Typically, you would say that your parents or siblings have helped shape you, but for me, it's also been a small army of people who might not be blood related but whom I consider family. I wouldn't be who I am today without this exceptional group of angels, who have supported me through both the mountains and valleys. With great reverence, I thank you all.

To my one and only Mikey Purewal, for being my rock and encouraging me to follow my heart three times over. For bringing home the bacon while I tried to figure out life and being my biggest cheerleader to boot. I couldn't have done it without all your love. I so admire your level of integrity and kind heart. You're a dream come true.

To my firecracker Bianca Purewal. You came along full of light and wonder. It's you who teaches me how to be present. I love you to all galaxies and back, my sweet butterfly. Your understanding of life is far beyond mine.

To all my teachers, who have given me life's greatest gift, knowledge. I am forever humbled in your presence knowing I have just scratched the surface: the enlightened gurus at the Chinmaya Mission, Sadhguru Jaggi Vasudev at the Isha Foundation, and the lovely Tanya Porter at The Inner Space.

To my soul sistas, Susan Mann and Dusty Bisla, for teaching me how to stand in my authentic truth and cultivate my intuition. Your deep understanding of life never ceases to amaze me. I don't know what I would do without our endless heart-to-hearts.

To my bros and new sis, Ankit, Avi, and Caitlin Mehta, for walking me down the aisle, intriguing conversations, and always having my back.

To my "Cadbury Mom and Dad," Susan Parsons and Unni Krishnan, for your unconditional love. I could not survive without your infinite wisdom. You are simply embodiments of the truth itself.

To my precious girlfriends, for brightening my life with your limitless sunshine and for loving with a whole heart. My one and only wifey and mom whisperer, Tracey Baker. My Laurier gems, Lauren Bone, Sara Curto, Jacqueline Grahek-Charles, Kirby Kittel, Lynn Manders, and Kelly McGregor. My halo-top life twin, Shahina Rhemtulla. My adventurous beauty, Serena Everingham. My vanilla, Dawn Mason. My RWPS bestest buddy, Carol Johnston. And of course my badass mama, Alicia Katsavos.

To stellar friends who keep me laughing with countless good times: Bill Katsavos, Marc Beauchemin, Laurie Verbruggen, Rob Baba, Lisa Hoo, Julie Spurrell, Arti Kashyap-Aynsley, Geoff Hartley, Lianne Barr, Nathan and Sarah Kumpf.

To my life mentors and to those who have stepped up as B.'s grandparents when we needed the support. There is no shortage for love for her, and we are so grateful for that: Neil and Laxmi Ohm, Rajiv and Sweety Mehta, Cathy Doutsas, Garnet Parsons, Ranjana Kiran, Barb Munro, Rama Dave, and the FGMs: Rita Bruni, Archana Seth, and Ann Woo.

To Mom and Dad, my wonderful in-laws: Bahadar and Resham Purewal, for teaching me the value of hard work and loving with a pure heart. Thank you for raising a remarkable son and being the sweetest grandparents to Bianca.

To my hive-mind rock star and partner in crime, Kate Petriw. Thank you for asking me to conduct my very first mindfulness workshop. You are so full of life, and your love glistens through your stunning smile. The way you approach life despite any adversity thrown your way is inspiring. Writing this book has been both a blast and a blessing. I'm so grateful the universe brought us together.

To all my clients, both corporate and public, for being advocates of mindfulness and partnering with Pure Minds. For also joining me on this journey to inject more peace and happiness into this world.

To my brother, Vijay Nayar, whose generous spirit and zest for life always moved me. Physically here or not, you have *no doubt* been here for your big sis. There isn't a day that goes by where I don't think about our inexplicable love.

To my mama, Rita Nayar, my hero and guru. I couldn't have done this without you. Your single, pointed focus to seeking truth along with your massive perma smile and unwavering approach to positive living still has me in awe. You taught me that with strength and resilience anything is possible. You are my greatest inspiration. I know you reside within the depths of my soul, but I still miss you.

Kate

This book contains much of the knowledge I've gained through all the beautiful peaks and the stormiest of storms these past five years. Meditation and mindfulness have helped me to move through them, but I couldn't have done it without the support from all the amazing people in my life.

To my dad, for your unwavering love and kindness, which inspires and lifts me in so many ways. Who knew all our countless discussions and musings on things "new age-y" would lead to a book and business that have allowed me to speak my heart.

To Cam, my caring baby bro, for always making me laugh and thinking I'm funny.

To my mom, for inspiring me in so many ways and always cheering me on.

To the Bear, who has always believed in my wild ideas, and encouraged me to throw as much spaghetti as possible until something sticks. Thanks for being a rock and always knowing how to make me smile. And thanks to LDH for your loving support.

To Robyn Keystone and Alison Fosbery, without whom

Mind Matters workshops would have never seen the light of day. Am so grateful to you both!

To Ashley Mulvihill, Dave Elliott, and the whole team at the Drake Hotel, who believed in our idea of changing the way people see mental health. We couldn't have imagined a better location to host our workshops.

To all the instructors and other partners at Mind Matters who make our workshops possible: Or Har-Gil, Alison Fosbery, Tony Tie, Luis Serrano, Mark Freeman, April Miranda, Palak Loizides, and Kanae LiCerda.

To my career partner, Nina. Everything we tackle together just feels right. I couldn't imagine doing this with anyone else. Your peace is also a part of what inspired me to follow this amazing path, and I am so glad and grateful you said yes to running our Mindful AF workshop! It's been such a beautiful journey writing this with you, and I am lucky to have you as a dear friend.

Thanks to Jackie Moss, for letting me take time off to write this book and letting me ride two waves at once.

To Dylan, whose light reminds me not to take it all too seriously. Thank you for introducing me to the wonderful world of yoga and meditation twelve years ago.

To the McArthur family, for their encouragement, love, and laughter: Cam, Shelley, Claire (fierce supporter of Mind Matters), and Will.

To my wonderful Nana, I am so grateful for our chats. Thanks for always lifting me up with love and kind words.

To my sweet Baba, whose humour, lightness, and deep love lightens my life.

Thank you to the Thomson-Opolko family (Karen, Frank, Christina, Erin, and Mary), who treat me like of one their own. I appreciate all that you do.

To Roxanne Ramjattan, whose wise and thoughtful words have helped me through so many storms.

To Patrizia Mola, your remedies and vivacious spirit have helped to heal me in so many ways. I can't thank you enough.

To Anita Horner, thank you for your healing sessions and letting all the good stuff flow in.

To Hilary Shea, for being such a kind, hilarious, and thoughtful cheerleader; and Lindsay Roxon, for your loving support and helping me push myself beyond my boundaries.

To all my friends who continue to amaze me by their bottomless well of compassion and love: Michelle O'Brien, Tiffany Willson, Jeff Ross, Mike Choptiany, Kathleen Ryan, Justin Reingold, Kelsey Rutherford, Kiri Ellis, Rose Schonblum, Nicole Steffan, Jennifer James Davis, and Ainsley Mourin. Am beyond grateful you are all in my life!

WE WOULD BOTH LIKE to thank the whole team at HarperCollins, especially Kate Cassaday and Laura Dosky, for your insightful feedback and supportive encouragement. And thank you to Linda Pruessen and Stephanie Conklin for your edits, which helped take our book to the next level—in record time!